Pelican Sociology
Editor: R. E. Pahl
Industrialism and Industrial Man

Clark Kerr organized the Institute of Industrial
Relations at the University of California just after the war.
He became Professor, in 1952 became the first
Chancellor of the Berkeley campus, and from 1958 to
1967 served as President of the University. His career
has included important work both in industrial relations
and as a governmental adviser.

Charles A. Myers is Professor of Industrial Relations
and Director of the Industrial Relations Section at the
Massachusetts Institute of Technology.

Frederick Harbison is Professor of Economics and
Director of the Industrial Relations Section at Princeton
University.

John T. Dunlop is Professor of Economics and Chairman
of the Wertheim Committee on Industrial Relations at
Harvard University, and is also Dean of the Faculty of
Arts and Sciences. He has served on many committees
concerned with management and labour relations at both
local and national levels.

Industrialism and Industrial Man

The Problems of Labour
and Management in
Economic Growth

WITH A POSTSCRIPT

Clark Kerr,
John T. Dunlop,
Frederick H. Harbison
and Charles A. Myers

Foreword by Roy Haddon

Penguin Books
in association with
Heinemann Educational Books

Penguin Books Ltd, Harmondsworth,
Middlesex, England
Penguin Books Australia Ltd, Ringwood,
Victoria, Australia

First published by Harvard University Press 1960
Published in the United Kingdom by
Heinemann Educational 1962
Second edition published in the United States as an
Oxford University Press paperback 1964
Postscript first published in Switzerland in the *International
Labour Review*, vol. 103, no. 6, June 1971
British second edition with Foreword and Postscript
published in Pelican Books 1973

Made and printed in Great Britain by
Cox & Wyman Ltd, London, Reading and Fakenham
Set in Monotype Times

Contents

TABLES

CHARTS

Preface

to the 1964 Edition

Industrialism and Industrial Man was first published by the Harvard University Press in 1960. In the Introduction to the volume, we characterized it as 'a progress report on our explorations to date, a report that is subject to change, for we have become acutely conscious of our own changing views'.

The present edition remains generally unchanged in its major concepts and outlines, but it does include some of the revisions we had come to expect. A few sections have been dropped; others have been condensed or re-ordered; some new illustrative material has been added.

These changes are partly the result of further reflections and research by the four of us, but also partly the result of helpful critical response by our readers. We hope that this new edition, reaching a new audience, will elicit additional suggestions and so help us to cast further light on a significant aspect of the changing world around us.

We wish to express our grateful appreciation to Abraham J. Siegel and Virginia T. Norris for their most helpful assistance in preparation of this edition.

Clark Kerr   John T. Dunlop   Frederick H. Harbison
Charles A. Myers

Foreword

The optimism which pervaded so much of the writing and reflection on industrial society and industrial man in the late 1950s and early 1960s can be seen now with the benefit of hindsight to have been a reflection of but a brief interregnum in western social thought. The fact that it was optimistic in tone betrays of course the value position from which it was written – western social scientists thought they could perceive social and economic developments which accorded with their own values; there is a sense of relief that after the traumas of the Depression, the Second World War and the Cold War, capitalism had not destroyed itself and did not seem to be in danger of doing so in the foreseeable future; the working class were not making a revolution in the advanced capitalist societies despite the appearance in Britain of 'socialized medicine' as it was called by some; the social problems of mass unemployment, poverty and inequality (especially inequality of opportunity – to become unequal) were thought to have been overcome by a combination of post-war prosperity, full employment and welfare services, so much so that voices in Britain were emboldened even by the early 1950s to pronounce that we should soon be able to do away with the apparatus of public social services.

The self-confidence with which social scientists and politicians alike advanced their interpretations of what was happening ('We're all becoming middle class now' and 'You've never had it so good') marks a decisive point in that aspect of western sociology which has been referred to as the 'debate with Marx'. For perhaps the first time since the nineteenth century social observers began to feel that underlying social conditions were working against the proposition that capitalism would destroy itself and the working class seize power. Hitherto, the failure of the working class and the political left to carry through a socialist revolution in western capitalist society had seemed to be a matter requiring explanation. Now the absence of a socialist revolution and the trends in the development of social and economic conditions within western capitalism seemed to be in harness.

A number of theses were advanced in an effort to explain and interpret what was taking place. Amongst the more popular of these theses were embourgeoisement, various versions of managerialism, and the end of ideology. In sum they amounted to a theory of the incorporation of the working class into the mainstream of affluent capitalism, both a political and an economic incorporation.

If the theories were unsatisfactory, it was not because the various national working classes in western societies were insurgent. The unsatisfactoriness of the theories in the first instance turned on the association between political insurgency and social conditions, since later researches began to reveal that the assertions about redistribution, reduction of inequality, elimination of poverty and the expansion of educational opportunities and social mobility, and the propensity of affluent workers to vote Conservative, were much exaggerated or even downright wrong.

The phenomenon of affluence was poorly understood (and those excluded from it disappeared temporarily from sight). Many parts of western industrial society returned (almost literally as the motor car and motorways became more pervasive) to a state of affairs described by Engels in the 1840s:

The town itself is peculiarly built, so that a person may live in it for years and go in and out daily without coming into contact with a working-people's quarter or even with workers, that is so long as he confines himself to his business or to pleasure walks . . . And the finest part of the arrangement is this, that the members of this money aristocracy can take the shortest road through the middle of all the labouring districts to their places of business, without ever seeing that they are in the midst of the grimy misery that lurks to the right and the left.[1]

In more gentle English tones, and with appreciation of the greater complexity of society in the mid-twentieth century, Titmuss makes the same essential point:

> By 1960 England had become a more muffled society. The condition of its people ... concealed by a combination of myth and computer incompetence.[2]

Sociology had to await the publication in 1966 of W. G. Runciman's *Relative Deprivation and Social Justice* before it began to get a finger-hold on an understanding of the possible forms of association between social conditions and political action in the mid-twentieth century.

By the middle of the 1960s (if no earlier), the interregnum was coming to an end. It was, nevertheless, an interregnum which left us facing in a new direction. For it was not simply the 'rediscovery' of inequality and poverty in Britain and North America which brought it to an end. If this alone had been responsible, we would have probably reverted to the 'debate with Marx' and see the interregnum as a premature celebration. What in fact also happened was that a new series of deep and bitter conflicts affecting both the internal and external relations of western society grew into prominence: racial conflicts, Vietnam, the poverty of the Third World and the threat to the environment presented by technological and economic developments.

The interregnum marked a point of discontinuity between the old political and theoretical discourse and new phenomena of social reality and social consciousness. Despite certain changes in western society and associated shifts of consciousness, inequality and poverty remained and may even have been growing, yet the working class as classically conceived was not generally insurgent. To this extent the working class did not present themselves as a fundamental social, political or economic 'problem' to the system. On the other hand, shifts in the consciousness and expression of grievance by black people, even though their basic situation was far from wholly new, projected race as a 'social problem' into the political arena.

Society thus found new social and political preoccupations (in

3

addition to race relations, students and other counter-cultural movements fed into this), and neither Marxist theory nor the sociology of the interregnum were able to handle these developments very easily. A new global sociology of industrialism and imperialism, able to handle simultaneously structural relationships within industrial society and their articulation with the structures of relationship between industrial society and the Third World, has become an urgent need. Like social thought in general, sociology must be responsive to changes in social structure and social consciousness and their interrelation.

On a less global scale, attempts are being made to give a more coherent account of the ways in which capitalism has modified itself, and to understand its contemporary dynamics. In particular emphasis is being placed on the implications of the high productivity, high consumption equation of the affluent society and the social stresses that this occasions. We may cite one example at random of the way in which this theme has assumed a central place in recent social thought, to which many varied social phenomena are related. A paper by Jock Young in a recent collection of papers on deviancy observes:

... the reaction against the drug-taker springs from moral indignation engendered by an economy which dictates the necessity of maintaining both productivity and high consumption. The ideal citizen of the post-Keynesian age is one who is disciplined in his work yet hedonistic in his leisure. For we are taught to value the deferred gratification of hard work, although seeking our identity within the hedonistic consumption patterns which shape our free time. As a result we feel guilty about both, and the consequent fundamental ambivalence is deeply ingrained in our social relationships. Thus the bohemian fascinates us because he seems to us to be acting out our fantasies of unrestrained hedonism, while at the same time he angers us because he disdains hard work and does not *earn* his free time.[3]

For Keynesians the essential problem was to find the means of maintaining economic equilibrium at a socially acceptable level of employment. Today our question has become: can we survive economically *without* artificially stimulating the level of consumption, without built-in obsolescence, and without the modern 'potlatches' of the space race? The *political* dimension of this question is clear. Can we use our productivity to eliminate poverty and inequality (national and international); and how far is high consumption the means by which the bulk of the working class are kept incorporated into the western capitalist (and welfare state) societies?

The thought that we may have started on an economic treadmill based on the fiction of permanent scarcity in order to contain the political and egalitarian thrust of the working class in the metropolitan societies cannot be far from our minds. It is a device, however, which seems to necessitate the close coordination and management of both work and leisure, of both production and consumption, of both the economic and the social – coordination and management designed to maximize economic performance. These developments seem to be the dominant ones regardless of whether they take place under the banner of sharper economic competition or under the banner of government sponsored rationalization and technological innovation. The versions of efficiency represented by competition and the 'white heat of technology' differ of course, but in either case they seem to demand a reduction of that margin of 'inefficiency' which preserves the human dimension of society.

*

In several respects *Industrialism and Industrial Man* is a product of that period we have characterized as the interregnum. The reader will find embedded in the book elements of embourgeoisement, managerialism and the end of ideology. It is a book which is securely anchored in the tradition of the 'debate with Marx'. It would be unfair to dismiss the book as no more than this, however. In the first place, as John Goldthorpe, one of the major critics of the theses advanced in *Industrialism and Industrial Man*, has pointed out:

. . . we are . . . much indebted to the authors . . . for showing us a way to escape from the cramped quarters of trivialized empiricism without falling victim to highly speculative building with 'empty boxes'.[4]

Foreword

The authors have indeed attempted to deal with large-scale societal developments on a global canvas, and in the process they have made use of a conceptual framework which embraces rather more than a concern with the developments of western capitalist societies. In particular they have sought to interpret what was happening in the Third World – though in my view they have done so from the standpoint of a distinctively western perspective. Although therefore the book begins in Chapter 1 within the framework of a debate with Marx, it seeks to break out of the straitjacket of the argument about the future of capitalism by substituting for Marx's idea of the 'process of capitalist production', the concept of the 'industrialization process'. By virtue of this fact alone, *Industrialism and Industrial Man* stand apart from much of the work of the interregnum since it anticipates our present-day preoccupation with another two thirds of the world.

The sceptic may reply that the substitution of one concept for another is a sleight of hand rather than a convincing argument, and that conjuring tricks with concepts tell us more about the sociologists concerned than about the real world. There is undoubtedly some substance in this view, reflected in the observation:

Sociologists are increasingly becoming traders in definitions: they hawk their versions of reality around to whoever will buy them.[5]

There is no doubt that the key concepts used in analysis and description do reflect ways of thinking about society, and that this is a major element in the study of the sociology of knowledge. Definitions of reality and concepts are not somehow conjured out of the sky and put on offer like so many varieties of ice-cream. They derive from the social experiences and values (including indirect experience transmitted through various media of communication) of the individuals who develop them, and they are differentially taken up and used (and rejected or ignored) by individuals and groups in society.

Concepts are central to establishing and maintaining the 'reality' of the world we live in and as such they are abstractions which represent ways of thinking about and responding to society (and new concepts or new accretions of meaning to existing ones reflect changed perceptions and responses to social change), as well as constraints upon our observation, perception and thinking. In their capacity of both providing new vision and blinkers, the concepts we use prompt us to ask certain questions and to fail to ask others. These abstractions are, as Raymond Williams has pointed out, 'necessary to establish the reality of social life' but are also 'under continual pressure from experience'. 'Our thinking about society is a long debate between abstractions and actual relationships.'[6]

The reader of *Industrialism and Industrial Man* should accordingly keep two things in mind. On the one hand he must attempt to abstract the theoretical structure which unfolds from its beginning in the employment of the concepts of 'industrialism' and the 'industrialization process'. On the other hand, he must attempt to discern what experiences of change in the real world are pressing in on the authors' attempt at conceptual and theoretical exposition.

The overview of the industrialization process and its ultimate destination is presented by Kerr *et al.* in order to provide a context for their study of labour problems, and the development of systems of industrial relations, in the course of economic development. They set out originally with the intention of examining the recruitment and commitment of a labour force to industrial life, the patterns of worker protest which developed in the course of economic development, and the impact of the policies and practices of management and the state. They report however that they soon came to the view that worker protest did not have a determinate effect on the course of societal developments; instead they formed the view that industrial workers were a conditioning force, and that it was management which held the 'seed of the future'. Moreover, they assert, the 'peaking of protest' occurs relatively early in the process of industrialization, and is not difficult to control. In other words, it does not offer a fertile seedbed for socialist revolution. Rather than the 'labour problem' being defined as the response of unions to capitalism, they redefined it as the structuring of the managers and the managed under

7

industrialization. 'The protest of today is more in favour of industrialization than against it.' The focus of their interest in industrial relations systems is therefore on the development of the web of rules which regulate and institutionalize the conflicts of interest between industrial workers and management within the framework of the authority structure of the productive enterprise. Three parties – organized labour, management, and the state – are seen as participating in this process of institutionalization of conflict, which takes on the form of an eternal bureaucratic contest over details, rather than a class conflict over the nature and arrangements of industrial society as a whole. Labour organizations will take the form of occupational associations rather than component parts of class movements.

The source of the dynamic for these developments, through the process of industrialization to a future state of what they refer to as 'pluralistic industrialism', is the uniformity of the basic technology of an industrial society. Very briefly, their thesis is that the inherent logic of the industrialization process is leading societies which start from many different points (and follow a variety of pathways of industrialization) towards a common future – 'pluralistic industrialism'. The exposition of the thesis is organized in terms of the interplay between the 'universal', the 'related', and the 'unique'. By the 'unique' they mean the diversity of cultural, environmental, demographic and historical starting points of the march to industrialization; the 'universal' refers to the uniformity of basic technology – 'the character of science and technology and the requirements inherent in modern methods of production and distribution'; the 'related' refers to a typology of industrializing élites whose characteristic strategies and ideologies guide societies from their diverse starting points along the variety of pathways to industrialism. Each of these élites tends to have its own natural history of evolution as industrialization proceeds. The authors seek to specify, in a general way, the kinds of social conditions which they think are most conducive to any one of these types of élites getting into the saddle.

The significance of concepts like 'industrialism', 'industrialization' and 'pathways to industrialism' as these are used by

Kerr *et al.* is that they represent an attempt to provide the basis for a single theoretical framework capable of embracing a range of historical experience over time and space. They are used as essentially unifying concepts. The substitution of 'the industrialization process' for the 'process of capitalist production' is central to this attempt, since it seeks to distinguish between an historical configuration or epoch (capitalism in nineteenth-century Europe) and an analytical concept (industrialization). Because, to a degree, the theorists of industrial society have been participants in the debate about the future of capitalism, it has sometimes been argued that the idea of industrial society has been substituted for the concept of capitalism for less than scholarly reasons. The gist of this attack is that the concept of industrial society serves to defuse the critical content embodied in the notion of capitalism.

The issue is rather more complex than this, however, since we are not confronted with a simple substitution of concepts in the analysis and description of the same historical configuration. What is also involved here is the question of the usefulness of the notion of the 'process of capitalist production' in the analysis of the development of the eastern bloc and the Third World. The convergence theory, which is the name that has been applied to the theses advanced in *Industrialism and Industrial Man*, must be seen as one which confronts a world characterized by two divisions – that between East and West (or between socialism and capitalism), and that between North and South (or between the industrial and non-industrial, modern and traditional).

Historically, both these contrasts have been drawn upon in the sociological analysis of social change *within* western society. Thus as Robert Nisbet[7] has argued, the key ideas of sociology took the form of a series of antitheses which had their source in the confrontation of two social orders: the feudal-traditional and the democratic-capitalist. It was not the transition of Europe from one to the other, but the *confrontation*, Nisbet argues, which provided the spark of creativity that produced the distinctive unit ideas of classical sociology. They were the product of the brief period of confrontation when the two social orders were 'of almost equal power in the loyalties they inspire and the incentives they arouse in reflective minds'. The confrontation was not between societies based on different principles of social organization, but between two principles of social organization competing for dominance within the same group of societies.

Similarly, the other major preoccupation of western sociology – the 'debate with Marx' – was also not in origin a contrast between two societies, or groups of societies. It was concerned with the confrontation of groups (classes) *within* capitalist society. The importance of these points may be highlighted if certain essential features of Marx's theory are outlined very briefly.

According to Marx's theory a number of historical types of society could be distinguished. Three of these – feudalism, capitalism and socialism – are of immediate interest in the present context. Marx defined types of society on the basis of the dominant mode of production, an inclusive concept which referred to both the *forces* of production (a society's productive capacity or relationship to nature, including scientific knowledge, technological equipment and the organization of collective labour), and the *relations* of production (the legal and political framework within which the forces of production operated – the most significant aspect of this being ownership of the means of production).

The forces and relations of production were conceived as being in dialectical relationship, so that the potential inherent in the productive forces could only evolve so far within the system of the relations of production that had initially developed them. Beyond this point the relations of production became 'fetters' on the further rational development of the forces of production. Historically, therefore, capitalist relations of production were seen as a progressive force *vis-à-vis* feudalism, but as a barrier to further development of the forces of production that capitalism had sponsored. Capitalism was considered by Marx as a necessary stage in the succession of societal types (feudalism to capitalism to socialism), a stage in which the essential functions of primary capital accumulation and development of the productive forces were carried through. Until the material conditions were appropriate, however (i.e. until the forces of production had reached the limits of their development under the given relations of production), the transition from one historical type or epoch (capitalism) to the next (socialism) was not possible. One of the senses in which capitalism was held to contain inherent contradictions and to carry the seeds of its own destruction was that as capitalism matured the conflict between the forces and relations of production would sharpen.

Nevertheless an historical agent was required to achieve the transformation of society, and in the case of capitalist society, Marx located this agency in the proletariat. He argued that as capitalism developed it increasingly polarized society into two antagonistic classes (bourgeoisie and proletariat), which were defined in terms of their relationship to the means of production. On the basis of the labour theory of value and the theory of surplus value, Marx argued that the proletariat would become pauperized even as the wealth generated by the productive forces under capitalism increased. The conditions of work and life associated with the factory system of production and with urbanization would provide the conditions for a growth of class consciousness on the part of the proletariat. From a class-in-itself, the proletariat would become a class-for-itself capable of collective class action. A fully class-conscious proletariat would transform the class struggle into a political struggle, and would develop a consciousness of its historical location and mission as the agent of the transformation of society from capitalism to socialism. The revolutionary proletariat would not simply seize power but would eventually destroy the capitalist relations of production, including the state and the politico-legal framework that underpinned the capitalist notion of private property rights in the means of production. In so doing they would liberate again the forces of production.

The generation of a proletariat thus represents a second sense in which capitalism would develop within itself the seeds of its own destruction. It is possible to see, therefore, how Marx's theory synchronized the class struggle and the proletarian revolution on the one hand, with the removal of the 'fetters' on the development of the forces of production on the other.

Marx's theory was essentially a theory of social change through conflict. The conflict of classes and of ideologies was envisaged as taking place *within* capitalist society, and the outcome would be a revolutionary transformation of capitalist society. This is the original form of the debate about the future of capitalism; but since the Russian revolution of 1917, there has been superimposed upon this formulation an international conflict between whole societies, and the conflict between socialism and capitalism has become one which has also been embodied in the conflict of the official ideologies of whole societies. Moreover, these societies which now proclaim socialism as their official ideology did not arise out of the ashes of mature capitalist societies, and mature capitalism has nowhere been overthrown by an indigenous proletarian revolution. Nevertheless, both groups of societies have established an industrial, factory-based, system of production employing and developing modern technology. It is in the context of these developments that the comparison of the political, economic and social structure of capitalist and socialist societies, as variants of the more general industrial type of society, has become a meaningful and popular sociological exercise.

With reference to the antitheses between traditional and modern, Nisbet[8] suggests that in western society we are living 'in a late phase of the classical age of sociology' since the two revolutions (the French and Industrial) have been accomplished. 'We *are* urban, democratic, industrial, bureaucratic, rationalized, large scale, formal, secular and technological.' Because of this the substantive empirical referents of the classical antitheses are no longer extant within western society. At the same time, increasing interest has been focused on the processes of modernization, industrialization and economic development within the Third World; and many of the formulations of classical sociology have been applied to the process of social change in these societies. In addition, however, they have been used to highlight the contrast *between* the industrialized North (East and West) and the non-industrial or industrializing South.

The concepts of industrialism and the industrialization process serve to enable the authors to transcend any given historical time and place. They seek to distinguish the development of an industrial and factory system of production, and the use of technology and science in the processes of production and distribution from the variety of historical societies in which they have been and are found. They go considerably further than this, however, to suggest that it is precisely these former elements which are growing in significance for an understanding of the structure of society. This creates some conceptual difficulty in moving from a concern with an analytical *element* of society, to the characterization of historical societies as moving toward a common form – 'pluralistic industrialism'. That is to say, there is some difficulty in moving from the element, to the concrete processes of social change. The authors seek to resolve the difficulties by asserting that modern technology is much the same from one society to another, and that the emerging social structures are increasingly determined by the exigencies of technology.

It may be useful at this point to refer to Dahrendorf's justification for the view that the notions of 'capitalist society' and 'industrial society' are not simply different terms for identical concepts. He argues that the historical definition of capitalism combined two elements: firstly, those factors connected with industrial production as such, independently of its social, legal or economic context; and secondly, those elements which characterize merely the particular form of industrial production displayed by the industrializing countries of Europe and North America in the nineteenth century. These two analytically distinct elements were combined in the particular historical configurations of the latter. Dahrendorf introduces the concept of industrial society in order to refer to factors 'which cannot disappear, therefore, unless industry itself disappears'. This analytical distinction is employed by Dahrendorf in the course of considering whether classes and conflict are phenomena of the specifically capitalist type of industrial society, or whether their existence is a consequence of industrial production itself, and therefore a lasting feature of all industrial societies.[9]

There are a number of objections to Dahrendorf's larger thesis. For example I do not subscribe to his views about the significance of the alleged separation of ownership and control; and his concept of class as turning on the participation or not in the exercise of authority in imperatively coordinated associations seems to lose sight of the *societal* dimension essential to the notion of class. At the same time he is surely correct in drawing our attention to the authority structure of the productive enterprise under a factory system, and forcing us to inquire into the wider social ramifications of this, and to ask whether this authority structure is really peculiar to capitalism. The nature and significance of the issues raised here, both theoretically and politically, were clearly recognized by Bukharin in 1920:

Here before all the entire sum of the newly arising production relationships must receive theoretical consideration. For there arises here a question of basic significance; how is an entirely different combination of persons and elements of production possible, if the logic of the production process itself brings forth relationships of a specific type? An engineer or a technician must of course give orders to the workers, and must therefore stand *over* them. In exactly the same way must the former officer in the Red Army stand *over* the common soldier. Here as there an inner, purely technical, objective logic is involved, which must remain in any given social order. How should this dilemma be solved?[10]

With reference to these sorts of questions, Dahrendorf and the convergence theorists take the requirements of the industrial productive system as the focal point of reference from which to trace out the ramifications in society of the logic of industrialism. Analysis of this kind is perhaps most explicitly presented in J. K. Galbraith's[11] dissection of 'the industrial system' and the 'technostructure' which is a central text in the corpus of work on both the convergence thesis and the managerial revolution.

The concentration of focus on the authority structures of the productive enterprise, and on the eternal bureaucratic contest between managers and the managed (or the semi-managers and semi-managed as Kerr *et al.* refer to them), are common to both Dahrendorf and the convergence theorists. Like Dahrendorf, Kerr *et al.* see these conflicts as essentially institutionalized and generally segmentally contained.

It is true that contemporary analysis of social stratification in

14

industrial society has elevated occupation (with its various dimensions of income, skill, prestige, authority and work conditions etc.) to being the most significant index (and determinant) of social class position – Parkin,[12] for example, suggests that this is perhaps even more true in relation to eastern European societies than in relation to western capitalist ones – but we should perhaps be wary of translating too simply from the internal structure of the productive enterprise (and the type of occupations associated with it) to the social structure of society as a whole. For one thing, this analysis of stratification as essentially a system of (occupational) *positions* ignores some of the more important aspects of 'class', in particular the development of groups organized for conflict; and furthermore it substitutes essentially static sociographic data for the study of social relationships.

One difficulty here is that the productive enterprise cannot be considered in isolation from the economy or polity, since it is essentially an organization operating in an economic and political environment. For this reason, even at the core of the productive process, it seems difficult to conceive of the productive enterprise as being structured (and as operating) merely in consequence of technology. Technology is a human artifact that has to be used, that is to say it has to be introduced by human beings and is a factor which has to be taken account of in human organization. Only in this context can it be considered to have any effects on societal structure, organization and process. In this sense technology can be a 'potential' or 'effective' environment in a way that is analogous to elements in the physical environment.[13] To make this point, however, is to suggest that what is sometimes attributed to the exigencies of technology ought properly to be attributed to a fundamental system of values and orientations to the world, or to the political economy in which technology is embedded and utilized, and not to technology *per se* as though it were autonomous.

Part of the confusion here seems to stem from the juxtaposition of capitalism as an historical configuration and industrialism as an abstraction; and associated with this is the attempt to assert a radical separation of the ideas of the forces and relations of production. In respect of the latter, emphasis is placed on the forces of production (industrialism) and the significance of the relations of production is de-emphasized, since the thesis of convergence suggests that it is the industrial system of production and distribution *per se* which is the more salient in shaping the societal structure.

Dahrendorf is somewhat ambiguous as to whether industrial society is a general type (with sub-varieties: capitalism, post-capitalism) or an analytical element in historical societies. There is some ambiguity of a slightly different kind in Kerr *et al.*'s formulation:

> Industrialization refers to the actual course of transition from the traditional society towards industrialism. Industrialism is an abstraction, a limit approached through historical industrialization. Industrialism is the concept of a fully industrialized society, that which the industrialization process inherently tends to create. Even the most economically advanced countries of today are to some degree and in some respects underdeveloped. They contain features derived from earlier stages of development which obscure the pure logic of the industrialization process.[14]

In this formulation, 'industrialism' is somewhat akin to the Weberian idea of an ideal type (e.g. bureaucracy), and the concrete process of industrialization is seen as an historical development which through time increases the relevance of the use of the ideal type (industrialism) as a template against which to measure different societies. The equivalent of the historical concept in this thesis, however, is not industrialism which remains essentially an abstract limiting case, but the idea of 'pluralistic industrialism'. As the authors make explicit in a later postscript to their book, however, the idea of 'pluralistic industrialism' is lacking in specificity as an historical concept.

> We noted the 'diversity' of arrangements that is possible within pluralistic industrialism. This diversity lies between the alternative of pure state socialism and pure market capitalism, both of which emphasize the role of the manager: and between the guild socialism of G. D. H. Cole and private anarcho-syndicalism, both of which emphasize the role of the working group. Each of these four possibilities

constitutes a 'pure' model with clear sovereignty for one group or another. Pluralistic industrialism, by contrast, emphasizes mixed sovereignty and there are many possible mixtures . . . We see pluralistic industrialism as a range of alternatives rather than a single arrangement. [15]

The thesis that the logic of industrialism derives from the exigencies of a common basic technology is worked out in *Industrialism and Industrial Man* at two interrelated levels. At the first of these it is argued that convergence between societies will be greatest along those dimensions of social structure which are most closely related to technology:

Social arrangements will be most uniform from one society to another when they are most closely tied to technology: they can be more diverse the further removed they are from technology. [16]

The second of these levels deals with the degree of behavioural conformity, its occupational and organizational structures. In this case the focus is on the internal organization of a society, and the differential degrees of independence allowed to the individual in different parts of it; again this is related to closeness to technology.

The areas closest to technology will be the most conformist; those farthest from the requirements of its service the most free. [17]

Both of these issues are returned to in the postscript. In the case of the former the authors spell out the need to distinguish the differential degrees of constraint exercised by technology in different areas of society; and in the case of the latter they take up with renewed emphasis their earlier discussion of the 'new bohemianism'.

Whilst these and other denials by the authors that they conceive of the future state of pluralistic industrialism as one of complete identity between industrial societies – they claim to recognize 'limits' and even 'exceptions' and to be suggesting 'two-way partial convergence' rather than 'one-way total convergence' [18] – must be respected in any interpretation of their work, there is undoubtedly a certain sense in which the concept of industrialism carries with it the imagery of a 'total' environment. There are two aspects of this. Firstly, the question of the creation and maintenance of consensus ('an integrated body of ideas, beliefs and value judgements') in which sphere they see the intellectuals and industrializing élites playing a vital role. In the second place, however, their concept of industrialism and the industrialization process implies a continuous movement towards the establishment of internal *structural* consistency. It is this latter which we wish to explore further here because it pinpoints the fact that the convergence thesis is a rather curious amalgam of structural-functionalism and a tendency toward a single-factor theory of social change. The logic of the convergence thesis seems to be that other parts of the social structure are conceived as having to change in order to meet the requirements of the industrial system of production and distribution. Causal primacy, at least, in this theory of societal change is given to technology and the industrial economy, and the drift of the thesis is that society moves toward re-establishing an equilibrium anchored around the requirements of the new industrial system of production and distribution.

W. E. Moore[19] has suggested that at the back of much thinking behind the search for uniformities in the impact of industry on society is a three-stage model of pre-industrial (traditional) society, a transitional (industrializing) phase, and industrial (modern) society. Moore's objection to this model is that there is a tendency to overstress the relatively static and integrated properties of the pre-industrial social order, and *implicitly* (implicit, argues Moore, because if it were made explicit it would be seen to be patently false) to assume that the industrialized society is also a static social order.

In the strict sense there is some doubt as to whether the latter objection in particular can be laid at the door of the authors of *Industrialism and Industrial Man* since the overriding impression conveyed to the reader by this book is that pluralistic industrialism is all flux, change and bureacratic contest. The use of the concept 'industrialism' as an abstraction enables the authors to suggest that as yet *all* societies (including the most economically and technologically advanced) are in some degree underdeveloped. There is nothing in the book to indicate that the authors envisage technological and industrial development coming to a halt. Thus in accordance with the causal primacy given to technological and industrial change, one would suppose that the social institutions and social structures of industrial society will continue to change and adjust to the exigencies of a developing technology.

Because industrial society is in this respect itself conceived of as dynamic – it is the fact of apparently continuous change which marks off modern rational scientific societies from traditional ones – it is not easy in fact to draw a distinction between industrialization and industrialism. Yet there is an implicit distinction between the two which makes Moore's criticisms of more relevance. The distinction is this: the transitional period of industrialization is one in which there is held to be a *fundamental* lack of structural congruence between the institutions of traditional society and an emerging industrial economy. Industrialism on the other hand is a concept which envisages much wider participation of all sectors of society in the industrial economy; it implies not a static social order, but at least a coherent principle of social organization whereby social institutions and structures maintain a much greater degree of structural consistency with a technologically advanced economy. Whereas in the transitional stage, pre-industrial elements of the social order remain insufficiently changed or eliminated for society to be represented as a coherent social order anchored around the new industrial technology, in the industrialized stage the lack of perfect fit between industrial economy and social structures is one of degree not of kind. In so far as industrial society is economically and technologically dynamic, the achievement of a workable and acceptable degree of structural consistency is unlikely in any finalized form, any more than social policy, for the same reason, reaches a point of finality; but in so far as structural consistency with the industrial economy is the principle of coherence in the social order of industrialism, the more dynamic the industrial economy, the more visible will be manifestations of that principle in the form of pressures for change of social institutions, and urgent diagnoses of the 'What's wrong with . . . ?' variety. In terms of the movement through the industrialization process toward industrialism, therefore, the question raised by the convergence thesis is what ranges of variation in institutions and social structures are possible as industrialization advances?

*

The world-wide empire of industrialism portrayed by Kerr *et al.* is a curiously depoliticized world. It is so not merely in consequence of the idea that ideologies will wane under the impact of technical necessity, but also in the more general sense of there being little place for effective purposive human action aside from the role of élites in the course of the industrialization process. At one level this fact of the convergence thesis has been commented upon by Goldthorpe who has objected to the primacy given to the economic over the political in Kerr *et al.*'s work, on the grounds that the stratification system in Soviet society can be seen to be significantly shaped by political regulation, whereas in western society 'economic, and specifically market, forces act as the crucial stratifying agency within society'. He argues that whatever the phenotypical similarity, stratification in Soviet society is genotypically different from stratification in western society.[20]

It was noted above that the convergence thesis left us with the question of what variation in social institutions and structures was possible as industrialization advanced. Stated rather differently, this raises the question of whether once the 'decision' to industrialize has been taken, and it is decided to continue with economic development, the consequences for society as a whole can be shaped by political and social action. We confront here the question of human control.

It is interesting to note that Dawe[21] has recently drawn attention to the fact that one of the problems which has fascinated men since the Enlightenment period has been 'how human beings could regain *control* over essentially man-made institutions and historical situations'. In addition to that strand of sociological thought (having its more general counterpart in the conservative reaction) which has taken the *problem of order* as its focal concern, Dawe suggests that there is a second sociology which has taken the *problem of control* as its focal concern.

In the modern world, however, the problem of control has a dual meaning. Firstly, there is the modern thrust to dominate nature in which science and technology has played a vital role, and which has expressed itself in the industrial system of production and distribution. In the form of a vast industrial-urban complex this has had the effect of removing whole societies from direct relationship and dependence upon the natural environment. Secondly, however, the problem of control has to do with men's (collective) control over their own social institutions and relationships, and it is not possible to grasp fully the meaning of the problem of control in this second sense without regard to the democratic dimension. The most difficult issue which confronts us, however, both in theory and practice, is the link between these two meanings or aspects of the problem of control.

When we consider the nature of this link we are forced to return to the study of human society in terms of the interrelation between the organization of society on the one hand and the man-nature relationship on the other. The significance of this for modern sociology is that the radical separation of these two things which underlies much of the effort to define sociology as concerned only with 'the social' has to be rejected. Instead we should be looking at the social anthropologists' concept of tribal social structure as representing the maintenance of social relationships at a given level of ecological adaptation,[22] and try to see whether a comparable notion can be employed in relation to the social arrangements of modern societies where the 'ecology' is in large part a man-made industrial-urban one.

Formulated in terms of the convergence thesis the issue becomes one of the extent to which human societies can choose how to organize the collective effort to subjugate nature and create for themselves a largely man-made industrial-urban environment; and whether, having created such an environment, the task of maintaining it in being, and servicing (or administering and managing) it determines the structure of institutions and patterns of social organization. The answer implied by the convergence thesis is that it is no longer sensible to try and shape society according to 'utopian' ideals; we are told, in effect, that in order to achieve mastery over the natural environment, and maintain or improve our standards of living, it is necessary to forego the ideal of seeking to exercise human control over the quality and organization of human society.

What is significant about the discussion in *Industrialism and Industrial Man* is not so much the absence of human actions and conflicts of interest, as that the long-run outcome of these is portrayed as being essentially predetermined whatever the participants themselves may pretend. In this respect the thesis is a rather grand statement of the priority to be given in social analysis to the unforeseen, and unintended consequences – a viewpoint which of course fits conveniently with certain assumptions about external, objective social analysis divorced from any engagement with value-orientations and purposive actions of human beings. Primacy is inevitably given in such an approach to 'social forces' and the 'logic' of social structures, which represents the sociological expression of the loss of control. But this rests rather uneasily alongside another proposition sometimes expressed in the sociological literature on industrial society to the effect that one way in which industrial societies are more alike is that they 'exhibit a degree and extensity of deliberate and administered social change that is historically unmatched'.[23]

It may be that the idea of inevitable outcomes is a necessary device for mobilizing and gaining consensus for efforts at planned social change (which can be thus represented as working in the direction of historical trends), and discouraging opposition to what is 'inevitable' and 'necessary'. Alternatively it may be that the ideology of planning hides the true state of affairs which is that people feel impotent not 'because they are dominated by a well-organized system of social control' but because it is 'lack of control which is at the heart of the social order'. This latter view is one that MacIntyre[24] has put forward:

The most impressive political fact of our time is the accidental character of most of the policies which government is forced to embrace, an accidental character where peculiar quality springs from the combination of the uncontrolled nature of the events with the insistence of those who govern, dominated as they are by the ideology of planning, that events are in fact directed by their deliberate and willed purposes.

It is necessary of course to distinguish between the argument that most ordinary individuals feel, and are, powerless to control the things which affect their lives, and the argument that history is all drift and not amenable to any sort of control by any group of the population. The former argument could well be true whilst the latter was not. It must be recognized that the outcome of purposive social action may be different from what was anticipated or intended, simply because complete knowledge of all the ramifications of a given action or event is not possible beforehand (it is difficult enough to evaluate consequences after the event), and because in any case the outcomes of action are in part the result of the interaction of a plurality of potentially conflicting purposive actions. Although some groups, individuals or interested parties will be able to exert greater power and influence over what happens in society than others, no society can be viewed adequately as a complete command system, nor can social change be wholly absorbed into the framework of a crude 'engineering' model. But simply because these facts must be recognized, it does not permit us to retreat to a position in which we see everything causing everything and see a complete lack of control where society is abandoned to 'social forces', and abandon all notion of powerful groups and 'command posts' in society.

It is impossible to grasp the significance of the problem of control unless it is fully realized that the effort to subjugate nature is a *collective* effort, and since this is so it is also essentially political. The organization of this collective effort involves relationships of power and class between men. Similarly the physical, economic and industrial-urban environment is not an abstract world unpopulated by human beings, so that when we 'manage' the economy or the urban system we are using power to force people to participate in the industrial economy in a certain way. Control in the sense of seeking to increase the domination of nature is therefore not separable from control of human action and social institutions. Yet because it is very easy to emphasize the man-madeness of the industrial-urban environment, and to conceive of the industrial economy as something apart from human action, there is also a continuing temptation to employ techniques of management and

T—B

control which ignore the fact that these are essentially political actions in the broadest sense.

With these points in mind we can return to the question of structural consistency, by commenting further on the relationship between the economic and the social in industrial societies. For in this context it can be suggested that the thrust towards control (or the phenomenon of 'deliberate and administered social change') in modern society has taken the form of an intensification of the dominance of the 'economic' over the 'social', rather than a reassertion of social control over the industrial economy.

Burns[25] has argued that in the second half of the twentieth century industrialization has become a major *political* goal, and in consequence social and political changes that were once conceived of as being the *consequences* of industrialism are today thought of as a necessary *pre-condition* for creating or revitalizing the component factors of industrialism. The interventions of governments to regulate the economy, overcome 'bottlenecks' and stimulate technological and economic change – interventions which are primarily oriented to the 'needs' of the national economy – are a major factor in this intensification of the subordination of society to the economy. We might hypothesize that the greater the saliency of economic and technological objectives in the range of societal goals, and the greater the effort and competence at deliberate and administered social change, the greater will be the pressure for a relatively high degree of institutional integration around the requirements of the industrial economy. For from the point of view of a subjective concern with economic goals, the functional autonomy of parts of a society represents a potential source of hindrance to the achievement of these salient societal goals.

The implication of this argument is that the problem of order and the problem of control in this context are hard to distinguish, for technology and the requirements of an industrial economy making use of technology have replaced the king as the starting point of description to which everything else is related. Or at least social institutions are so related in so far as they are perceived to have any bearing on economic performance. Leaning heavily as they do on continued economic success in a competitive international economy for their political and social stability, and employing ever more sophisticated and costly technology which creates complex interdependencies, modern industrial societies in the cause of regulating and managing their economies are pushed towards recognizing the económic relevance of an increasing range of social phenomena. The situation is paralleled in industrializing societies where economists engaged in planning economic growth and industrial development have been forced to include more 'non-economic' variables in their models. In this situation there is no clear or static boundary between the 'economic' and the 'non-economic', for as long as economic objectives are accorded priority, the twists and turns of economic policy seem likely to reveal repeatedly the economic relevance of aspects of society that have hitherto been considered outside the realm of economic interest.

Industrial man is in danger of finding himself continually under pressure to give up his attachments to valued institutions and ways of life in the cause of growth, productivity and efficiency. It may be that for the moment many people are willing to make these sacrifices for the chance of higher material consumption, but we ought perhaps to ask how long this 'exchange' of costs and benefits will be acceptable, and for how long they will be considered as exchangeable equivalents. The world of industrial man is in danger of being denuded of the formal and informal social devices that have grown up at each stage of industrial development to act as protection against exposure to impersonal, external economic and technological forces over which many of the people affected have little or no control.

The notion of internal structural consistency is to be seen therefore as a subjective matter – what is consistent is consistent with the achievement of certain objectives. If there is a discernible strain toward structural consistency we should look for its source in industrial society not in some self-regulating mechanism restoring equilibrium, but in human agency and its location in the social system. The impact of industry on society is not to be understood, today, as merely the result of the unregulated impact of a highly differentiated and self-regulating market economy, but as the result of coordinated political and economic management.

In other words, rather than talking in value terms that imply that the system as a whole exerts control over its parts, it is preferable to conceive of society in terms of structures of power and decision-making, and to examine empirically in any given society which groups and agencies have an interest in promoting (their subjective definition of) structural consistency; and what sanctions they have at their disposal to implement it. When we speak of sanctions in this context we should not be thinking merely of power, in a positive sense, to insist on certain kinds of behaviour on the part of the population, but also of the ability to undermine alternative means of organizing the supply of basic needs. Thus we are not merely concerned with the recruitment of an industrial labour force, but with the devices used to try and detach people from their existing, or prevent the formation of alternative, systems of social organization which are conceived as obstructive to the achievement of the dominant societal goal.

The classic model of course is the depriving of the population of nineteenth-century capitalist society of access to the means of subsistence except via participation in the labour market. The substitution of the 1834 Poor Law in England for the Speenhamland system of poor relief is to be seen in this light, and as an early example of the coordination of social policy and economic policy in which the latter dictated to the former. Another example is the insistence of colonial powers that African tribes should pay taxes in *monetary* form, thus precipitating a part of the population into at least a limited and specified participation in a commercial economy.

Populations and social institutions are not simply so many billiard balls on the historical table, propelled in a purely passive way by the impact of industry and technology. They are themselves capable of action, though the effectiveness of their actions will vary. If we are to preserve a humanistic view of man and society it is essential to insist upon this capacity for action and to see the development of society under the impact of industrialization as a process involving social and political conflict; and furthermore to insist upon the authenticity of the actions and responses of those affected by the pressures for large-scale social change. As sociologists we must seek out and understand these responses and resistances, whether they take the form of the preservation of the colour bar in the context of industrialism (surely the most telling denial of the assumption that modern societies replace ascription with achievement), the rise of millenarian movements, machine-breaking, or the establishment of extended kinship networks and obligations in the urban-industrial society. The responses may be defensive and protective rather than insurgent; but in an age when anything less than unrestricted enthusiasm for technological and economic growth and expansion is suspected of being Luddite, the distinction between defence and insurgency may be increasingly difficult to establish.

Roy Haddon
York, September 1971

Introduction

The world is entering a new age – the age of total industrialization. Some countries are far along the road; many more are just beginning the journey. But everywhere, at a faster or slower pace, the peoples of the world are on the march towards industrialism. They are launched on a long course that is certain to change their communities into new and vastly different societies whose forms cannot yet be clearly foreseen. The twentieth century is a century of enormous and profound and world-wide transformation.

An age of change is an age of speculation and of decisions. The African nationalist lawyer in prison in Southern Rhodesia, the young intellectual studying at Tokyo University, the economist working on the next five-year plan for India, the party intellectual in Belgrade, the aristocrat in Teheran, the military commander in Karachi, and thousands of others are seeking to divine the course of history and to make decisions in the light of some understanding of the time, the place, the forces, and the goals.

Throughout history men have sought to place the immediate events of their times in a longer vista and to relate the developments in their communities to those in other areas. It is by this process that we give meaning to what happens. The task is never finished, for we must continually reassess perspectives and ideas in the light of changing developments.

It is always difficult for one age to see its own place in the stream of history. The interpretation of contemporaneous events suffers from myopia and distortions. The course and potentialities of the Renaissance in western Europe or the Industrial Revolution in England were not well understood by contemporary observers.

Introduction

Nor is our day likely to perceive with clarity the full implications of the great events of our time.

Yet it is vital to seek coherent interpretations of these developments and to expose each new analysis to critical review and revision. This is more than a speculative exercise. The interpretation placed upon past and present events often determines current policies and courses of action. And these, in turn, give new directions to the ongoing stream of history.

This book is an attempt to analyse and to place in a meaningful setting those contemporaneous events which fall within the authors' particular field of interest: labour economics. We wish to speak in this volume to many persons of many persuasions and in a number of countries. In particular, we hope to speak to the intellectuals, the managers, the government officials, and the labour leaders who today or tomorrow will have a role in running their countries, now in the midst of the great transformation. Originally we planned to speak on the subject of labour-management-state relations alone. But these relations are not discrete phenomena in society; they are, by and large, determinate results rather than determining forces. To study these relations, accordingly, it is necessary to study their contexts. This has led us to examine the industrialization process and to develop a view of industrialism itself.

We offer here, consequently, a view of the nature of the metamorphosis which everywhere is bending and shaping the lives of men into new channels; a view particularly related to the roles of the managers and the managed in new societies, but extending also to the inherent nature of these industrializing societies themselves. To grasp what we wanted to understand we found we needed a more general interpretation of current social processes. This led us to create a framework of our own which draws on the ideas of many others but which is, in its totality, new and different.

It may be of some interest to note how we came to write this book, how we abandoned some ideas along the way, and how we developed new ones to take their place.

As American labour economists, the four of us had done the usual things, particularly in the period of the Second World War and the years immediately following. We had worked for the government in manpower, wage stabilization, and dispute settlement programmes. We had made studies of American wage structures, labour-management relations, and labour markets. We had taught from the standard textbooks; even written some. We had arbitrated labour disputes in many industries and throughout the nation. But it was all largely related to the here and the now – the contemporary American scene.

We had learned from Commons and Perlman about the importance of 'job control' unionism; and from Hoxie about the variety of unions in the United States. But 'job control', rather than being a universal principle, was almost specific to our own country, and business unionism was hardly known elsewhere. Marx had said that the labour movement would get more radical all the time; but, in fact, it was becoming more conservative. 'Should American unions be more job-centred or more active in politics?' – this was the great issue in debates over the 'Theory of the Labour Movement'. The debate divided the Perlmanites and the Marxists; but it became a less exciting debate. The works of standard economists drew our attention to imperfections in the labour market and the role of wages in depression and in inflation. As labour economists we talked about these problems too; but the problems existed in a much larger and a changing context. Yet in most earlier analyses of labour problems there was little historical perspective for the broad sweep of industrialization. Some comparative perspective was, of course, possible and achieved; and we had piecemeal information on industrial relations in a number of countries. The experience of Britain, as the 'mother country', was well impressed on our minds, particularly because of the classic work of the Webbs. But Britain and the United States have served less and less as the models for industrial society and for its labour movements.

We began wondering whether we really understood the American system of industrial relations and particularly its uniqueness. Why was it so different from others elsewhere – Germany, Israel, the Soviet Union, Argentina? And why were they sometimes so different from one another? We became

Introduction

increasingly aware that we had no adequate intellectual framework to understand what happened and why.

The four of us, working at different universities, had come to share the same general concerns. We joined ranks to discuss these problems with Dr Thomas H. Carroll, then Vice-President of the Ford Foundation, who took an interest in our ideas and has continued to do so throughout. We told him we would like to help bring a more international perspective to American labour economics. Through an understanding of other industrial relations systems we might then understand our own better; and, as Americans worked abroad in the labour relations area, there might be, hopefully, some new suggestions for an appreciation of other situations and a consequent greater ability to work within them effectively.

This was the origin of the project which came to be known as the 'Inter-University Study of Labour Problems in Economic Development'. We conducted the project jointly and developed our ideas together. That it progressed at all is a testimony both to our intolerance of each other's pet ideas and to our tolerance for each other as individuals. We had almost endless and often heated discussions in which each developed his views; but they always ended up as 'our views'.

This volume is only one of the many results of the project, as the Appendix demonstrates. Some of several separate studies were undertaken by one or another of the four of us, but most were the work of other scholars drawn from several American universities and from among scholars abroad – in Great Britain, Sweden, Lebanon, India, Egypt, Germany, Italy, Argentina, Brazil, and Chile. We divided the studies into 'country studies' (Japan, West Africa, Indonesia, India, Egypt, and others) and into 'cross-cut studies' (wage structures, management organization and ideologies, the American corporation abroad, industrial relations systems, among others). In addition, there have been a number of conferences conducted in the United States and abroad – Istanbul, Beirut, Teheran, Karachi, New Delhi, Jakarta, Tokyo, Rio de Janeiro, São Paulo, Buenos Aires, Santiago, Bogotá, Lagos. In some of these conferences abroad we brought together in the same room for the first time representatives of labour, management, government, and the universities for discussion of common problems.

Consequently, this book must be viewed as a part of a project. To begin with, it stands as a summary of the views of the four of us at this particular stage. It is not documented in detail because the output of the total project largely supplies the documentation. Beyond that, the ideas are partly ours, but partly they are the summation and restatement of views of other authors in the series and of the many participants in the numerous conferences. They particularly reflect the impact of the late Lloyd Fisher, who was our colleague in planning the study in its initial stages. One of his favourite sayings was that 'truth is more likely to emerge out of error than out of confusion'. Lloyd Fisher was never confused; and we benefited both from the exploration of his errors and the lucidity of his truths.

This volume, moreover, should be considered a first rather than a final effort at outlining a general framework for the reconsideration of industrial relations issues that arise in the course of a society's economic development. Although the scholars who have worked with us on this project have produced a substantial amount of new information, we feel that we have just begun to explore what is still largely frontier territory. Our studies together are, in fact, still continuing; the assessment of manpower needs, the development of human resources, the priorities in reshaping educational systems – these are some of our present concerns in our ongoing desire to relate experiences from many industrial and industrializing nations in a common network of understanding.

In the studies encompassed in this book, we had started with these questions:

1. How is an industrial work force recruited and settled into industrial life?

2. What is the pattern of worker protest in the course of developing an industrial work force?

3. Who gets proprietorship over protest and who controls it?

4. How do the policies and practices of management affect the

development and expression of protest? What are the policies and practices of the state and what effect do they have?

5. How does the culture of a country affect the process of recruiting a labour force and the nature and pattern of labour protest?

We did not end up with these as our central questions. In our exploration of what was to us *terra incognita*, we failed to find some things we expected to find, but we found some other things instead. Among the concepts we discarded along the way were some of the ideas we cherished most dearly at the start.

The major point we 'unlearned' had been one of our central themes at the outset. Worker protest was not such a dominant aspect of industrialization, and it did not have such an effect on the course of society as we once thought. Marx, of course, had said that protest peaked in the inevitable revolution. But it was not only Marx who emphasized labour protest. Labour historians generally had concentrated on strikes and labour's political activity. To the anti-Marxist 'Wisconsin school' of Commons and Perlman also, labour protest was a crucial force. The question was who should control its use – the workers themselves for their own purposes or the intellectuals for theirs?

But labour protest, on a closer look, is on the decline as industrialization around the world proceeds at an ever faster pace. In the mid-twentieth century, workers do not destroy machines. The protest of today is more in favour of industrialization than against it.

In fact, as a number of recent re-examinations of the early stages of British industrialization have stressed, much of the intensified worker protest that has been associated with early industrialization was principally political in origin and reflected desires to widen political participation[1] and was not so closely related to economic development as it once appeared to be.

Instead of concentrating so much on protest, we turned to a more universal phenomenon affecting workers – the inevitable structuring of the managers and the managed in the course of industrialization. Everywhere there develops a complex web of rules binding the worker into the industrial process, to his job, to his community, to patterns of behaviour. Who makes the rules? What is the nature of these rules? Not the handling of protest, but the structuring of the labour force is *the* labour problem in economic development.

Who sets the structure? Commons and Perlman said that the demands of labour today were the rules of society tomorrow. But in some places labour did not participate in rule-making at all and yet the labour force was given its form. Elsewhere, labour organizations participated in the rule-making system but within the context largely given by the surrounding society. Who then gave the context to society? This led us to an examination of the various industrializing élites* – who they were, what strategies they followed, how they approached the worker. To examine the structuring of the labour force is thus to note the political realignments which define the respective roles of different groups in the rule-making processes of the society as well as the evolution of the substantive rules themselves which govern the world of work.

We changed our original views in other less crucial but still important ways. On closer examination, the recruitment and development of a labour force did not seem so difficult as we once thought. Men from the 'bush' drove trucks. Up to a certain level, skills came easily – social as well as technical. Rather than being difficult to recruit, the would-be workers more often were found pounding on the gates to be let inside the new factory system.

Nor were pre-existing cultures serious 'impediments' to economic development. Witnessing some transformations, it would appear that nothing changes so fast as customs. Family and religion, the two immutables, made their adaptations. When cultural factors were significant, their significance was usually greatest at the earlier stages of industrialization. The new culture, even without the draconian methods of the communists, sooner

---

* In this volume an 'industrializing élite' refers to the leaders of the industrialization process. These leaders vary from one society to another, but they include the political leaders, industrial organization builders, top military officers, associated intellectuals, and sometimes leaders of labour organizations. Every industrializing élite will require technicians, administrators, and bureaucrats.

or later took the place of the old. Instead, more crucial determining factors for the formation of the labour force and the development of management appeared to be the population situation, the starting point of industrialization, the pace of economic growth, and the strategies of the industrializing élites.

It was obvious that there was an East and a West. Which would come to dominate the industrializing world? At first this was for us a great policy issue. But the East, it turned out, was several things and not static; the West even more diverse. Instead of two worlds, there were several in the middle of this century of great transformation; and each of these several worlds was in transition. Certainly Britain, the United States, and the Soviet Union were not the only models in the world for the newly emerging economies. We began to develop, in particular, a sense of the importance of nationalism as a very real force at this stage in the history of the world. We also developed a sense of the decline of the importance of competing ideologies. More and more, the questions are technical as well as philosophical. How can this problem best be handled? How can the transition to industrialism best be made, given these conditions? The ideological differences are of great importance; but there is a new realization of the similarity of many problems and of the similarity of some solutions. Rather than two fixed points, there are several changing ones; and technicians are taking their place along with the social theorists.

Like ideologies, the great personality – the one great figure around whom historians so frequently weave their story – began to seem less important. Instead of ideologies and dominant personalities, we became increasingly attentive to the inherent nature of the particular industrializing system and the basic strategy and forces at work within it.

With the gradual abandonment of many of our earlier assumptions, a new design began to emerge from our efforts to organize what we knew about industrialization into the 'universal', the 'related', and the 'unique'.

We found that we could identify a number of processes and trends which occurred everywhere. There was always a web of rules, and some rules were repeated again and again. There were some quite obvious uniformities in the several patterns of industrialization. Generally these uniformities seemed to arise out of the uniformity of the basic technology itself.

Other things, although not universal, began to fall into related patterns. There were plant-oriented organizations of workers in both Germany and Japan; the worker was treated as an 'independent' person in both Great Britain and the United States. Labour organizations were under strong government control in both Egypt and Pakistan. We began to organize this diversity into systems characterized by the nature of the different guiding industrializing élites. We identified five generalized types. Developments in several countries were related to each other because of the similarity of the strategy and approach of their industrializing élites.

There were also developments which were unique to the individual situation. These seemed to have their explanation too, mostly within the cultural pattern of the particular country or in its historical, economic, and demographic setting. We sought to identify the major forces at work.

Thus we identify the universal with the 'logic of industrialization'; the related with the strategies of the 'industrializing élites'; and the unique with specific cultures and environments. In all this we were trying to go beyond the topographical studies describing the lay of the land in the individual countries; to go beyond saying that in Nigeria it was this way and in Turkey that. Looking at one country at a time, each situation appeared historically unique and the totality of the detail was almost incomprehensible. We sought a system of ideas which would help to make it more nearly comprehensible.

Having gradually developed our system of explanation, we proceeded to examine the nature of management, the process of developing the labour force, the response of the workers to the process, and the patterns of labour-management-state relations that emerge.

And, finally, we turned to some long-term speculations about the industrial society of the future. Industrialization today follows several diverse routes. Where do they all lead? Do they converge in the end, and, if so, where? In the contest between the uniformity dictated by the nature of the industrialization process and the diversity of approaches among the industrializing élites, which wins out?

We had begun with five questions centred about the recruitment of a labour force and the development of labour protest. As the project progressed, these gave way to a longer and much broader list. It now seems to us that any general interpretation of the industrialization process and its relation to workers and managers must provide answers to the following groups of questions:

1. Does industrialization have an inner logic? What are the inherent tendencies of the industrialization process, and what impact do they necessarily have upon workers, managers, and governments?

2. Who are the leaders who plan the strategy and direct the industrialization process? What are the implications of each strategy for the relations among workers, managers, and governments? What are the origins and evolutionary trends of these groups?

3. What are the pre-existing cultural factors and the economic constraints that uniquely shape the industrialization process in every nation? What are the major questions which confront a country seeking to industrialize, and how do the ways in which these questions are decided influence the relations among workers, managers, and governments?

4. What is the role of enterprise management in the industrializing society? What are the consequences of alternative policies and philosophies of managements upon economic development and the pattern of industrial relations? How are enterprise managers generated and developed?

5. How is an industrial labour force recruited, developed, and motivated in the course of industrialization?

6. What are some of the universal impacts of the industrialization process upon workers? What are the responses of workers? Who organizes them? Are there any general patterns of worker response that emerge over industrial time?

7. Into what types of institutions are workers organized, and what are the major patterns of interrelations that are established among workers, managers, and governments in the industrialization process?

8. Do industrializing societies, regardless of their origins and leadership, tend to become more similar to each other, or do they retain the variations of their pre-industrial background or develop new diversities?

These eight groups of questions are considered in turn in the eight chapters of this volume. The discussion of these questions taken as a whole is designed to provide a coherent and general framework for the consideration of industrialization's impact on managers and workers.

We offer here an approach to an understanding of industrial relations which seeks to draw on the experience of several countries rather than of one or a few; and a way of looking at the problem which seeks to place labour-management-state relations in the context of the imperatives of industrialization, the desires of the controlling élites, and the demands of the particular environment. We offer this approach as one more attempt to comprehend the swirl of events around us. It is a progress report on our explorations to date, a report that is subject to change, for we have become acutely conscious of our own changing views.

This approach runs against tradition; against Marx, the Webbs, Commons and Perlman, and Mayo, alike. We have redefined the labour problem as the structuring of the managers and the managed under industrialization rather than as the response of unions to capitalism; we have suggested several lines of development rather than a single one – towards communism or socialism or job control or human relations. The followers of each of the standard traditions will of necessity take issue with our approach. We acknowledge this in advance and gladly. They all share, however, our concern to comprehend the world-wide variations in industrial relations systems and the great historical changes affecting them.

We live in a diverse and moving world and the description, alone, of the here and now is not enough.

1 The Logic of Industrialization

Industrialization refers to the actual course of transition from the preceding agricultural or commercial society towards the industrial society.

Great Britain is the first and the classical case of industrialization. 'What is certain is that by 1830 Britain had, in one way or another, obtained a body of wage-paid workers, acclimatized to factory conditions and able to move from place to place, and from employment to employment, as occasion required.'[1] In the years before the First World War, the industrialization process spread widely from its British centre through the western world and to Japan. The international commodity, capital, and labour markets were decisive mechanisms in the propagation of economic development to the United States, Canada, Australia, and parts of South America, not only from Great Britain but also from other emerging industrial countries, notably France and Germany. Industrialization spread out largely by diffusion rather than by independent social invention.

In the inter-war years the Soviet Union embarked on a rapid and harsh industrialization programme, building upon a base from the old régime, under new leadership and creating new institutions. After the Second World War, ambitious industrializing programmes were adopted by nations and regions in Asia, Africa, and the Middle East. The relatively backward areas of economically advanced countries, such as southern Italy, have also embarked on a course towards industrialism.

In the 1850s the world had essentially one model of successful industrialization: that led by middle-class capitalists. Today the newly industrializing countries have a wide variety of prescriptions, a range of political and economic forms, and a growing body of industrializing experience from which to choose. Experimentation with methods of achieving the industrial society continues to grow, as the recent history of India, Yugoslavia, China, Brazil, and Egypt illustrates. The next century is likely to see, despite the obstacles and masses of people involved, an even more dramatic transformation in the countries recently embarked on industrialization than occurred in England in the century after 1750 and in the United States after 1850.

The industrializing nations have a sense of urgency, even of desperation – some more than others. They have come to recognize, as did the Japanese leaders of the Meiji restoration, that industrial technology overwhelms; they must master it or face oblivion. A military defence now requires a relatively advanced industrial technology. The military bases and operations of the great powers have demonstrated to the farthest corners of the globe, no less than the truck and the tin can, the invincibility of the giant of industrialization. Non-industrial societies are ultimately destined to be consigned to the rear ranks of nations.

To recognize the invincibility of the industrialization process is not necessarily to approve or to advocate industrialism. It may be argued from some value systems that economic development is undesirable or secured at too high a price of social and political changes in the traditional society. As individuals we may not approve of all the implications of an industrial society. But an argument against industrialization in general is now futile, for the world has firmly set its face toward the industrial society, and there is no turning back.

Although industrialization follows widely differing patterns in different countries, some characteristics of the industrialization process are common to all. These 'universals' arise from the imperatives intrinsic to the process. They are the prerequisities and the concomitants of industrial evolution. Once under way, the logic of industrialization sets in motion many trends which do more or less violence to the traditional pre-industrial society.

In the actual course of history, the inherent tendencies of the industrial process are never likely to be fully realized. The pre-existing societies and conditions shape and constrain these inherent features. The leaders of economic development influence the directions and the rate of industrial growth; and the existing resources and the contemporaneous developments in other countries are also likely to affect actual events. These influences will be important in every case of industrialization. They do not, however, deny the validity of searching for some of the fundamental directions in which industrialization will haul and pull. Indeed, an understanding of these tendencies is requisite to a full appreciation of the influence of historical, cultural, and economic factors on the actual course of industrialization.

What, then, are some of the imperatives of the industrialization process? Given the character of science and technology and the requirements inherent in modern methods of production and distribution, what may be deduced as to the necessary or the likely characteristics of workers and managers and their interrelations? What are the inherent implications of industrialization for the work place and the larger community? What, in sum, do the actual histories of those societies with either brief or more extensive industrializing experience suggest about the principal forces implicit in an 'industrial revolution'?

The Industrial Work Force

[The workman] becomes an appendage of the machine, and it is only the most simple, most monotonous, and most easily acquired knack, that is required of him (*Manifesto*, p. 65) . . . Hence, in the place of the hierarchy of specialized workmen that characterizes manufacture, there steps, in the automatic factory, a tendency to equalize and reduce to one and the same level every kind of work that has to be done by the minders of the machines (*Capital*, p. 420) . . . The more modern industry becomes developed, the more is the labour of men superseded by that of women (*Manifesto*, p. 66) . . . The various interests and conditions of life within the ranks of the proletariat are more and more equalized, in proportion as machinery obliterates all distinctions of labour, and nearly everywhere reduces wages to the same low level (*Manifesto*, p. 69) . . . The essential division is, into workmen who are actually employed on the machines (among whom are included a few who look

43

after the engine), and into mere attendants (almost exclusively children) of these workmen ... In addition to these two principal classes, there is a numerically unimportant class of persons, whose occupation is to look after the whole of the machinery and repair it from time to time, such as engineers, mechanics, joiners, etc. (*Capital*, p. 420).[2]

These quotations from the *Manifesto* and *Capital* envisage as the consequence of capitalist production the destruction of the hierarchy of specialized workmen in pre-industrial society and the subsequent levelling of skill, a minor number of skilled labour, engineers, and managers, and the use of women and children for a growing number of unskilled tending and feeding jobs. The historical evidence of the past century, however, suggests a quite different pattern of evolution for the industrial work force.

Industrialization in fact develops and depends upon a concentrated, disciplined industrial work force – a work force with new skills and a wide variety of skills, with high skill levels and constantly changing skill requirements.

The industrialization process utilizes a level of technology far in advance of that of earlier societies. Moreover, the associated scientific revolution generates continual and rapid changes in technology which have decisive consequences for workers, managers, the state, and their interrelations.

The industrial system requires a wide range of skills and professional competency broadly distributed throughout the work force. These specialized human resources are indispensable to the science and technology of industrialism, and their development is one of the major problems of a society engaged in industrialization. The absence of a highly qualified labour force is as serious an impediment as a shortage of capital goods. The professional, technical, and managerial component of the labour force is particularly strategic since it largely carries the responsibility of developing and ordering the manual and clerical components.

Mobility and the Open Society

The dynamic science and technology of the industrial society creates frequent changes in the skills, responsibilities, and occupations of the work force. Some are made redundant and new ones are created. The work force is confronted with repeated object lessons of the general futility of fighting these changes, and comes to be reconciled, by and large, to repeated changes in ways of earning a living. But there may be continuing conflict over the timing of change and the division of the gains. The industrial society requires continual training and retraining of the work force; the content of an occupation or job classification is seldom set for life, as in the traditional society. Occupational mobility is associated with a high degree of geographical movement in a work force and with social mobility in the larger community both upwards and downwards.

One indication of the extent of occupational shifts which occur in the course of industrialization is reflected in Table 1 for the United States in the period 1900–60.

Industrialization tends to produce an open society, inconsistent with the assignment of managers or workers to occupations or to jobs by traditional caste, by racial groups, by sex, or by family status. There is no place for the extended family; it is on balance an impediment to requisite mobility. The primary family provides a larger and more mobile labour force. The function of the family under industrialism is constricted: it engages in very little production; it provides little, if any, formal education and occupational training; the family business is substantially displaced by professional management. '. . . Economic growth and a transference of women's work from the household to the market go closely hand in hand.'[3] In the industrial society the primary family is largely a source of labour supply, a unit of decision-making for household expenditures and savings, and a unit of cultural activity.

This society is always in flux and in motion. As a result of its science and technology, it is continuously rearranging what people do for a living, where they work and where they live, and on what they spend their incomes. Their children come to expect to live different lives from their parents. But mobility in the industrial society is not random; it comes to be organized and governed by a complex of rules of the work community.

Table 1. OCCUPATIONAL DISTRIBUTION OF
EMPLOYMENT, UNITED STATES, 1900–60

(Thousands of people, 14 years of age and older)

	1960	1900	change 1900–60	% increase 1900–60
Total	66,159	29,030	+37,129	128
OCCUPATIONAL GROUP				
Total farm employment	5,037	10,888	−5,851	−54
Total non-farm employment	61,122	18,142	+42,980	237
White-collar workers	28,507	5,115	+23,392	457
Professional, technical, and kindred workers	7,418	1,234	+6,184	501
Managers, officials, and proprietors	7,032	1,697	+5,335	314
Clerical and kindred workers	9,710	877	+8,833	1,007
Sales workers	4,347	1,306	+3,041	233
Blue-collar workers	24,280	10,401	+13,879	133
Craftsmen, foremen, and kindred workers	8,606	3,062	+5,544	181
Operatives and kindred workers	11,988	3,720	+8,268	222
Labourers	3,686	3,620	+66	2
Service workers	8,335	2,626	+5,709	217
Service workers excluding household workers	6,134	1,047	+5,087	486
Private household workers	2,201	1,579	+622	39

Source: U.S. Department of Labor, Bureau of Labor Statistics, *Employment and Earnings, 1960*; and U.S. Department of Commerce, 'Occupational Trends in the United States', Bureau of the Census Working Paper No. 5, Washington, 1958, pp. 6–7.

Education – The Handmaiden of Industrialism

Industrialization requires an educational system functionally related to the skills and professions imperative to its technology. Such an educational system is not primarily concerned with conserving traditional values or perpetuating the classics; it does not adopt a static view of society, and it does not place great emphasis on training in the traditional law. The higher educational system of the industrial society stresses the natural sciences, engineering, medicine, managerial training – whether private or public – and administrative law. It must steadily adapt to new disciplines and fields of specialization. There is a relatively smaller place for the humanities and arts, while the social sciences are strongly related to the training of managerial groups and technicians for the enterprise and the government. The increased leisure time of industrialism, however, can afford a broader public appreciation of the humanities and the arts.

As in all societies, there is debate over what the youth is to be taught. The largest part of the higher educational system tends to be specialized and designed to produce the very large volume of professionals, technicians, and managers required in the industrial society. There is a case for some degree of generality in the educational system because of the rapidity of change and growth of knowledge during the course of a career. A technically trained work force needs to be able to follow and to adapt to changes in its specialities and to learn to shift to new fields. Generality is also requisite for those coordinating and leading the specialists.

The industrial society tends to create an increasing level of general education for all citizens, not only because it facilitates training and flexibility in the work force, but also because, as incomes rise, natural curiosity increases the demand for formal education, and education becomes one of the principal means of vertical social mobility. It will be observed that the industrial society tends to transform drastically the educational system of the pre-industrial society. Further, the high level of technical and general education requisite to the industrial society cannot but have significant consequences for political life. The means of mass communication play a significant role both in raising standards of general education and in conditioning political activity and shaping political control.

The Structure of the Labour Force

The labour force of the industrial society is highly differentiated by occupations and job classifications, by rates of compensation, and by a variety of relative rights and duties in the work place community. It has a form and structure vastly different from the more homogeneous labour force of the traditional society.

The variety of skills, responsibilities, and working conditions at the work place requires an ordering or a hierarchy. There are successive levels of authority of managers and the managed, as well as considerable specialization of function at each level of the hierarchy. Job evaluation and salary plans symbolize the ordering of the industrial work force by function and compensation.[4]

The work force in the industrial society is also structured in the sense that movement within the work community is subjected to a set of rules; hiring, temporary lay-offs, permanent redundance, promotions, shift changes, transfers, and retirement are applied to individual workers and managers according to their position, station, seniority, technical competency, or some other measure of status in a group rather than in random fashion. Not all jobs are open at all time to all bidders. The ports of entry into an enterprise are limited, and priorities in selection are established. Movement tends to be relatively easier within than among job families in an enterprise. Delineation of job families may also vary and will often depend upon whether movement involves promotion, lay-off, or transfer.

The industrial system changes the hours of work that prevail in predominantly agricultural societies. The silent night of pre-industrial society yields to the sometimes insistent requirements of continuous operations. The work force is geared to shift operations and the community to a changed attitude towards working at night. Even the holidays and religious days of the traditional society do not escape transformation.

Scale of Society

The technology and specialization of the industrial society are necessarily and distinctively associated with large-scale organizations. Great metropolitan areas arise in the course of industrialization. The national government machinery expands significantly. Economic activity is carried on by large-scale enterprises which require extensive coordination of managers and the managed. A wide variety of rules and norms are essential to secure this coordination.

Urban Dominance

The industrial society is an urban society, concentrated in metropolitan areas with their suburbs and satellite communities. While substantial cities have arisen in pre-industrial societies as commercial and religious centres,[5] urban ways come to permeate the whole of industrial society. Rapid means of transportation and mass communication reduce the variance of subcultures, particularly those based on geography and the contrast between farm and city.

In the industrial society agriculture is simply another industry; it is not a 'way of life' to be preserved for its own value or because it constituted a traditional and antecedent form of society. Agricultural units of production (farms) tend to be specialized according to products, and the general farm, substantially self-sufficient, has little place. Indeed, the proportion of the work force engaged in agriculture is a rough index of the degree of industrialization of a society.[6] 'To the economic eye a community which needs to have the majority of its people working on the land is merely demonstrating its inefficiency.'[7]

Table 2 shows the relative role of agriculture in a number of countries; it reflects the low proportion of agriculture in the economically advanced countries and the high percentage of agricultural population in the less economically advanced societies.

Industrialization tends to promote the values, folkways, and heroes of the city and to weaken those of the farm. Even the art and music of the highly industrialized society can be expected to be substantially different from that of the pre-industrial society.

Table 2. AGRICULTURAL POPULATION

Country	% of active population in agriculture
United Kingdom (1951)	5
United States (1950)	12
Sweden (1950)	20
W. Germany (1950)	23
France (1957)	26
Italy (1957)	31
Japan (1957)	39
U.S.S.R. (1950)	50
Brazil (1950)	58
Egypt (1947)	65
India	71
Iran (*c.* 1953)	80
Afghanistan (1954)	85
Nyasaland (1949)	90
Nepal (1952–4)	93

Source: Norton Ginsburg, *Atlas of Economic Development*, Research Paper No. 68, Department of Geography, Chicago, The University of Chicago Press, 1961, pp. 32–3.

Large role for Government

The industrial society is necessarily characterized by a substantial range and scale of activities by the government. In a society of advanced technology there are a larger number of activities for government; for instance, roads and highways, airports, the regulation of traffic, radio and television. Urban development has the same consequences. Technology also creates a more complex military establishment, extending in many directions the activities of government. The more integrated character of the world increases governmental activities in the area of international relations. The scale of some scientific applications and the capital needs of new technologies, such as atomic energy development or space exploration, increase the scope of public agencies. As income rises, the demand of consumers may be for services largely provided by governments, such as education, parks, roads, and health services.

The role of government in countries entering upon industrialization, regardless of political form, may therefore be expected to be greater than before. There is wisdom in the observation: '. . . it is extremely unlikely that the highly modernized systems of the world today could have developed indigenously on the basis of any system other than ones that relied very heavily indeed on private individual operations, and it is extremely unlikely that latecomers can carry out such development without relying very heavily on public operations.'[8]

The industrial society and individual freedom, however, are not necessarily to be regarded as antagonists. A high degree of discipline in the work place and a large range of governmental activities is fully consistent with a larger freedom for the individual in greater leisure, a greater range of choice in occupations and place of residence, a greater range of alternatives in goods and services on which to use income, and a very wide range of subgroups or associations in which to choose participation. It is a mistake to regard the industrial society as antithetical to individual freedom by citing ways in which the scope of public and private governments has increased without also noting ways in which industrialization expands individual freedom.

THE WEB OF RULES. The production of goods and services in the industrial society is largely in the hands of large-scale organizations. They consist of hierarchies composed of relatively few managers and staff advisers and a great many to be managed. The managers and the managed are necessarily connected by an elaborate web of rules that is made the more intricate and complex by technology, specialization, and the large scale of operations.

At any one time, the rights and duties of all those in the hierarchy must be established and understood by all.

The web of rules of the work place concerns compensation, discipline, lay-offs, transfers and promotions, grievances, and a vast array of matters, some common to all work places and others specialized for the type of activity – factory, airline, railroad, mine, or office – and to the specific establishment. The rules also establish norms of output, pace, and performance. Moreover, the web of rules is never static, and procedures arise for the orderly change of these rules. The industrial system creates an elaborate 'government' at the work place and in the work community. It is often observed that primitive societies have extensive rules, customs, and taboos, but a study of the industrial society reflects an even greater complex and a quite different set of detailed rules.

The web of rules depends partially on those technological features and market or budgetary constraints of the work place which are generally common to all types of industrializing countries, and partially on the particular resources and the political and economic forms of the country. The relative strength of these factors, and their mode of interaction, is important to an understanding of any particular industrial society. Cultural and national differences are less significant to the substantive web of rules, the more a country has industrialized. The impact of cultural and national heritage is more clearly discerned in the differences to be found in the process for formulating and promulgating the rules affecting men at work than in the content of the rules themselves.

The tug of industrialization – whatever these initial differences – is towards a greater role for the state in an eventual pluralistic rule-making system. The state does not evolve simply as a class apparatus and instrument for the oppression of another class, as Marx asserted.[9] Nor does it 'wither away' in the ultimate 'good society'.[10] Governments have a significant role in determining the substantive rules of the work community or in establishing the procedures and responsibilities of those with this power. In the highly industrialized society, enterprise managers, workers, and the government tend to share in the establishment and administration of the rules. The industrial relations system of the industrial society is genuinely tripartite.

Consensus in Society

The industrial society, like any established society, develops a distinctive consensus which relates individuals and groups to each other and provides an integrated body of ideas, beliefs, and value judgements. Various forms of the industrial society may create some distinctive ideological features, but all industrialized societies have some common values.

In the industrial society science and technical knowledge have high values, and scientists and technologists enjoy high prestige and rewards.

Taboos against technical change are eliminated, and high values are placed on being 'modern' and 'up-to-date', and in 'progress', for their own sake.

Education also has a high value because of the fundamental importance of science and the utility of education as a means of social mobility.

The industrial society is an open community encouraging occupational and geographic mobility and social mobility. Industrialization calls for flexibility and competition; it is against tradition and status based upon family, class, religion, race, or caste.

It is pluralistic, with a great variety of associations and groups and of large-scale operations; the individual is attached to a variety of such groups and organizations.

Goods and services have a high value in the industrial society, and the 'demonstration effect' is very strong on the part of individuals and groups seeking to imitate the standards of those with higher income levels.

The work force is dedicated to hard work, a high pace of work, and a keen sense of individual responsibility for performance of assigned norms and tasks. Industrial countries may differ with respect to the ideals and drives which underlie devotion to duty and responsibility for performance, but industrialization requires an ideology and an ethic which motivate individual workers. Strict supervision imposed on a lethargic work force will not suffice; personal responsibility for performance must be implanted within workers, front-line supervisors, and top managers.[11]

Industrialism and Industrial Man

It is not by accident that the leaders of industrializing countries today exhort their peoples to hard work. 'This generation is sentenced to hard labour' (Nehru). 'We shall march forward as one people who have vowed to work and to proceed on a holy march of industrializing . . .' (Nasser). 'The chief preoccupation of every Communist régime between the Elbe and the China Sea is how to make people work; how to induce them to sow, harvest, mine, build, manufacture and so forth. It is the most vital problem which confronts them day in, day out, and it shapes their domestic policies and to a considerable extent their attitude towards the outside world.'[12] There are many counterparts for the Protestant ethic.

The western tradition has been to harness the drive of individual self-interest; the communist method combines in varying proportions at varying times, money incentives, devotion to a revolutionary creed, and the compulsion of terror. Regardless of means, industrialization entails a pace of work and an exercise of personal responsibility seldom known in economic activity in traditional societies.

The function of making explicit a consensus and of combining discrete beliefs and convictions into a reasonably consistent body of ideas is the task of intellectuals in every society. There are probably more intellectuals in the industrial society because of the higher levels of general education, income, and leisure. There are also new patrons to the intellectuals – the university, enterprise, labour organization, voluntary association and government – in place of the old aristocratic patrons. The function of formulating and restating the major values, premises, and consensus of a society from time to time, of reconciling the new industrial processes with the old order, plays a significant role in industrialization. The intellectuals accordingly are an influential group in the creation and moulding of industrial society.

World-Wide Industrialism

The industrial society is world-wide. The science and the technology on which it is based speak in a universal language. '[Science] is nonnational, nonlocal and, although one would not say non-cultural, singularly independent of the form of government, the immediate tradition, or the affective life of a people.'[13] There can be few technological secrets, at least for very long, as the atomic field has well demonstrated. The industrial society is an integrated world, to use Myrdal's phrase.[14] The differences in language and dress, which themselves are much reduced, are in contrast to the common characteristics produced by the automobile, airplane, tin can, electric lights and power, and other features of industrialization. It is a common experience that the metropolitan centres of the world appear so familiar and so similar. The same might be said more often of the work places of modern industry, save that they are much less frequented by tourists and travellers.

Industrialization spreads out from centres of advanced technology in a variety of ways. The normal channels of trade in the markets for commodities, services, and capital may not be relatively as significant today as they were in the propagation of industrialization from England, Germany, and France before the First World War, but they are still important. Governmental development programmes constitute a channel of growing importance. The training of students, the temporary resort to foreign experts, and the demonstration effect produced by exchanges of persons are further means of spreading the industrial society. The character of military defence and the world-wide scope of military conflict have been a significant means of diffusing modern technology. The training of a work force to build bases and to maintain motor vehicles and aircraft involves the establishment of important beach-heads for industrialization.

The extreme discrepancies in the methods of production which now exist between more and less highly industrialized countries will tend to decrease over time, although significant differences in income levels and in the specialization of activity are likely to remain for a very long time.

Industrialization transforms an old society or an empty country and creates a new form of society, some of whose major characteristics have been outlined in this chapter. Pre-existing conditions will often obscure the underlying processes at work to some degree.

Industrialism and Industrial Man

But the logic of industrialization prevails eventually, and such similarities as it decrees will penetrate the outermost points of its universal sphere of influence. Each industrialized society is more like every other industrialized society – however great the differences among them may be – than any industrial society is like any pre-industrial society.

Not one, however, but several roads lead into this new industrial society.

Chart 1. The Logic of Industrialization

Work force	Increased skills and widening range of skills.
	Increasing occupational and geographic mobility.
	Higher levels of education more closely related to industrial function.
	Structured work force.
Scale of society	Urbanization and decline of agriculture as a way of life.
	Larger role for government.
Consensus in society	Increasing ideological consensus in a pluralistic society.
World-wide industrialism	Industrial society spreads out from the centres of advanced technology.

2   The Industrializing Élites

Industrialization is introduced by either native or alien minorities, by groups of men who seek to change or to conquer the society through the superiority of the new means of production. A war between the old system and the new takes place whether the conquest is internal or external. The new, in the long run, is always bound to win. The dramatic issue is not whether industrialization will emerge supreme but rather which minority will assume and maintain control of the process and what its strategic approach to the organization of industrialization will be.

The ideological conflict which is so characteristic of our age is a natural accompaniment of the diverse routes taken toward industrial society under the leadership of diverse minorities. Contending ideologies are fashioned as men seek to guide this historical process by conscious effort, to explain it to themselves, and to justify it to others. But the ideologies are used not only to guide, to understand and to justify, but also as weapons of war among the proponents of the several routes; and thus the inherent conflict is sharpened and the lines are hardened. The routes become crusades as well as diverging pathways. Men debate and protest and fight with each other almost every step of the way. This has been a large share of the history of the past century and will be a good share of the history of the next.

The Dynamic Élites and Social Conquest

Industrialization is always of necessity undertaken by a minority group – the colonial company, the indigenous entrepreneur, the government agency, the military unit. It cannot come into full bloom overnight except, perhaps, in small societies with unusual natural resources which attract external capital, like Kuwait. Usually industrialization starts in a restricted geographical area or sector as a small subculture, which then spreads until it is the dominating system of production affecting almost all the relations of men within the society.[1]

At the start of the industrialization process there are some important minorities which do not wish to move in this direction at all. They are the static minorities, usually found among the leaders of the older society: the landowners, the 'medicine men', the higher artisans, the aristocrats. They can delay and thus affect the location within society of the new initiative, but they cannot prevent the transformation in the long run; and their delaying efforts are only likely to make the inevitable transition more traumatic.

The technology of industrialization requires dynamic élites for its introduction and extension into a society. The human agents who successfully introduce and extend the new technology come to have great influence in the society. They can guide and direct it within reasonable limits to suit their wishes.

Thus a crucial factor in any industrializing society is which élites become the initiators of industrialization, and how they view their role and the nature of the 'good society'. The universal questions are these:

1. Who leads the industrialization march?
2. What is the purpose of the march?
3. How is the march organized?

The answers to these three basic questions depend in part on the conjuncture of economic and cultural variables that gives rise to the development of a particular élite and that shapes its values and strategies. The answers also depend in some measure on the aspirations of the newly emerging group of industrial employees, ever more numerous and more powerful. They wish progress, and they also wish participation. Some élites promise more of one or the other or of both than do others. Much of the turmoil of the last century was caused, and much of the turmoil of the next century will be caused, as this group debates its preferences, as it changes or is led to change its preferences, and attempts to assert them. The industrial workers, however, are usually a conditioning, not an initiating influence. But they can have a clear impact on the selection, the performance, and the survival of the dynamic élites. The peasants, however, are, except at certain times of crisis, a more passive force in the industrialization process and are also a declining element.

To this point in history there have been five generalized types of élites who may take the leadership of the industrialization process:

1. The middle class
2. The dynastic leaders
3. The colonial administrators
4. The revolutionary intellectuals
5. The nationalist leaders

The third group, at least in its pure form, is particularly transitory in its span of leadership; and the longer range competitors are probably found among the other four. But they also may turn out to be transient instruments of the transformation; for industrialization is relatively new to man and what form it will take in the more distant future can only be a matter of speculation.

Each of these élite groups may be composed of several elements – political leaders, industrial managers, military officers, religious figures, top civil servants, leaders of labour organizations, associated intellectuals, among others. Thus when we speak of a certain élite we refer more to the character of its central orientation than to the individuals who constitute it at any moment of time.

Each of these élite groups has a strategy by which it seeks to order the surrounding society in a consistent fashion. This strategic perspective, if the society is to end up with a cultural consistency, must pervade the entire culture. Otherwise there is internal tension, conflict, and restlessness. It is partly because the colonial managers do not have in their positions and in their outlooks the possibilities for developing a cultural consistency that they are perishable elements; their base of operation is too foreign and too narrow.

An internal conflict between the new culture, with its dominant theme set by the industrializing élite, and the old culture is inevitably fought on many fronts – the economic, political, religious, intellectual. An external conflict among alternative ideologies of industrialization tends to be fought on all fronts at once. Consistency at home and compatibility abroad, since industrialization will come to be world-wide, are two imperatives felt in greater or lesser degrees by each dominant group; imperatives which press on the instinct to survive. Each industrializing system becomes a 'way of life', and a 'way of life' demands internal acceptance and external protection. The only ultimate external protection is a world organized along reasonably compatible lines. These are the internal and external aspects of the historical battle over the character of the industrial society.

Management types, protest forms, labour organization typologies, rule-making relationships, taken as individual phenomena may appear largely unrelated to each other and explained singly only by history. But they are all bound more or less firmly together by an internally consistent theme, as set by these five alternative approaches to industrialization, and the elucidation of this consistency is the first step in the analysis of the separate types, forms, typologies, and relationships. All things are not possible in all situations.

To understand the different forms and paces of industrialization and their varying impacts on labour and management, we need first to take a closer look at the five generalized types of élites. What are their distinguishing attitudes and characteristics? How do they typically work – and with what results?

In this initial discussion of these 'ideal' types, we describe the major strategies of industrialization as they appear to have emerged to date and are currently discernible. The five types are depicted here essentially as snapshots of a contemporary slice of time – from approximately post-World War I to the present – and in the poses that are relevant for analysis today and for projection from this date forward. These ideal types of industrializing strategies ignore much important detail in individual cases. Most actual cases are mixtures, and several societies have changed and will continue to change their essential type over time. Moreover, some élites have developed at an earlier point in history than others and would be described somewhat differently then than now. Consequently, comparison at the same point of time imputes no 'timeless' value judgements relating to each of the strategies. But most individual cases may be understood better in relation to one of these types. They abstract from reality, but by reducing complexity they can also illuminate reality. They give order to our task of comprehending the forms of industrialization and their varying impacts in the area of labour-management-state relationships; and they provide a base for judging the future turn of events in a world embarked on the quest for effective industrial evolution.

The Middle Class and the Open Market

The human agents here are members of a new class rising, as in England, in opposition to the old élite, but able to live in co-existence with it. They are most likely to be drawn initially from existing commercial or artisan groups often composed of religious or national minorities. Such groups, never entirely integrated into the old society, are sensitive to the gains to be had from the new means of production. They do not advance on the wings of a rigid ideology; rather they tend to be pragmatic. They favour a structure of economic and political rules which best permits them to pursue their gains. This brings them into conflict with the old order, but they seek to impose their will piecemeal, and their assault is carried out through concentration on specific issues rather than as an explicit social revolution. In their conflict with the old order, the new group may find allies among the intellectuals wanting more freedom and the workers wanting more opportunity, particularly for political participation.

The middle-class ideology is economically individualistic and politically egalitarian. Each individual is held to be morally accountable to and for himself, within the limits of the law, which is supposed to apply equally to all members of the community. Each man's responsibility begins and ends with the injunction to make the best use of his opportunities. In practice the rigour of this doctrine is softened by the social and religious beliefs embodied in the culture, but the emphasis is on progress and on the individual. Each man is his own 'Lord Spiritual'. Instead of the old and the community, there is the new and the self.

Upward mobility in society is fairly directly related to knowledge of opportunities and capacity to make use of them. Family background and wealth are important, not for themselves, but only in so far as they tend to affect the range of opportunities open to men. No one is born to rule, but some must manage; and management relies more on policies and rules than it does on personal preference. The system is based heavily on consent, and the appeal in politics and in economics is to self-advantage. Every manager is, in part, a politician adjusting, within the rules of the game but with some rapidity, to the pressures of individuals, groups, and institutions. Mobility and self-interest are at the centre of the social process, in practice and in theory.

The 'good society' is an indistinct and shifting shadow. It is more a series of means than an end; and the means are reason, self-interest, and a relatively broad toleration of dissent. Relative emphasis is placed on many centres of decision-making power and on a system of checks and balances. The checks and balances in political life involve the separation of church and state and of the legislative, administrative, and judicial authorities. In economic life, economic units are typically separated into discrete and competitive entities.

In industrial relations, the worker is relatively independent and is expected to be self-sufficient economically and politically. '. . . He knows that he is the political equal of his employer and he has no intention of subordinating himself by incurring a debt of gratitude. He is in the workshop by virtue of a business transaction and he does not consider the personnel as a family group of which the entrepreneur should be the patriarchal head.'[2] The worker may indeed be in organized opposition to the enterprise manager – some degree of conflict is built into and accepted by the system; and a whole series of economic and political institutions is in fact devised to channel and settle such conflicts. Rule-making may be more or less equally shared – by management, by organizations of workers, and by the state in a pluralistic arrangement.

Progress is taken for granted in the belief that it flows naturally out of the day-to-day decisions of many people. It should not be retarded nor should it be forced unduly by state action. The incentive of self-interest in a competitive and materialistic society is relied upon as a sufficient spur to progress. Thus economic advance is not centrally planned. Such a system will be intermediate in its record of economic growth. It will not be held back by the built-in resistances of some dynastic élite systems but it also is not geared to the forced-draft industrialization of which the revolutionary-intellectual type is capable.

Such a system depends for its more specific aspects on its origin. It may find its origin in an established society (England, Sweden, India). Here there will be more initial conflict between the old élite and the new entrepreneurs,[3] and also more of an attitude of class warfare between capital and labour because of the heritage of ruling-class attitudes. The old generally will have a greater hold and the new will have to struggle harder to gain acceptance. All this conduces to more participation by the state as the arbiter of these conflicts and as a carrier of the aspirations of the working class.

Such a system may originate in a new and relatively classless society (United States, Canada, and New Zealand). From the beginning there is more social mobility and a freer hand for progress. The middle class reigns supreme and eventually nearly everyone is or believes himself to be middle-class; and the market is as open as markets are ever likely to be. This is the more or less pure model of the 'middle class and the open market'; and economic progress is likely to be reasonably rapid – the new business and industrial class is given its head. Internal cultural consistency is comparatively readily attained; in contrast to the case of origin in a class society, where as many as three subcultures may develop beside each other – the subcultures of the aristocracy, the business class, and the working class.

The evolution of the new industrial managers may not be the gradual process experienced in England and the United States. It may instead be abrupt, as in Pakistan; and this is an increasingly important phenomenon. In a rapidly industrializing nation, if the state is not to be the universal entrepreneur, private entrepreneurs must be deliberately developed. They are most likely to be drawn from among the larger merchants who have some capital and some managerial experience. Almost overnight, instead of operating a shop, they are running a modern factory. But they have not had time to accumulate experience, and this leads to inefficient use of the new facilities. Nor have they had an opportunity to change their orientation from concentration on a quick profit to the development of a continuing organization concentrating on production, and this leads to an attitude of short-term exploitation of the new situation. Nor has a competitive market grown up around them to restrict greed and compel efficiency, and so the state must step in to control the situation. The state may have an additional claim to control through its partial provision of the necessary capital.

In these cases, the new industrial managers must be as much oriented towards the state as towards the market – towards the bureaucrat as toward the consumer; and stifling bureaucratic controls and the possibility of corruption may be among the most insistent problems. Middle-class leadership so created is subject to special strains – the task of learning its new assignments and new attitudes quickly, the likelihood of worker and consumer protest against 'exploitation', and the complications associated with dealing with the state as well as the market. The success of the new class will depend, in part, on how fast the industrialization proceeds and thus how soon the discipline of the market can replace that of the state in controlling prices and forcing efficiency. Only when the market has largely taken over as the regulating mechanism can this new class be certain of its future.

Middle-class leadership, extending as it does from the merchant just reaching into production in a newly industrializing economy to the formally trained manager of the long established enterprise in the highly organized society, covers a wide span of managerial types and attitudes. Both the men and their environments are widely different; but there is the same search for profits, the same acceptance of a role for private initiative, the same emphasis on piecemeal adaptation and change. Managerial performance, worker attitudes, and labour-management relations, however, will vary quite considerably.

The Dynastic Élite and the Paternal Community

The members of the dynastic élite are originally drawn from the landed or commercial aristocracy, since agriculture and commerce are usually the pre-existing forms of production. Less often, they are drawn from the military caste (as the samurai were in Japan), a religious hierarchy, the government bureaucracy, or tribal chieftains. This élite group is held together by a common allegiance to the established order. New recruits may be added from time to time from other strata of society, but the emphasis is on a closed system based on family and on class. Its orientation is predominantly towards tradition and the preservation of tradition.

The 'realists' within this élite acknowledge the rise of the industrial system and its eventual dominance. They seek to identify the essentials of the past and to preserve them in the face of the new form of production. However, they will make whatever compromises are necessary to permit industrialization to proceed under their guidance. This was essentially the approach taken by the samurai during the Meiji restoration which sparked Japan's drive to industrialize.

By contrast, the 'traditionalists' in the group may denounce and seek to fend off the new industrial system as in some Latin American countries such as Peru, or as in Iran, where the '1000 families' resist industrialization's violation of tradition. Thus the 'realists' and the 'traditionalists' in the early stages may find themselves locked in combat. Only if the 'realists' triumph (and they will start out as a minority within the élite) can this élite avoid liquidation at worst or oblivion at best.

A dynastic élite may also include 'decadents' who are oriented towards personal indulgence, which may be expressed in high living, corruption, attachment to a foreign culture, or personal security through foreign investment, rather than towards national tradition or national progress. Only if the 'realists' are dominant, and are also strong, competent, and patriotic, is a dynastic élite likely to master the industrialization process, as in Japan and Germany.

If the 'realists' get control of the industrialization process, their approach to it is quite distinctive.

The emphasis is on personal rule which involves perpetuation of the family which is 'born to rule' and of the class within which alliances are made and from which managerial recruits are usually obtained.

The system rests on tradition but ultimately on the use of power. Such a system under sufficient pressure can become fascist in an effort to maintain internal control, since fascism is oriented towards the élite and the use of force and action. But the normal emphasis is on the approach of the patriarch towards his family or the benevolent monarch towards his subjects.

The 'good society' cherishes the virtues and the symbols of the past and its institutions – the family, the church, private property, the national state. It changes from past forms only to the extent necessary for survival. Consequently, it is inherently anti-intellectual except for the 'Lords Spiritual' who interpret and reinterpret the essence of the past and assess the present in the light of this essence. These 'Lords Spiritual' may hold a high place in the society.

Law and order and firm administration are prized in this system, and there are often cartels and a mixture of 'private' and 'public' affairs in the conduct of economic life.

The political system is paternalistic and so also is the economic system. The worker is to be cared for and in return he is expected to be loyal. He is dependent on the manager for his welfare and his leadership.

The idea of tension between the enterprise manager and the worker is abhorred; and 'harmony' is devoutly sought.

Rule-making is held, as far as possible, solely in the hands of management; prerogatives of management are sacred.

The social and economic systems alike have a clearly stratified hierarchy of superiors and subordinates and a reciprocal series of duties and obligations.

Industrial progress will be no faster than necessary to meet the pressures placed on the élite. These pressures may be external or internal, and they may produce quite different results. If external from foreign economic or political and military competition, they may stimulate rapid economic progress. Germany and Japan again come to mind as examples. The dynastic élite, given strong incentives, can select goals and has the mechanism to achieve them. It may exhibit substantial internal change, although the motto is likely to be 'no faster and no farther than necessary'. If the pressure is internal, it is less likely to arise from economic competition (since the system is usually structured against it) than from political pressure from a class-conscious working class or a strong group of independent and alienated intellectuals, or both. Checked and balanced this way, the dynastic élite may be unable to maintain its control over the total culture or wield enough power to be able to set and attain economic goals. Consequently, internal pressure is likely to be against economic progress. External pressure aids economic progress and internal pressure supports political instability.

The Colonial Administrator and the 'Home Country'

The colonial élite has been a major instrument for the introduction of industrialization in many areas of the world – supplying capital, techniques, and leadership. The colonial administrator, however, is an alien 'alien'; he not only represents a new system of production but also an external society. Consequently he must carry the weight of two justifications – the justification of the new system and also of his personal intrusion into the indigenous culture. Thus his role as prime mover can be an unusually difficult one.

The other aspect of the externality of the colonial approach is the essential service to the home country rather than to the indigenous population. The home country may be served by a supply of raw materials, a market for finished products, a source of profits, an outlet for 'younger sons' or surplus population; or by an opportunity to extend an ideology and political and military suzerainty. An alien élite and an alien purpose are the twin features of all colonialism; and because of this foreignness, the use of force is latent or actual in the direction of the society.

We are not concerned here with simple political control (Cyprus),[4] or with the populating and industrializing of largely empty lands (Canada, Australia). Nor are we concerned with foreign investment, foreign management, and foreign technical assistance under the rules and within the system of the indigenous population; for this is a separate phenomenon. Rather our concern is with foreign control and administration of a society in the course of industrialization.

The colonial approach to industrialization has been and is a diverse one, and so it may be better to identify it as a series of approaches related by the theme of external conquest or attempted conquest of an indigenous culture.

Any colonial power must make several basic decisions. First, is its rule a transitional or a permanent one? Its views on this may change from one period to another. Second, should it develop only a segment of the society (the plantations or copper mines) or should it try to absorb and remake the total society? Should it make the natives 'Portuguese' or communists? Third, should its nationals reside temporarily in the area, as 'expatriates', or should they become permanent 'settlers', maintaining their own separate cultural patterns and dominant economic and political power? Immigrants who adopt the indigenous culture are neither expatriates nor settlers.

1. 'Segmental colonialism' is the result when the external power develops only a small segment of the society – more often the extractive and commercial rather than the manufacturing segments. The external power may plan to stay only temporarily and to use expatriates. Examples are cocoa exports from Ghana and sugar cane production in the Philippines and the complementary sale of manufactured goods in return. This is the lightest form of colonialism and seldom has severe political repercussions, but it does serve to introduce contact with the irreversible process of industrialization.

Of greater impact is a segmental form of colonialism which aspires to be permanent. The colonial power makes the investment in transportation, communications, a civil service, and the like, which is requisite to permanent participation in the economy, but attempts to develop only segments of the productive system (jute in India, sugar cane in the Fiji Islands and Jamaica, tropical fruits in the Ivory Coast). Segmental colonialism has varied considerably in the depths of its penetration; and the depth of penetration is usually related to the prospective advantage to the home country.

2. Where 'settlers' from the home country become an important element, a new and particularly difficult dimension is added to colonialism ('settler colonialism'), for it takes on an aspect of true permanence; and, to service to the home country, is added service to the 'settlers' who may have quite contrary interests to those of the home country because their views, of necessity, are more rigidly tied to the *status quo*. Rather than concentrating on profit, settler colonialism comes to concentrate on preservation of the settlers' 'way of life'. Settler colonialism may seek to encompass only part of an economy (plantations in Indonesia, farms in Kenya) or it may seek to absorb the total society as part of the home country (Algeria before de Gaulle). A dual economy and a dual society are created, whereas industrialism requires unity and consensus for its fullest development.

3. The heaviest form of colonialism occurs when the home country seeks to transform the subject area into its own image, using indigenous leaders and a few expatriates as its human agents ('total colonialism'). The purpose is the complete assimilation of the economy and society of the indigenous area, and its permanent attachment to the home country. This may happen with fairly general consent (Hawaii) or grudging acceptance (Mozambique) or general resistance (Hungary). If successful, the subject country has been totally conquered. Industrialization and its guiding élite have become indigenous and, after a time, the system ceases to be 'colonial'.

The characteristic colonialism of the dynastic élite or the middle class is quite different from that of the revolutionary intellectuals. It has been more apt to be directed towards profit or access to raw materials or outlets for 'home' products, or to economic advancement for the individual settlers. The revolutionary intellectuals, as we shall see, have been more politically oriented, and through the use of indigenous associates more intent on conquering the cultural totality of the dependent area. The dynastic élite and the middle class are oriented towards the 'home market' and the revolutionary intellectuals towards the 'home ideology'.

All colonial administrators, however, have in common service to the home country or ideology, above all. The power of the government and of the management of enterprises is likely to be great in order to handle an indigenous labour force; the worker is likely to be viewed as in a dependent or at least semi-dependent status, since the management represents a superior culture. Conflict between labour and management, subject to exacerbation by nationalistic sentiments, is likely to be severely controlled or suppressed. Labour organizations, when they exist, tend to be oriented towards nationalist goals.

The indigenous worker, however, is likely to be treated quite differently from one form of colonialism to another. Settler colonialism allows him to rise until he competes with the settlers; the segmental, until he reaches the level of the expatriates; the total, once he is politically reliable, to the very top. Total colonialism is most interested in full and rapid development of the economy, including manufacturing; and the segmental generally the least. Total colonialism also attacks the old culture most aggressively; while settler colonialism may even insist on the maintenance of the old culture (South Africa), and segmental colonialism may more or less ignore the existing culture.

The Revolutionary Intellectuals and the Centralized State

A new class of intellectuals and associated activists may take over the industrializing process and society in its entirety, and sweep away, as fast as it can, the old élite and the old culture. From the beginning it intends to eliminate the former leadership groups and the pre-existing cultural arrangements and to replace them with a new ruling class and a brand new culture. The new wine shall be in totally new bottles. The principal new bottle is the centralized state. The contrast with the middle-class élite is as sharp as the difference in the industrialization approaches of, for instance, Canada and Communist China.

These intellectuals are self-identified for the task of leadership by their acceptance and espousal of a theory of history. This theory of history specifies for them the place to act, the time to act, and the means to act. Acceptance of this theory of history sets them off from other persons. They are, they contend, the bearers of the virtually inevitable historical process, the possessors of an ideology which will make it possible for them to create the future.

The ideology is the cement which holds this class together. It states that the new society is inevitable – a society fully committed to the new technology and the economic and social relations which are thought to be most compatible with its fullest development. Since an ideology is at the centre of this class, there must be 'high priests' to interpret and apply this ideology to current developments. The faithfulness with which one follows these interpretations is a main determinant of who belongs to the ruling class and who does not. New recruits to the class are drawn on the basis of ability combined with political reliability.

Once the new class has attained full power to control society in a centralized fashion, then the original revolutionary intellectuals within it give way increasingly to high-level political administrators and bureaucrats as the leaders of the system. It is still the new class that controls the new society but over time the new upcoming bureaucrats may run it rather differently than the original revolutionaries. In fact, the revolutionary intellectuals and the bureaucrats to whom they give over power may be almost the antithesis of each other. Emphasis on constant change gives way to greater conservatism; debate over basic policy yields place to reinterpretation of received doctrine. We see something of this happening today in the U.S.S.R.

This transition is of great importance in the evaluation of this system. But, with both the old intellectuals and the new bureaucrats, instead of the self, there is the ideology, the party, and the state. Once the influence of the original, or old, revolutionary intellectuals is gone, the centralized state remains.

If the first type of élite may be said to spring from commerce and the second from the land, then the third finds its source in the manifesto. The 'vision' is the animating force along this road to industrialization. The system rests on the cohesive force of a common ideology among the leaders; the manipulation of economic class interests among the masses; and the use of force when necessary at both levels. Collective thinking and collective force are central to the system.

The world conflict is seen in large part as a test of which system can make the best use of the new technology. This society is considered 'good' by its proponents because they believe it follows the logic of industrialization to the full and thus has the greatest survival value. Above all, the new technology must be served. This means forced-draft industrialization and the construction of a culture which is consistent with the new technology and its fullest utilization; thus education, labour organization, art and literature must all be geared to the system of production in a single-minded fashion. The centralized state is the only mechanism which can fully conquer the old and create the new culture, and undertake the forced-draft industrialization – the centralized state under a disciplined bureaucracy supported by the political police.

The society, of necessity, is monolithic – there can be no real separation of economic, political, and religious institutions.

Rule-making, generally, and in industrial relations, specifically, is inherently in the hands of the dominant class – the managers of this historical process. The worker is dependent on the enterprise manager, who is in turn dependent on the state, both economically and politically.

The worker's highest attribute is a sense of duty. 'The Productivity of Labour, in the final analysis, is the most important, the main tool for the victory of the new order.' (This quotation from Lenin appears on the front of a collective agreement in the Soviet steel industry.)[5] The worker is a 'citizen' with many duties and few rights.

Overt conflict between the enterprise managers and the workers is suppressed.

History is viewed as a conscious process, subject within limits to central control. History makes its demands in fits and jerks. Not only are there strategic constellations of class interests to be manipulated, but also strategic moments of time; and it is part of the task of the ideology to identify these constellations and these moments. As a consequence, a chiliastic view of history is forced on the followers who must respond to these crucial moments: expectation of the millennium is used as a force in society. This type of society is particularly capable of forced-draft industrialization, and this may turn out to be both its pre-eminent survival characteristic and its greatest historical impact.

The system, however, is subject to a gap between the assertions of the ideology and the aspirations of the masses. Individual variations within this general approach may be identified depending on the attention paid to each of these factors. In the more orthodox version (Soviet Union and China), the ideology and thus the centralized state are pre-eminent. This calls for a heavy-handed bureaucracy and a strong police arm to get rapid industrialization and to control unrest. The original intellectuals are likely to be most committed to this approach.

The orthodox version may have its costs in internal opposition and sabotage and in external criticism; and so a revision of approach may take place where the masses are served to the extent permitted without endangering minimum adherence to the ideology (Poland and Yugoslavia). There is some decentralization of the bureaucracy, some relaxation of police control, some increase in goods and services available to consumers, some more permissive attitudes towards older cultural and nationalistic traits, even at the cost of some resultant slowing of the pace of industrialization. But the central commitment remains to the ideology, the party, and the state. This version is likely to be adopted by the more politically and practically oriented members of the new class, but it is viewed by the more orthodox as a miscellany of expedient concessions which will lead over time to a forsaking of the true faith.

The Nationalist Leader and the Guidance of the State

The agent of industrialization may also be the nationalist leader, though the mantle of nationalism may be worn by many different types of persons. There is no single social base for nationalism and no single outlook on the nature of the industrial system. Historically important as a mechanism of transition, the nationalist leader may point his society in any one of several directions. Nationalism is more a sentiment than a system of thought, more a method of motivating than of organizing industrial society. Some other element must enter here before the choice can be made and this other element usually is the social orientation of the nationalist leaders. Beyond the fact of nationalism is the great question of who rides to power on its magic carpet. In this sense 'nationalism' is more an opening of the gate towards industrial development than a specifically demarcated road towards industrialization.

Still, nationalism does predispose a society in certain directions.

A nationalist revolt against the old order or a campaign against colonialism usually raises a leader or a small group of leaders to the forefront; men who are the symbols of the new independence and who carry with them the aspirations of the populace; men who are, at least at first, national heroes. They are often charismatic personalities. Their personal influence is great and given the unstructured situation at the start of a period of great national development, they can guide or form a society within broad limits in accordance with their will. Some of the newer nations in Africa, in the Middle East, and in South Asia are examples.

Instead of classes of people there tends to be a chiliastic mass – a mass with great expectations for sudden improvement but little appreciation of how that improvement will come about; a mass subject to ecstasy and to despair. And the earlier the stage of economic development and the lower the level of education and material standards of the population, the more chiliastic the mass. The goals are extravagant and the means ignored. The attitude of this mass is open to sudden and erratic change, and thus the total situation is an unstable one.

This chiliastic attitude pervades nationalism. The view of history is a climactic one – that men can 'take fortresses of history by storm'.[6] There is not only the Man but also the Moment. The act of independence is such a climactic event, and the tendency is to rely on other climactic undertakings (the Aswan Dam approach). This tends to lead industrialization into difficulties arising from an over-extension of total efforts and some grave imbalance among individual efforts as the startling advances (a new steel mill or an elaborate new university) are placed ahead of the more prosaic; and industrialization, instead of being a flow, becomes a series of episodes. Political and economic activity is organized around patriotic zeal instead of duty or self-interest.

While nationalism itself has no social philosophy, and is usually more pragmatic than ideological, it does predispose towards state-directed effort. Nationalism initially is negative – against the old order or the external enemy. This is enough of a platform to gain power but not to rule an economy. There may be no theory in advance as to how to proceed, but there must be a practice, a practice which will almost inevitably involve the state as the only available mechanism for a great national effort. This tends to lead to the planned economy, to state or state-sponsored investment, to state-controlled labour organizations, to workers dependent on the state for economic benefits and political direction, to state guidance of the new industrialists, to state appeals for hard work and saving, and to a call for unity.

The nationalist state requires a civil service in a crucial location in society, and the quality and the source of the civil service is a strategic factor in the development of the society.

With the state assuming the responsibility for the guidance of the new industrial managers, the new labour force, and the new labour organizations, rule-making is largely in the hands of the state, the worker is likely to be viewed as a 'patriot' serving a national purpose, and labour-management conflict is likely to be controlled or suppressed.

The nationalist leaders may be found among the indigenous hereditary élite, as in Iran; among the liberal-democratic or quasi-socialistic intellectuals, as in India; or among the military commanders, as in Egypt. The first two sets of leaders may be more inclined towards reliance on private capital and initiative and the last towards state capital and initiative; liberal-democratic and quasi-socialistic intellectuals towards freedom for the individual and persuasion, and the hereditary élite and military commanders towards force and discipline and duty and personal rule. Where labour organizations have been important in the independence struggle, as in Indonesia, and particularly if they are under left-wing influence, the emphasis may be additionally upon state activity. In any event, the nationalist economy is likely to be a mixed economy lying somewhere between the private initiative preferred by the middle class and the state control preferred by the revolutionary intellectuals. Where the leaders have risen through nationalist political or military channels and have had little prior contact with the theory or practice of managing a society, they tend to seek out what works best at the time with few preconceived ideas.

The 'nationalist society' is particularly a plaything of history. Its recent past is of especial significance. If the nationalist leaders arise out of a violent rejection of a hereditary dynastic élite or of settler colonialism (e.g. Indonesia), the emphasis is particularly likely to be a negative one stressing hates and fears. But if the transition is a more peaceful one, as, for example, a transition out of segmental colonialism (e.g. India), elements of the old system are more likely to be retained and attention to be turned to positive developments. In any event, there is likely to be a negative period when independence from the old and a lack of social discipline (slack work and heavy consumption) will be the dominant themes. The more violent the act of independence, the longer this period is likely to last with its uncertainty and lack of national consensus about anything except distaste for the old, as in Indonesia and Iraq. More fortunate is the society which can move quickly and firmly into a positive programme of national economic development. But even here, as in Turkey, there are likely to come periods of rapid forward progress and periods of relative stagnation. The need for clear direction is great. Yet this clear direction is particularly difficult to attain. The leaders come out of a political background rather than a solidly anchored class or group and are 'personalities'; and as the leadership shifts so does the 'personality'. The mass may alternately expect too much and then too little. And there is no single ready-made ideology for the nationalist conduct of an economy. Consequently, the nationalist approach tends to be a wavering one following an unsteady course. This is particularly true if regional, tribal, or religious differences are added to the uncertainty over social direction. If the nationalist approach is to be successful, it must attain a sense of national unity and substantial forward momentum. The tests are how soon the national purpose can be moved from the negative to the positive phase, and then how much effort can be pulled out of the nation, and how sustained that effort will be.

Any society at any moment of time probably needs some reasonably well-settled theme for its development if it is to move ahead, as is so well illustrated by the case of Indonesia, or of Poland when it was immobilized between Stalinism and revisionism. Economic progress awaits a firm decision as to the specific approach to be followed; in the case of the nationalist economy, in particular, how much state guidance there will be. There is no good substitute for a strategic concept.

Chart 2 summarizes the major elements in the strategies of the five generalized types of élites.

In order to contrast the major contemporary patterns of industrializing strategies, the foregoing descriptions of the five generalized types of industrializing élites have been essentially static. In actuality, of course, industrialization under any élite leadership is a constantly growing and shifting process. To provide more reality to the portrayal, it is now essential to consider the dynamics of the total situation, and to examine briefly the sources of the several élites and the natural history of their developments.

The Sources of the Élites

Some élites have achieved supremacy in some places and others in others; some for one reason and some for another. How did they happen to get this authority? In each single case the explanation involves a great deal of historical detail. Viewed broadly, however, there appear to have been four major considerations variously involved: the nature of the pre-existing society, the role of geography, the stage of history, and the accidents of history.

The Pre-existing Society

Industrialization began in western Europe. It is one of the mysteries of history why it began there and at the time it did. Ancient Greece and Rome and before them Mesopotamia and Egypt had developed a capacity for new ideas and new ways of doing things. In each of these societies, they could build buildings, organize men, engage in elaborate commerce, develop transportation, keep accounts. But they never did develop science or get the machine capable of repetitive operations, nor did they find the secret of constant sources of power other than man or beast. The Chinese and even the Mayan civilizations also had many of the conditions necessary for the start of industrialization; but it never started.

In the cities of western Europe, commerce and craftsmanship rose to high levels. When the new machines and the new sources of power came along there was already a substantial urban middle class oriented towards profit and sufficiently independent of the older feudal order to undertake the industrializing process. The early industrialization in England and the Lowlands was led by

Chart 2. The Industrializing Élites and their Strategies

Strategic concepts	Middle-class	Dynastic
Central strategy of the élite	Individual self-advancement.	Preservation of traditional society.
Central characteristic of the society	Open market.	Paternal community.
Sources of variations in the approach	Origin in class or classless society; or in rapid industrialization.	Nature of external and internal pressures.
Basic rule-making authority in labour-management relations	Employer, union, state.	Employer and state.
Élite's view of worker	Independent.	Dependent.
Élite's attitude toward conflict	Accepts within rules of game.	Suppresses.

the new middle-class entrepreneurs already accustomed to a market economy and a democratic polity. Here was a new and better way of getting things done and making profit. The new held no terror for them because they were already in opposition to the old feudal order. No other élite group at this time could so easily and quickly have embraced and encouraged the new productive techniques.[7]

The new industrialization found acceptance elsewhere, and sometimes in the most unlikely places. Dynastic élites still in control of their societies, as in Germany, Japan, and more recently Iran, saw the success of the new technique and came to use it. In Germany with the competition of England, in Japan with its fear of foreign conquest, and in Iran with its fear of social revolution,

Revolutionary intellectuals	Colonial administrators	Nationalist leaders
Centralization of power in forced-draft industrialization.	Servicing the 'home country'.	National independence and progress.
Centralized state.	Alien system under alien control.	State 'guided' development.
Comparative responsiveness to ideology, or to desires of masses.	Segmental or total approach; and absence or presence of 'settlers'.	Negative or positive stage of development.
Largely state.	Colonial administrator and employer.	Largely state.
Dutiful producer.	Dependent.	Patriot.
Prohibit.	Suppress.	Control.

the obvious hand of the future impelled the established élites to accept the unaccustomed methods while still seeking to preserve as much as they could of the old order. Some dynastic élites elsewhere, however, either refused to come to terms with the new modes of production or were so ineffective they could not make proper use of them. By a strange turn of fate, in recent times, the old has come to embrace the new. The old dynastic élites which once scorned commercial and industrial pursuits have come to seize upon industrial endeavour, as in parts of Latin America and the Arab world, as the source of their salvation. The old dynastic élite has taken the place of the new middle class as carrier of change.

The middle-class and dynastic élites alike, and for much the same reasons, took industrialization into many more primitive societies in the interests of the home country. These societies were sufficiently primitive economically so that they could not develop, or at least had not developed, industrially. In some cases the idea of industrializing was totally new to them. In any event, they did not have the means of effective resistance in the face of the weapons placed in the hands of the colonial powers by their machines. Thus industrialization initially came to Indonesia, India, the Congo, and many other parts of the world under colonial auspices.

In reaction to colonialism or to a resistant or ineffective dynastic élite or a combination of both, nationalist leaders have seized control, as in Egypt, Mexico, Indonesia, and now lead the industrializing process. Again, reacting to precisely the same forces, revolutionary intellectuals have also captured nations for the sake of industrialization; as they took over in Russia from a crumbling aristocracy and in China from a society too often run by war lords in the country and foreign firms in the treaty ports. Never have the nationalist leaders or the revolutionary intellectuals attained control, by means of internal action, from a vigorous middle class or dynastic élite. In areas and times mutually conducive to their ascendancy, the nationalist leaders and the revolutionary intellectuals often stand as alternatives to each other, and are thus inherently competing for power.

Thus a successful commercial society is predisposed towards middle-class leadership of industrialization; a feudal or semi-feudal system towards continued leadership by the dynastic élite if it is realistic enough and forceful enough; a truly primitive society towards guidance, although often involuntarily, by the representatives of a colonial power; the evolving colonial or the decaying feudal society towards either nationalist leaders or revolutionary intellectuals. The middle-class leadership attains supremacy by its mere existence and its inherent temperament; the dynastic, by the right of its hereditary authority; the colonial, by virtue of its technical and military superiority; the nationalist and revolutionary intellectuals through the weakness of others and their own will to power.

The Fact of Geography

This factor affects the advent to power of each of the several élites through the influence of propinquity, of discovery, and of conquest. The British system had its impact in western and northern Europe, the North American in Latin America, the Soviet in China; in each case both through example and through influence. The British colonized North America and Australia. The British conquered India; the Dutch, Indonesia; the Soviets, eastern Europe; the Chinese, Tibet. Africa was divided up by western European powers. Each dominant nation favoured its own system of industrialization.

The Stage of History

Before the First World War, industrialization was undertaken by middle-class, dynastic, or colonial élites; since the First World War, and particularly since the Second World War, by nationalist leaders and revolutionary intellectuals. They have risen against alien control and against backwardness. By 1918, colonialism had passed its zenith as an international influence and in many colonial countries, with the spread of skills and education, a new class of indigenous leaders was arising. By 1918, industrialization was so obviously the road to power, to better health, to higher standards of living, and to education that it became the goal of mankind and the essence of national aspiration. Turkey was among the first to seek modernization under nationalist leaders.

Industrialism and Industrial Man

By 1918, the Bolsheviks had attained power in Russia and set about the successful and rapid industrialization of that country, with visions of ultimate world-wide conquest. Also by 1918, middle-class elements and most dynastic élites which had the vision and the vigour to industrialize their countries had already begun to do so. Thus the large new areas for industrialization since 1918 have fallen under the leadership of the nationalists or the revolutionary intellectuals; except that, as noted earlier, some still reigning dynastic élites have in recent times undertaken industrialization in the interests of self-preservation.

The Accidents of History

Finally, among our four considerations, the accidents of history help explain who seizes the reins. War and depression have determined a great deal of history. The revolutionary intellectuals would not so certainly have taken over Russia except for the First World War and China except for the Second World War. Colonialism came to a quicker end in India and Indonesia because of the Second World War. The chief beneficiaries of violent eruption have been the nationalists and the revolutionary intellectuals.

The Natural History of the Élites

The actual industrializing élites are seldom if ever pure or ideal types, as we have noted earlier. They are often both mixed and changing by type. But there is usually enough resemblance to an ideal type to permit differentiation and classification. At this point in the mid-twentieth century, we can still identify many countries which adhere to one or another of these types. Each type seems to have its own natural tendencies for evolution, and thus there exist more or less parallel evolutions for countries equally patterned after a certain type.

The Middle Class and the Organization Society

The middle-class system is the most stable of our several types, partly because the middle class is also the mediating class in society and makes its adjustments a little at a time rather than in dramatic bursts. In fact, the middle class once in full control of the industrialization process has never in history lost its authority for internal reasons. This does not mean, nevertheless, that the middle-class system does not itself change significantly.

The size of enterprise becomes larger. A separation takes place between ownership and management. Workers add to their power through their own large-scale organization. The state takes on ever new duties. It provides social security, regulates competition and industrial conflict, redistributes wealth, assures a minimum level of economic activity and employment, and enters the internal life of private organizations to guarantee equality of treatment and opportunities for participation. It becomes the biggest single employer.

The market loses some of its influence. Decisions are supplied by rules and by group actions as well as by atomistic interchanges in the market place. The worker becomes more closely tied to his particular employment through seniority rules and security benefits. Individual self-advancement gives way increasingly to efforts at group advancement. The middle class becomes less and less a definable leadership élite, as many elements in society share urban middle-class status. The middle class still rules, but less obviously so; and the markets are still major instruments for making decisions, but they are no longer so open.

The Erosion of the Dynastic Élite

Where the dynastic élite governs ineffectually, as it frequently has done, the country will, in modern times, shift to either nationalist or revolutionary intellectual leadership. If it governs effectively, however, it is also subject to changes. As industrialization proceeds, the hereditary élite expands, recruiting new members from lower strata in its society and particularly by the process of selection through the mechanisms of higher education.

Industrialization requires a great deal of mobility in the labour force, from one occupational level to another, from one area to another, from one enterprise to another. This tends to break down the paternal plant community, as does the growth of social services provided by other institutions than the enterprise. Class lines are softened. The political parties and labour organizations of the working class become gradually less ideological, although this can take a long time and involve many conflicts between the traditionalists and the revisionists. Both the managerial and working classes converge towards the upper and lower ranges of the middle class in their habits and beliefs. Tradition and status mean less; competition and contracts mean more. The worker becomes more independent and the manager more professional. Attitudes towards industrial conflict also soften. The labour organizations come to share more of the rule-making authority.

The society is moving towards the middle-class type, as Germany has done and Japan seems to be doing. But it may retain for a long time remnants of the earlier ideological struggle which is so typical of such societies: permanently enhanced power for the state, a heightened attention to the role of occupation in determining the standing of an individual. The society, however, is no longer so traditional and the managers no longer so paternal.

The Fate of all Colonies

The colonial system is the most transient of the several ideal types of élites. 'Colonialism spawned its destroyer – nationalism.'[8] Segmental colonialism has not penetrated deeply enough to make possible its continuing hold on the economy and the society. It carries the seeds of industrialization and the seeds of its own destruction. It may continue, however, in a new and changed form: a segment for foreign ownership and management in the economy within a compatible political system operated by the indigenous people. The colonial enterprises may retain their profits by giving up their control of the society. Settler colonialism has more tenacity and also creates a greater need for tenacity. Whether it can survive anywhere is still in doubt. Past history would indicate that settlers only survive by ceasing to be 'settlers', giving up their separate and dominant 'way of life', as in the case of the colonies of ancient Greece. The colonialism with the greatest survival possibilities is total colonialism because it ceases, once it is effective, to be colonialism. It becomes the system of the country itself under its own indigenous leaders.

All colonialism, in the end, is either overthrown by the 'natives' or ceases to be colonialism by becoming the 'native' system or a component part of it. No advanced industrial society has ever yet been run by aliens.

The 'New Class' of Intellectuals

The revolutionary intellectuals are committed to the view that the climactic change through which they seize power is the last great change in social relations. The classless society will emerge, and, according to Marx, the only other really substantial change in prospect is the 'withering away of the state'. Thus far it has not withered, and it is highly unlikely it ever will. But other changes can and do take place.

There is in communist society, as noted earlier, the great contradiction between the demands of the ideology and the desires of the populace. These desires are particularly hard to deal with if they arise from a subjugated people (Poland, Hungary) who are resistant to essentially alien rule by an alien system. They have their nationalism around which to rally opposition and pressure. Aside from the pressure of nationalism against the 'total colonialism' of the communists, there may also be the antagonistic interests of some national minorities, as in the Soviet Union itself.

The desires of the populace, however, are basic under any circumstances, whether encouraged by nationalism or not. The ideology calls for an attack on the old culture, and there are those who cherish it. The ideology requires an immense national effort of hard work and austerity, and there are those who resent it. The ideology calls for a great centralization of power, and there are those who seek to share it. The most persistent drive is probably in the direction of sharing power. The military makes its demands. The scientists and the new managers make theirs. Even the workers, as they get more skill and responsibility, and thus power, can make demands of their own. These groups may come to have their own areas within which they can govern. While they may not share authority over society, they may be able to bring greater influence to bear upon those who do. Universal education, which is an imperative of successful industrialization, may even open up an eventual possibility of diffusing political power widely throughout the society.

The requirement of efficiency itself may force some fractionalization of power. As there are more enterprises and particularly as more enterprises are involved in the production and distribution of a myriad of consumer goods and the provision of an increasing range of personal services, central control becomes less possible. The more successful the process of industrialization, the more reliance has to be placed on localized decisions and on markets, instead of on centralized decisions and plans; and markets bring the middle-class approach in their wake.

The new generations of leaders become more secure, more professional, more bureaucratically interested in standard performance than in all-out effort, further removed from the old ideological considerations and the traditions of the revolution. The wolves give way to the watchdogs. With greater educational opportunities and a less desperate need for trained people, the class stratification of the society declines and a new equality seeps into the society.

The masses also will come to crave more of the product of their own labour; and the drive for more consumer goods and better housing will change the society too.[9]

The revolutionary intellectuals appeal particularly to the 'transitionals'[10] in societies in the very early stages of industrialization. They promise an end to the old ruling élite or the colonial power, to the old tribal or feudal culture, to economic and educational backwardness. They have much less to offer to others than to the 'transitionals', and particularly have they little to offer to the members of a developed middle-class society. They may have some continuing appeal to the workers in a class society under a dynastic élite, but if this élite is successful in managing industrialization and moves over time towards the middle-class approach, the appeal lessens. In the nationalists, they meet competitors who offer the same things and can hold the allegiance of the 'transitionals' if they are reasonably successful in delivering what they promise.

The revolutionary intellectuals have programmes for handling the problems of the transition – rapid commitment of a labour force, the fast build-up of an educational system, the quick encouragement of labour discipline and productivity, the enlargement of the gap between current consumption and current production for the sake of investment, development of an export surplus from the agricultural segment to feed the cities, suppression of industrial conflict.

Again, however, they have much less in the way of programmes for an advanced industrial society. They are handicapped, because of the rigidity of their ideology, in handling diversified production, in responding to the insistent calls for fractionalized power, in giving the freedom for inquiry which goes along with highly developed educational and research institutions.

Their historical message may be only to the 'transitionals' anxious to leave behind them a decaying feudal or alien colonial society; and their greatest historical impact may be, not the creation of the 'classless' society, but the firm, even forceful handling of the economic and political problems in the immediate transition from the traditional to the technological society. They respond to the problems of one stage in history and to the defaults of others in handling those problems. Their rule is neither inevitable nor necessarily everlasting. It may be communism itself that withers away. However that may be, any society they run, despite any reluctant tendency towards gratification of the desires of the masses, will be comparatively disposed towards the managerial state, the use of force, the service of technology, the supremacy of the party and the suppression of conflict so long as their ideology has any hold either in theory or in continued practice and acceptance.

The Nationalists as Experimenters

Nationalism relies heavily on the state, but not so rigidly as the revolutionary intellectuals. Consequently, private enterprise and markets not only have a chance to survive, but the opportunity to take over larger areas of the economy as they are capable of doing so. Nationalism often conduces to one-party rule or domination, but again this is not based on ideology and, as consensus develops in the society and education spreads, a greater distribution of

T–D

political power can occur. The nationalist leaders, while having many of the same goals as the revolutionary intellectuals, are not bound by an all-pervading ideology. They are opportunists and experimenters. This has its disadvantages and its advantages. The lack of an effective ideology leads to much stumbling and uncertainty in the early stages; but it also helps avoid confining rigidities in the later stages of industrialization. Generally, nationalism, if successful, will tend towards a modified version of the middle-class approach, modified by heavier emphasis on the state; if unsuccessful, however, only the revolutionary intellectuals can readily attain leadership.

The natural history of each of our five types is to change: some completely (colonial), some drastically (dynastic élite and national-ist), and some substantially (middle-class, revolutionary intellec-tual); but they all do change. Chart 3 summarizes the natural history of these ideal types of élites.

Chart 3. The Sources of the Élites and the Natural History of their Systems

Industrializing élite	Middle-class	Dynastic
Pre-existing society	Commercial.	Strongly led feudal or quasi-feudal.
Stage in history	Relatively early.	Relatively early.
'Normality' of development	'Normal'.	'Normal'.
Inherent direction of change	More group and state action.	Less élitist and paternal.
Changing relation to markets	Markets lose some of their influence.	Larger role.

The Floating Forces – The Intellectuals and the Generals

Two forces – one representing ideas and the other power – are inherently socially unattached on any permanent basis in the struggle for supremacy in organizing industrializing societies. Both the politically minded intellectuals and the generals often can and do align themselves now with one and now with another élite and its strategy; and their alignments can be a crucial factor.

The intellectuals (including the university students) are a particularly volatile element, capable of quite rapid shifts of opinion, quickly sensitive as they are to the social climate. They are almost always divided among themselves. They have no continuing commitment to any single institution or philosophical outlook, and they are not fully answerable for consequences. They are, as a result, never fully trusted by anybody, including themselves as their constant and often bitter doctrinal and policy disagreements and quarrels testify. Yet they have power which can move society.

Revolutionary intellectuals	Colonial administrators	Nationalist leaders
Weakly led quasi-feudal; or colonial.	Primitive.	Weakly led quasi-feudal; or colonial.
Relatively late.	Relatively early.	Relatively late.
Development at a crisis point (war or depression).	Most transient.	Development often at a crisis point (war or depression).
Less ideological; more bureaucratic; more sensitive to the wishes of the masses and of other emerging élites.	Nationalism; and occasionally rule by revolutionary intellectuals.	More middle-class influence, if successful; revolutionary intellectuals, if unsuccessful.
Larger role.	Larger role internally and externally.	Markets qualified by nationalist state.

The intellectuals generate ideas and serve as constant critics of society. They help determine how men think about each other, about history, about the nature of the good society. They spin theories and ideologies; they can turn conflicts into crusades. In the modern world with its perfected communications, they are particularly influential since ideas travel fast. The new invaders are not the hordes breaking across a traditional boundary but ideas riding the air waves and the printed page around the world. What is the quality of the intellectuals on each side and how well are they used? This is an important question for social groups within a nation as well as for the contending systems among nations; and particularly in periods of internal or external crisis. The intellectuals speak the loudest and are heard the most at the crossroads of social history.

Each of the generalized types of élites, even the colonial in Kipling and others, has drawn its intellectual supporters – the romanticists and historicists supporting the dynastic élite and the old culture and the idea of community; the humanitarians and rationalists favouring the liberal-democratic theme and the open society; the revolutionaries aiding communism and destruction of the old order; and the chauvinists elevating the national state and national character. There have also been political intellectuals who have withdrawn to the side in disillusionment and bewilderment into nihilism, existentialism, or some other school of thought standing largely aside from the battle over the transformation of society into its industrial mould.

But intellectuals are not always free to float as they please, for they may be controlled, and the more authoritarian the society the more effective the control; and the communist as the most authoritarian has the most control. It is part of the essence of communism (and fascism) that the intellectuals must serve the ruling order if they are to serve at all. In these instances they are neither free-floating nor much of a force.

The generals influence society not through ideas, but through the ultimate power of the armed forces. In some societies, aside from the power at their command, they are and are recognized to be the best trained and most patriotic elements in the society. They may also be closest to the aspirations of the mass of the people, particularly when the army is one of the few channels for upward social mobility. They often have a reputation for being less corrupt than other elements, for being more dynamic in getting things done, for being able to make decisions, for having trained staff available. They also, like the intellectuals, can transfer their allegiance and support from one group to another, or from one system to another, but are more likely to be attached to the ruling element, whatever it may be. In fact, in some societies the ruling element is by definition the element with the support of the armed forces. The military tend to be more important in societies which rely heavily on force for their sanction than in the liberal-democratic society which relies more on consent. In the liberal-democratic system, the military almost of necessity must be under civilian control and is not a significant partisan political factor.

The generals normally stand for law and order, and serve as a reserve force either to back the ruling group or to take over from it if it breaks down. But they may also be a force for reform, often of a populist character, for they have a mass base in the soldiery; and so there may be a Cromwell as well as a Franco. Military reform when it comes tends to be nationalist, disciplinary, and responsive to a great mass wish – like independence or land reform – and not to have a full ideology or an intellectual base or even much knowledge of the complexities of civilian life. Whether supporting the ruling group or supplanting it, the military may insist on industrial modernization, as in Japan and Germany, for the sake of the strength of its armies and thus become an influential factor in economic progress.

The generals, like the intellectuals, are a more crucial factor in a critical period. A crisis, whatever else it may do to other groups, heightens the influence of these two elements; and tranquillity humbles both. Even if the military remains silent in a crisis, it is taking sides and affecting the outcome; while the intellectual attempting to influence events cannot be silent. Since force is most likely to be used internally in a period of social transition, the armed forces play a special role under such circumstances. The orientation of their leaders becomes a vital factor, and whoever captures the military leaders may well capture the system. This is particularly true in recent times when the armed power of the soldier so far surpasses the unarmed power of the citizen.

The general is more important at some times – the crises – and in some systems – those based on force – than at other times and in other places. Thus, in a dynastic system under severe internal pressure, the communist society in an internal power struggle, the colonial economy subject to unrest, and the nationalist régime looking for national unity, the role of the generals may be the single conclusive factor. This is not to suggest that they will always all see alike – some of the drama may lie in their internal rivalries. Their role, of course, is enhanced by external as well as internal warfare. Only the liberal-democratic system in peace can afford to ignore the generals.

These floating forces – the intellectuals and the generals – guide industrialization mostly when the process is faltering or changing course. On other occasions the guidance of the process is left to the other more persistent elements described earlier.

The middle class offers individual choice; the dynastic élite, continuity; the revolutionary intellectuals, high velocity industrialization; and the nationalist leaders, the integrity and advancement of the nation. None of them, however different their essential emphasis, can escape the imperatives of consensus and assimilation. In each case, starting as a minority, they must get the acceptance of the society and become broadly based within a culture which is compatible with their strategic approach. Once this has been done, internal ideological conflict in a society will slacken, for there is no longer a basic clash over the strategic approach to industrialization.

The decline of ideology in a society marks the rise in acceptance of the dominant strategy. But new minorities will arise from time to time to challenge the accepted strategy; and so the ideological weapons will be kept burnished, if not often actively employed. The decline of ideology in the world will come when there is only one accepted approach to industrialism; and that eventuality, if it ever comes, is still a long distance away.

3   Shaping the
                       Industrialization Process

The preceding chapter was concerned with the several types of industrializing élites and their characteristics: concepts which help describe both the differences among societies organized by different élites and the similarities among societies organized by the same élite types. Even where broad similarities exist, however, societies viewed in detail are unique. Each has grown within a pre-existing culture; each has encountered a series of historical and economic facts and been moulded by them. Not only are there societies whose characteristics reflect more a mixture of types than any single 'ideal' type, but there is an endless variety of realistic experience which inevitably blurs the boundaries of any 'ideal' typology. And this variety can be understood only by reference to the variety of cultural, historical, and economic settings. This chapter will deal with some of the important factors which give a uniqueness to each industrializing society, no matter how it is organized, and the ways in which these factors affect the decisions of the industrializing élites.

The Conflict of Cultures

The sweep of industrialization throughout the world transforms the cultures of the traditional societies. The nature of the conflict between the old and the new cultures, and the degree of penetration of the traditional by the industrial, depend both on the attraction of the new and the resistance of the old. The different possible outcomes of this conflict have significance for workers and managers in the industrialization process.[1]

Industrialism and Industrial Man

As the anthropologists define it, 'culture' is broader than those features we shall discuss here. In their definition, 'Culture . . . is that complex whole which includes knowledge, belief, art, law, morals, custom, and any other capabilities and habits acquired by man as a member of a society.'[2] The present discussion somewhat arbitrarily selects from this broad array five cultural elements which appear significant in the industrialization process and the strategies of the industrializing élites. They are: (1) the family system, (2) class and race, (3) religious and ethical valuations, (4) legal concepts, and (5) the concept of the nation-state.

The Family System

In the great majority of traditional cultures a number of nuclear families act as an aggregate in their social and economic pursuits. This composite or extended family is, more often than not, unfavourable in some respects to economic growth. It provides shelter and food for all of its members, regardless of their individual contributions, so that the indigent and the indolent alike are cared for in a sort of 'social security' system. Working members are expected to pool their earnings for the benefit of everyone; individual saving is discouraged. The behaviour and careers (including marriage) of its members are the close concern of the elders. Family loyalty and obligations take precedence over other loyalties and obligations. Thus, the extended family tends to dilute individual incentives to work, save, and invest.

There are some circumstances, of course, in which the extended family may facilitate the transition to an industrialized society. It may be the main source of initial capital for investment when only close relatives may be trusted or persuaded to lend money. It may offer security and means of adjustment in the industrializing urban areas to new recruits from the villages, as in India or the Congo. But these advantages are at best temporary; the enterprise must eventually tap a wider and less personal capital market; the industrial worker eventually becomes a member of an urban nuclear family. '. . . Economic change is always destructive to a joint family system.'[3] The industrializing élites are confronted with the prospect of adapting the industrializing process to the existing family system or of altering the family system in the course of industrialization.

Traditional Japan was family-oriented, and its industrial change under the guidance of a dynastic élite was geared to the preservation of existing family structure and values. A Japanese worker expected to remain with one industrial or commercial 'family' for the rest of his life. But post-war economic, political, and social changes in Japan have weakened family ties as compared to the pre-war period. 'The nuclear family is displacing the extended family and has come to be the dominant form in the cities of Japan. Where the extended family exists, it has everywhere diminished in size and functional importance.'[4] These changes have weakened commitment to a single enterprise as well. The labour market is coming to play a larger role.

In less economically developed countries, the dynastic élite has geared the structure and management of enterprises to the extended family. The role of the extended family in dominant Indian business enterprises is well known. In each case, the extended family's control of an enterprise or group of firms enables less competent members of the family to hold managerial positions for which their training and ability would not otherwise qualify them. The consequence is that outsiders, however competent, seldom advance to high managerial positions in the enterprise; although in some cases the extended family may concentrate on training and developing its more able members for these top managerial posts.

In contrast, the more advanced industrial countries place less emphasis on family connections and greater emphasis on competence, although family influence is certainly not unknown in enterprises in England, Sweden, and the United States. Preference for family members – whether in managerial positions or in industrial employment – is, however, criticized as 'nepotism'.

When the prime movers in industrialization are the revolutionary intellectuals, as in the Soviet Union and more recently in China, they set out deliberately to weaken loyalties and obligations to the extended family and to demand primary loyalty to the state as the principal instrument of industrialization. This is clearly evident in China, where establishment of 'communes' in the villages sought to break up the ancestral homes in which members of an extended family lived together and to which absent members returned periodically. This destruction of the extended family was evidently designed to require labour of all its members, as well as to replace loyalty to the family with full allegiance to the totalitarian régime.[5] The difficulties subsequently encountered by these communes may be an indication of the strength of family life.

The nationalist leaders also seek to modify the joint family, but less drastically and more indirectly. Their efforts to industrialize a newly independent country tend to break down the wider family affiliations as the nuclear family develops in the urban centres. The colonial administrators, on the other hand, have no uniform policy towards the pre-existing family structure. Their policies reflect particularly the problems of recruiting a labour force. In India during the British rule the joint family persisted as it had for centuries. Then industrialization under nationalist auspices after independence began to weaken it. On the other hand, colonial administrators seeking to exploit natural resources may recruit labour in ways which break family ties, as in parts of Africa where 'target' workers are employed.

The logic of the industrialization process requires that selection and promotion be made on the basis of ability and competence. It demands loyalty to the enterprise and to the work group (with its labour organization) and to a nationalist aspiration rather than to the extended family as such. The separation of loyalties from the family, the contract with the individual worker, the movement of production from the home to the factory were steps in the industrialization of the West. Later industrializations may not repeat the identical steps, but weakening or destruction of the extended family and the substitution of new loyalties and affiliations are apparently inevitable.

Class and Race

Most societies have distinct social groups composed of individuals with some common characteristics. Economic activity involves a division of labour, which results in stratification based on occupation, property, income, and so on. Thus, there is an 'economic order' which may be distinguished from a 'status order' stemming from family lineage, traditional styles of living, and other factors. In the extreme, as in pre-industrial India, the class systems resulting from these two orders may merge in a 'caste system' which combines the economic and status ordering – both cemented together by religious sanction.

Industrialization challenges the old hierarchy and replaces it with a new ordering of the classes; professionals, managers, administrators, and industrial workers replace the pre-industrial economic ordering of landowners, merchants and traders, master craftsmen and guild journeymen, apprentices, and peasants.

If traditional class and caste lines are relatively rigid, as in pre-industrial India, or nineteenth-century France and Italy, this newly ordered class structure of an advanced industrializing society may be slower in developing. This is particularly likely when the dynastic élite is the prime mover towards industrialism. In Japan, for example, the paternalism and authoritarianism of the old class structure have been preserved in the new factory system.

Societies such as those of the United States, Canada, and New Zealand which are much newer have had relatively open class structures compared to the earlier industrial societies of Western Europe and the later ones of Japan, the Soviet Union, India, China and others, which had pre-industrial class structures of varying degrees of rigidity. Industrial workers in the United States, for example, have had a much greater possibility of upward and horizontal mobility, particularly between generations, and the belief in 'equal opportunity' has persisted. The bitterness of class conflict has not plagued labour-management relations to the same degree in these newer societies. When the middle class directs industrialization, as in Britain or Sweden, it retains control, in part because it modifies the harshness of class distinctions – often under pressure from labour movements and labour parties which challenge the authority of the traditional ruling class. Where the latter has tried to hang on to its power at all costs, an intense class conflict has resulted in labour-management relations and in politics, as in the past in France and Italy.

When industrialization is under colonial auspices, the class and racial structure from an alien society is superimposed on or tries to subordinate the class and racial structure of the occupied society. This describes the impact of the British in India or Rhodesia and the Dutch in Indonesia, for example. Racial tensions become intermixed with nationalist conflicts, and spill over into labour-management disputes, especially when management is white and western, and labour is nonwhite and nationalist in sentiment. The explosive possibilities of apartheid in South Africa represent the extreme case in a spectrum which includes racial and national discrimination in varying degrees in most industrializing societies, whether it be in the southern sections of the United States, in pre-independent India, or in some of the South American nations with large indigenous Indian populations.

The revolutionary intellectuals' approach to industrialization involves complete overthrow of the pre-existing dominant class, as in the Soviet Union and China. The ruling groups may be physically liquidated, or forced to surrender their power and wealth as the price of physical survival. The 'managers of the economy' are a new class, and at the apex is the Communist Party which is dedicated to the perpetuation of its own power. Thus, the society which was to become 'classless' develops into one in which the ruling class has a power more absolute than most in history.

The nationalist leaders seek to exploit any evidences of class and racial discrimination to their political advantage both in the struggle for national independence and in the drive for industrialization. The difficult but successful effort of the Egyptians to show that they could build a textile industry despite the active discouragement of the British is parallel with the drive of newer nations today to build steel mills to prove their claim to national industrial vigour. The fierce pride of non-western peoples in their industrial achievements and in their future goals, fanned by nationalist aspirations, is the reaction to centuries of western domination and treatment of these peoples as backward and indolent. The current Chinese industrialization effort, no less than the present Soviet effort to overtake American productivity levels, is explained partially in these terms.

While the nationalist leader is mobilizing sentiment against the foreigner, he may also be seeking the subordination of divisive classes and groups within the new society and the dominance of the new state. Tribal rivalries complicate the national unity of Ghana, and long-standing regional differences pose problems to the leadership of the Yugoslav drive for industrialization. Independent India could not tolerate the continuance of the princely states within the new Indian nation, and it could not countenance that later agitation in 1955–7 for many separate linguistic states. Similarly, rigid caste distinctions are intolerable in a developing industrial society, and have been denounced by leaders like Gandhi and Nehru. More important than exhortations, however, are the eroding pressures of industrialization itself on caste lines, especially in the cities of India.

Religious and Ethical Valuations

In traditional societies, organized religion often obliges people to seek other-wordly goals, and the organized priesthood is the instrument in setting the pattern for the faithful to follow. The traditional religions, reinforced by the related social systems, also emphasize that each person has his 'place' and a 'duty' to fulfil that is not usually related to economic advancement. Religious and ethical valuations towards work, particularly with respect to manual labour, are generally not favourable to individual effort aimed towards material progress.

Furthermore, in the pre-industrial societies characteristic of much of Asia, there has been a 'cyclical theory of time'. 'If the nature of things is such that everything runs in a cycle, coming back at some later date to precisely where it is now, what is the point in trying to change the present state of affairs?'[6] Deliberately planned change is abhorred; the *status quo* is preserved in economic activity. The individual is directed to subordinate himself to a God or gods through the established religion and in accord with accepted doctrine.

Finally, religious and ethical valuations often influence the relationship between superior and subordinate, master and servant, manager and worker. In the pre-industrial society, the master has some obligations of a protective nature towards the servant. But the subordinate owes unquestioning obedience to his superior; he must carry out his orders and his wishes.

In varying fashion, the incoming industrial culture builds on, bends, or destroys these traditional cultural elements. In Japan, the traditional culture favoured the dynastic élite as the prime movers towards industrialization, and this élite in turn preserved as much of that culture as possible. The authority of superiors in Japan, stemming from the restoration of the emperor, was maintained, and the consequent employer-employee relationship in many Japanese factories is vastly different from that found in England, for example, or in other democratic western industrial countries. Yet the Japanese did not hesitate to adopt modern technology, and they borrowed heavily from the scientific and industrial knowledge of the West. Traditional religious beliefs did not handicap industrial development, and in modern industrial Japan many of the old customs persist side by side with advanced technology.

In such countries as Spain, and in parts of Latin America and the Islamic world, the power of organized religion has without question helped to preserve the hierarchical relations in the society and has been a factor affecting the slow pace of industrialization and the continued dominance of the dynastic élite.

The reverse of this situation is, of course, the importance of the 'Protestant ethic' for economic growth.[7] The revolution in religious ideas wrought by the Protestant revolution produced the personality of an inner-worldly ascetic, strikingly different from the personality of the other-worldly monk or the inner-worldly, luxury-devoted aristocrat. This inner-worldly ascetic is the prototype of the middle-class or bourgeois capitalist – pushed on by Calvinist predestination doctrine to accumulate more and more of the materialistic signs of grace. The middle-class capitalist leaders of industrialization in Britain, Scandinavia, and the United States found these spiritual doctrines congenial to doing what they devoutly believed was God's work on earth – practising the virtues of thrift, austerity, and capital accumulation. Because the spiritual and intellectual authority of the earlier established church was overthrown or rejected in these countries, the leaders of industrialization could therefore build on the new religious and ethical valuations towards work and accumulation. They helped spread the new gospel to the subordinate groups in the society – especially to the new industrial workers, who were urged to become 'independent' and self-reliant, rather than 'dependent'. Methodism in England, for example, helped industrial workers accept the harshness of the industrial system. Furthermore, the intellectual renaissance, combined with Protestant reformation and the religious dissent, was wholly congenial to the advancement of scientific inquiry and the development of advanced technology. Thus, the cultural stage was set for the world's first industrializing society.

In countries like the Soviet Union and more recently China, the pre-existing religious and ethical valuations of the traditional society seemed to block the prospect of rapid industrialization. So the new revolutionary intellectual élite set out deliberately to destroy these valuations. The revolutionary élite, of course, rejects private thrift and accumulation, substituting state investment; but they are no less 'Calvinist' than western European Protestants in their efforts to encourage hard work. They have clearly accepted for industrialization the valuations implicit in modern science and technology.

In Turkey, with its nationalist approach, 'Ataturk's genius as a social planner was to see "economic development" within a comprehensive behavioural matrix.'[8] He destroyed the political and temporal power of the organized religion; he established secular schools; he simplified the alphabet; and he degraded the traditional form of dress by ordering the wearing of western attire; he introduced radios into people's houses. Through such institutional changes he undermined rural isolation and encouraged modernization.

India has chosen a different route, under the direction of nationalist leaders who stress a 'socialist pattern of society' which leans heavily on the middle class rather than on a dynastic élite or on revolutionary intellectuals. Gandhi and Nehru have sought to modify the Hindu ethic in the industrializing society, but not to destroy it. Superficially, Hinduism with its other-worldly emphasis might seem to stultify economic growth, but Indian industrialists who are also devout Hindus do not seem to have been greatly inhibited in seeking economic gains. Similarly, the Muslim religion has not interfered with the development of banking, trading, or commercial and industrial institutions in Egypt.

Traditionalist religious values do not seem to have been as serious an obstacle to economic development in the long run as some anthropologists have thought.[9]

Legal Concepts

In the traditional society, custom and social norms are more important than written law in governing relationships between individuals and groups. But the advanced society has developed institutions such as legislatures to promulgate statutory laws and courts to interpret and apply them. There is administrative law by public agencies and, finally, a system of law affecting the work place, which may be developed by managers and labour organizations and by the government.

The early industrializing societies under the middle-class élite in Great Britain and the United States were characterized by laws which respected private property rights and enforced obligations concerning them. Legal concepts extended to the market and applied to functions rather than to persons as individuals. There was legal protection of contract rights growing out of economic activity, and the process favoured private capital accumulation and investment. Subsequently, in these industrializing societies, the statute and common law were expanded and modified to limit private property rights when they infringed upon the rights of workers (as well as other groups).

When the dynastic élites lead the industrialization process, the legal system is likely to support the existing élite and the national state above individual rights before the law. The Napoleonic legal code, a comprehensive set of rules affecting all types of conduct, has influenced the legal systems of industrial relations in such countries as France and Italy, where state regulation of the substantive terms and conditions of employment is much more detailed than in the countries with Anglo-Saxon traditions of law.

The German legal system, as applied to industrial relations, emphasized social justice more than individual rights, and this concept is found also in the administration of the detailed 'Labour Codes' which have developed in Chile and Brazil.

Colonial administrators impose the legal systems of the home country on the colony, as was common throughout Africa. The substitution of the laws of an industrializing state for the pre-industrial is designed to encourage foreign investment and the orderly handling of business affairs. In labour-management relations, the system of the colonial power may be introduced to settle disputes and possibly (as the Indians charge) to impose labour standards on new industry, thereby reducing competition with the home country. When ex-colonial countries win independence, they may take over the legal system of the colonial administrators, as the Indians have done. While compulsory adjudication of labour disputes in India has some distinctively Indian features, it is modelled on the pre-existing British court structure and legal system. Much of Indian labour legislation draws upon British experience. The contrast with China, which had no western-type legal system, is clear. Here 'people's courts' dispense a kind of justice quite unrelated to any western concept of established legal rights.

A nationalist leader seeking to destroy the pre-existing culture in order to further industrialization and national growth may adopt a western legal system in the modernization process. As one of his many revolutionary reforms, Ataturk abolished Islamic law in Turkey and substituted the Swiss civil code.[10] The Turkish labour code, promulgated in 1936 with 148 articles, was drawn largely from the French labour code, and was influenced by conventions approved by the International Labour Organization. Thus a different legal system, particularly as it applied to labour organizations and labour-management relations, was substituted within less than a generation for a traditional Islamic legal system which was found inadequate for a modern industrializing state.

The revolutionary intellectuals in Russia and in China rejected western legal systems as 'bourgeois' appendages of a rejected capitalist economic system. Soviet and Marxist legal theorists have held that 'law is no more than a social technique with some advantages and disadvantages in comparison with other possible ways of regulating human behaviour, but it is certainly not superior to what it should regulate'.[11] Thus the Soviet state may promulgate whatever decrees, laws, and rules are needed to suit the purpose of rapid industrialization and the growth of a powerful national state. There are no superior individual rights guaranteed by law against arbitrary action by the state or its agents.

With the exception of the communist states, the industrializing societies of the modern world have introduced legal systems which encourage economic growth through some protection to private property and individual rights. Rights and obligations of labour, management, and the state are developed through statutes, codes, court decisions, and administrative agencies acting under statutory power. The arbitrary power of the state or its agents is limited by these means. Private law, developed by management and labour organizations as part of a system of industrial relations, is a further limitation of the all-powerful state.

The Concept of the Nation-State

Pre-industrial societies are often divisive; tribal groups, language groups, and geographical regions assert their internal cohesiveness and their independence from central authority. Divisiveness is not such a serious handicap to agricultural or commercial societies, but the industrializing society requires the permanent nation-state. If the earlier society has been colonial, furthermore, the central state is the instrument of triumphant nationalism.

The late-comers to industrialization, like the Soviet Union, Turkey, India, China, and Egypt, are in a hurry, and state investment in basic industries of an industrializing society seems necessary to them – along with economic planning. The power of the state may also be regarded as necessary to destroy an impeding pre-industrial social structure (as in Russia or China), or to speed up a peaceful transition to an industrial society (as in Turkey under Ataturk and in Egypt since 1947). 'Statism' in this sense is a powerful political and ideological concept which appeals to industrially underdeveloped countries everywhere today. When this concept prevails, the state intervenes actively in the labour-management relationship.

Nationalism may be an integrating force in underdeveloped economies characterized by wide class and cultural differences between the élite and the masses. The Congress Party of India under Prime Minister Nehru was known as the 'Party of Independence' and was able to take the leadership in welding together India's many separate groups into a unified national effort to achieve more rapid industrial development. The experience of Israel serves as another example of nationalism harnessed for economic development, although in this case the same kind of prior colonial domination was not involved. Similarly, nationalism – fed by anti-western sentiments – was clearly a powerful force in the industrialization of Japan. Turkey is an example of a Middle Eastern country where national pride was harnessed by Ataturk to attempt economic development on the pattern of the West.

But nationalism may also be a hindrance to economic development if it requires for national pride alone such appurtenances of industrialization as steel mills or automobile assembly plants without sound economic justification. Extreme nationalism may also irrationally reject all forms of external aid, and drive out the technical and managerial resources identified with the former colonial power, as the Indonesians did with the Dutch, or the Iranians with the Anglo-Iranian Oil Company.

Finally, nationalism combined with revolutionary totalitarianism, as in the Soviet Union and China, merely reinforces those pressures for control of labour-management relations which are implicit in the ideology of totalitarianism. The managerial class and leaders of labour organizations are subordinate to the will and the interests of the state.

The nationalist leader in most industrializing societies is confronted with divergent group pressures in the cultures, such as tribal, regional, minority, and linguistic groups, as well as pressure groups like organized management or labour. The logic of industrialization compels a subordination of these groups to national survival and growth, and one of the dilemmas of modern industrializing societies is the conflict between freedom for these groups in the culture and the centralized controls which rapid industrialization requires.

The central themes in the conflict of cultures in the course of industrialization may be summed up as follows:

1. Industrialization imposes its own cultural patterns on the pre-existing culture. The culture of industrialization has the following general characteristics: (a) a nuclear family system which tends to accentuate individual incentives to work, save, and invest; (b) a relatively open social structure which encourages equality of treatment and advancement on the basis of ability; (c) religious and ethical values which are favourable to economic gain and growth, innovations and scientific change; (d) a legal system which encourages economic growth through general protection of individual and property rights from arbitrary or capricious rule; and (e) a strong central governmental organization and the sense of being a nation which can play a decisive role in economic development. If some of the necessary cultural factors are already present or if social revolt has already helped to uproot the older culture, the transition to the new industrial culture will be more rapid.

2. Conversely, the advance of the industrial culture will be impeded by: (a) an extended family system which weakens industrial incentives to work, save, and invest, and which reserves key managerial positions for family members regardless of competence; (b) a class or social structure based on traditional social status rather than on economic performance; (c) traditional religious and ethical values which emphasize 'place' and 'duty' unrelated to economic gain or advancement, and oppose change and innovation, particularly in science and technology; (d) traditional customs and social norms which deny individual and property rights and fail to guarantee observance of contracts; (e) divisive groups in the society which hinder or prevent the emergence of a strong nation-state.

3. Cultural impediments are not insuperable barriers to industrialization, but they are frequently significant in explaining the kind of industrialization which develops. The cultural patterns of industrialization may move in rapidly, advance slowly, or be sealed off in a particular society. They may penetrate deeply or

shallowly, depending upon the nature and strength of the pre-existing culture. In retarded or slowly developing industrial societies, the two conflicting cultures may persist for long periods side by side within the same society, or in different parts of it.

4. The faster the pace of industrialization, the more likely is the pre-existing culture to be modified or destroyed with the on-rush of the industrial society.

5. In the past, culture and social structure were changed by movements of peoples between countries. Today, ideas and institutions which affect culture are moving throughout the world with the speed of modern means of communication and transportation. Few pre-industrial cultures can be insulated for long from the spreading cultural patterns of industrialization.

6. The following generalizations are suggestive of the impact of cultural factors during the course of industrialization on labour-management-state relations (see also Chapters 4–6):

The greater the class distinctions in the old culture, the more intense the industrial conflict.

The less the emphasis upon work in the old culture, the greater the need for discipline at the work place.

The greater the emphasis upon the extended family, the slower the rise of professional management.

The greater the strength of the extended family, the slower the commitment of workers to industrial life.

The more diverse the groups in the old culture, the harsher the role of the nation-state.

The interrelationships between the industrializing élites and the major cultural factors discussed in this section are summarized in Chart 4.

Economic Constraints

The industrialization process and the élites that guide it must react to the economic realities of the present as well as to the cultural heritage of the past. Economic constraints are not the only nor necessarily the most serious impediments restricting economic growth. At any period, however, the economic constraints constitute parameters or conditions given to the industrializing élite that is leading the march. They shape the range of choice in economic policy that is available to the leaders seeking to push capital formation above the critical level of sustaining growth or beyond to ever more rapid expansion. They place in sober proportions the high flying aspirations to achieve industrialism. Among different countries, even at comparable stages of industrialization, there are very marked differences in these constraints upon the major decisions that shape the economy and the strategies of the élites. These constraints are outlined in the next two sections. The first considers economic limitations to development in the short period, and the second section indicates the constraints

Chart 4. Industrializing Élites and Cultural Factors

Pre-existing cultural traits	Middle-class	Dynastic
The family system	Weakens wider family; encourages nuclear family.	Preserves joint family.
Class and race	Modifies, develops fluid classes.	Preserves existing class structure.
Religious and ethical valuations	Modifies or builds on.	Tends to preserve.
Legal concepts	Developed to protect individual rights – and the law of the market.	National law developed to support existing élite and national state.
Concept of nation-state	Moderate emphasis.	Great emphasis.
The total culture	No policy towards the total culture.	Accepts for most part.

which arise from the historical timing and circumstances of the beginning of industrialization.

Economic Limitations in the Short Period

In every country, the industrializing élite confronts the following limitations in the short period:

1. the level of technology;
2. the known natural resources;
3. the educational development as it affects the skill, training, and experience of workers and the skill, organizing ability, and competence of the managerial and professional groups and government personnel;

Revolutionary intellectuals	Colonial administrators	Nationalist leaders
Destroy traditional family loyalty and responsibility.	Little change, unless breakup through labour recruiting.	Modify towards nuclear family.
Destroy, and substitute new élite class.	Substitute new superior class.	Modify existing structure – national state gives people sense of common citizenship.
Break or destroy – new valuations substituted.	Two cultures – slowly adapt.	Modify or break.
Administrative law – people's courts.	Two systems: national versus colonial.	Administrative – one system.
Great emphasis.	Little emphasis.	Great emphasis.
Drastically modify, or destroy.	Encourage dual culture, home and native.	Modify in part, accept in part.

4. the size of population, its age distribution, and the rate at which the population is increasing.

Since the above listing treats each country largely as a closed economy, a further factor accordingly needs to be added in an interdependent world:

5. the capacity to borrow funds or to secure grants or gifts from abroad and to export natural resources.

In the short period in which these dimensions are largely given, they constrict the possibilities of economic development, although they by no means uniquely determine the performance of an economy. In the short period, there is not very much which an industrializing élite can do about these dimensions except for grants from abroad. While some variations in style and size are possible, the economic suit must be cut to fit the given cloth.

The higher the level of technology, the richer and more highly utilized the natural resources, the higher the levels of education and applied skill in all sectors of the work force, the greater the availability of foreign capital and the greater the proportion of the population in education and in the active work force – in general, the greater the potential for economic growth.

The influence of the level of population and its rate of increase on economic growth depends largely upon the ratio of population to other resources. In relatively 'empty' countries a rapid rate of population increase may be essential to achieving a rate of capital formation compatible with any economic growth, as in Canada or Australia. But in relatively overpopulated countries like India or China, *per capita* economic growth is hampered by rising population.

Any comparison among countries reveals how large are the differences in the limitations which confront the industrializing élites, even if comparison be somehow restricted to countries in approximately the same stage of economic development. Some countries utilize the most modern technology, while technology in others is backward in many sectors. Some countries are richly endowed with a wide range of natural resources while others appear to be much less fortunate. The uneven world distribution of coal, oil, and water power is illustrative. Some countries have a skilled labour force with effective professional managers and public administrators, while other countries lack such resources. In some countries population is small relative to resources with an age distribution that results in a high proportion of the population in the working ages, while in other countries population is dense relative to resources, is increasing at a rapid rate, and the age distribution is relatively highly concentrated among children. Finally, some countries have ready access to scarce factors from abroad and secure generous capital grants or gifts, while other countries must rely almost exclusively on domestic resources. This range of limitations confronting industrializing élites may be expected to result in different rates of economic growth and in different economic policies among countries.

A brief illustration of the significance of these constraints is provided by a comparison of contemporary Iraq and Egypt. In agricultural land, Iraq is potentially rich and Egypt is desperately poor. Egypt must support today four times as many people as Iraq with less agricultural land than Iraq, whereas with even less new investment in dams and irrigation works and intensive land use than is contemplated in Egypt, Iraq could have an increase in agricultural production of three to four times that which would be technically possible in Egypt. Egypt's comparative position is even less favourable with regard to the availability of capital for investment in economic development. Iraq, in contrast, appears to have from oil resources an assured flow of funds for investment in needed development projects. Moreover, Egyptian population is increasing at a rate in excess of 2·5 per cent a year. These hard facts have convinced many Egyptians that it is practically and politically impossible to find an internal solution for the country's economic dilemma.

If the two countries are compared in terms of their human resources, the contrast is almost as sharp. But here the advantage lies with Egypt. Egypt has a large and comparatively well-trained body of civil servants, whereas Iraq is handicapped by an acute shortage. In the fields of social welfare, public health, rural community development, and agricultural extension services, Egypt is also far ahead of Iraq. Egypt eclipses Iraq in the field of education. Apart

111

from the foreign-managed oil companies Iraq has few skilled workers, technicians, or engineers. By contrast, Egypt has the high-level manpower for substantial industrialization. Human resources constitute the more serious restraint to economic development in Iraq[12] while natural resources are the more restrictive in Egypt. These strictures materially shape the direction of economic policies of any industrializing élite in the two countries.

While the five constraints noted above are relatively given and serve to limit and shape the potentialities of economic growth in the short period, they are not fixed over a longer period, and they frequently become the focus of policies designed by an industrializing élite to stimulate growth. The rapid and very high level of development in Japan after 1870 was made against the severe economic limitations of a high density of population, relatively poor natural resources, and a relatively low level of technology. Neither is the delayed economic development of Tsarist Russia[13] readily to be understood solely in terms of the short-period economic limitations noted above. As in other spheres of human experience, some handicaps may serve as an added incentive and may be compensated for by the development of skills in other directions. The economic development of Denmark, Switzerland, and England provide many illustrations of the stimulating character of some economic limitations and the compensating shaping of specialized skills and services.

Advanced technologies can be borrowed; systematic surveys and explorations may discover hitherto unknown natural resources; education, training, and health programmes raise the levels of skill and human performance; capital imports may be increased; and even the rate of increase of population may become the subject of public policies in some countries, although the independent effects of public policies are not well established. Indeed, the prospects for economic growth depend on the capacity of the industrializing élite to overcome these economic limitations and to provide fewer and less stringent constrictions to development. The short-period limitations are the principal locus of longer term economic development policies.

The Onset of Industrialization

The chronological date at which a country enters significantly the industrializing process makes a difference to the course of growth.[14] There are some advantages and some unfavourable consequences for industrial growth of early as compared with late starts. A late start has the frequently noted advantage of permitting industrialization with more advanced technology. It is likely to be more productive, to open up virgin territory with airplanes and modern equipment rather than with covered wagons and the technology of a century and a half ago. To an increasing degree, improvements in technology are capable of being rapidly distributed throughout the world; the present age is better organized for spreading knowledge and technology to those beginning industrialization. Technical assistance, relatively cheaper travel, technical journals, and the exchange of students are illustrative. The opportunity to plan the growth of cities for industrial society may result in many lower social costs relative to those involved in seeking to modernize older urban areas.

But a late start also involves many disadvantages and limitations to economic growth. In the past century the gap between the most advanced industrializing countries and those now just starting has widened appreciably. A late start has meant a relatively larger handicap and a greater distance to travel. The latecomer is particularly given to borrowing technology and machinery which may be poorly adapted to the relative distribution of resources of the country and which is likely to require a relatively larger importation than would have been necessary with more gradual and indigenous growth of technology. The latecomer is faced with the fact that modern technology frequently requires large-scale organizations, comprised in part of technical and professional groups, which cannot be created rapidly in a newly industrializing country. A late start frequently means a greater dependence on foreigners and a sharper change in social relations than would otherwise have been necessary. This is evident in almost all of the developing countries today.

In addition to these economic consequences, there are other major effects of an early or late start for managers or workers.

Industrialization at its formative stages in the modern world must now confront, to an extent that was not necessary among earlier starters, the economic and political organization of workers. Institutions as well as technology are borrowed, and they may not be well suited to the problems of countries at the early stages of industrialization. Labour organizations may be associated with a greater degree of industrial strife at the decisive formative stages, with relatively higher levels of wages, with relatively more advanced working rules and with a greater preoccupation with grievances than would have been likely with an historically earlier industrialization. 'While in other countries a period of very rapid industrial growth tended to be *followed by* a period of upward adjustments in the standard of living, in Italy the two processes tended to coincide. Had the industrial upsurge in Italy taken place one or two decades earlier, in all likelihood it would have been much less disturbed by industrial strife.'[15]

A study of the movement of real wages during the several most critical decades of early industrialization in countries now more advanced economically underscores the magnitude of the undertaking of many newly industrializing countries which promise one generation both industrialization and substantially higher real wages. Real wages may be increased in the sense that agricultural workers, usually with lower living standards, are absorbed into expanding industry at unchanged industrial wages. But some industrializing élites today promise immediate and substantially higher real wages to those already in industry; urban industrial workers are closer to the gains in productivity and are the more active and strategic group politically. But real wage rate increases of 1 per cent a year were a considerable achievement in the critical stages for economies at very much higher levels of development and without a substantial population problem. There was little, if any, rise in real wage rates in England between 1800 and 1830; and in the United States between 1840 and 1860 real wage rates increased less than 10 per cent a decade. The record for Sweden and Germany shows a higher rate in part because of the movement of world prices during the years of critical industrialization. In the Soviet Union after 1928 real wage rates declined.[16]

The role of I.L.O. conventions and resolutions is also a symbol of the change from an earlier period of industrialization. The drive for economic development and against backwardness often includes the adoption of the forms of modern labour legislation and social insurance. The international standards of the I.L.O. stimulate at the outset a full range of advanced labour standards which may impose a heavy burden on capital formation, even granting the difference between legal form and practice.

Any industrialization commenced after 1917, moreover, has had to face, and the more recent industrializing nations cannot avoid, the historically new problem that emerging workers' organizations may be captured or controlled by the communists. Industrializing élites must encourage or resist this development. The formation of the Indian National Trade Union Congress by the Indian Congress Party after independence (as a consequence of the capture of the All-India Trade Union Congress by the communists during the war) is a case in point. This response is a critical one at the early stages of an industrialization when the form and orientation of labour organizations have not been clearly established.

The magnitude of the economic constraints listed in the previous section at the time of the industrialization 'take-off' makes a difference in the process of development. The élite which seeks to steer an industrialization course starting from an exceptionally low level of technology and skills, with few developed resources and abnormally high rates of population increase, may be expected to have more difficult problems and perhaps require different methods than one which starts from a materially higher industrial base. Not all pre-industrial societies are equal. In some a political and a commercial revolution precede the industrial revolution, while in others these transformations are telescoped together.

The level of economic performance at which this break occurs may have far-reaching consequences on the process of industrialization that follows. It may be that the lower this initial level, the greater the strain called for by effective industrialization; the greater the burden put on the state in carrying through the necessary transformation; and possibly the pressure exercised by the state or other agents of industrialization upon the existing social institutions to effect the rapid change that is required. On the other hand, the higher the initial economic level, the easier it may be to secure the surplus necessary for facilitating the process of industrialization; the more gradual the transition may be; the less painful the pressures which the active agents of industrialization may be required to exercise upon those institutions and sectors in pre-industrial society that are likely to become less important as a result of the transformation.[17]

The timing of the initial thrust of industrialization and the level of productivity (or the degree of economic backwardness) from which a country starts are certain to shape the magnitude of the effort confronting the élite and the policies and decisions adopted to start the journey. The timing of industrialization and the starting level may also influence to a marked degree the chances of any particular leadership becoming the controlling élite to initiate industrialization.

Decisions of an Industrializing Élite

Any industrializing élite is required to make a series of major decisions – although the choices are not always conscious – within the economic constraints and the circumstances of the industrialization beginning. All alternatives of economic policy are not equally attainable, and these limitations and facts of history tend to shape in some measure the following basic decisions:

1. How fast shall the country industrialize, particularly in the earlier stages of the journey?

2. How shall industrialization be financed? What shall be the source of the funds used for the requisite capital formation?

3. What shall be the sequence in which industries are developed? What are the relative priorities to be given to heavy industries, social overheads, consumer goods and agriculture?

4. What pressures are placed upon enterprise management? How is the environment of the enterprise manager arranged?

5. What are the priorities in education and in the training of workers and managers? Education may be confined to a few or designed for the masses; the educational and vocational training system may be narrowly specialized or general; it may stress the

116

traditional culture or it may be more functionally related to the culture of industrialism.

6. What shall be the relation between industrialization in the one country and other parts of the world? Shall the country seek a relatively high degree of self-sufficiency or shall it specialize according to comparative advantage and substantially integrate its economy with others?

7. Shall public policy seek to do anything explicitly about the rate of increase in population? Are birth rates, death rates, and immigration to come within the purview of policy or to be treated largely as the result of uninfluenced decisions of households?

Taken as a group, the answers to these questions describe a programme and a time schedule for an industrializing élite. The answers are not isolated or independent of each other, and policies on one set of questions condition the others. Experience may show an élite that the separate answers are inconsistent, and the group of answers as a whole may need to be revised. The aspiration for rapid and immediate industrialization must deal with the costs of financing, the comparative advantage of raw materials, trade, external demands required for the growth of many industries, the social costs of industrial expansion, and the consequences of population increases. While these questions are discussed separately in this section, they must be considered by an élite simultaneously. The choices and answers must fit together more or less consistently if there is to be industrialization and if the élite is to survive.

Each of these seven major policy issues is considered in a subsection which also explores the answers to these questions provided by each of the ideal types of élites described in Chapter 2.

Pace of Industrialization

Perhaps the most fundamental decision of an industrializing élite concerns the pace of development. A decision on pace, resolutely pursued, significantly conditions and predisposes in large measure the other decisions confronting the élite. The middle-class approach asserts that speed should be determined by the individual choice of citizens between consumption and savings and by the decision of elected governments. The dynastic élite aspires to a pace no faster than essential to preserve itself and its traditional values or, if nationalistically oriented, to a pace as fast as required to achieve national goals. The colonial administrator sees the rate of colonial development as a by-product of the needs of the mother country for materials and of other claims for capital on the mother country within the limits essential to preserve his way of life. The revolutionary intellectuals regard it as their mission to attain the very highest possible rate consistent with the endurance of the population and continued control by the élite. The nationalist leader promises a rapid rate of industrialization to catch up with advanced nations and to remove the stigma of backwardness.

The greater the delay in industrialization, the more economically backward the country will be relative to others and the greater the gap to be narrowed. 'The rate of growth in a backward country during the early periods of its industrialization may be assumed to vary directly with the degree of the country's industrial backwardness. The more belated the big industrial upswing, the stronger it is likely to be when it comes.'[18] Countries recently starting to industrialize appear to begin from a materially lower pre-industrial base than the earlier starters. The late starters are likely to attempt to travel at a faster rate once they get under way. The example of Japan is a good illustration, for she became a modern industrial nation – the only one in Asia – in about eighty years.

Once an industrialization process gets under way, the more generous the resources and the less stringent all the economic limitations, the more rapid the potential rate of economic growth.

The more rapid the pace of development established by an élite, the larger will be the role of government in the industrialization process. 'In much of Southern Asia and the Middle East governments are impelled by forces largely outside their control to undertake tasks beyond their competence . . . A government that fails to seize the levers of economic development, or at least to make the attempt, is probably not long for this world.'[19] A rapid transfer of resources requires more central direction in an economy, as in wartime. A rapid rate of industrialization necessitates a higher rate of savings and capital formation than the individual members of the community choose to withhold voluntarily from consumption, requiring governmental action to secure promptly the requisite resources for expansion. Workers may not elect the occupations and private managers may not choose the types of output that are consistent with the rapid rate of industrialization, and the labour and product markets may operate too slowly or with too much dislocation, or they may not be sufficiently well established, to achieve the requisite resource reallocation or expansion in the limited time. The more rapid the disruption of the old society, the more extensive the governmental action to contain the dislocations, the opposition, and the resistance to the new industrial order.

Sources of Capital

Economic growth is directly related to an increase in capital relative to population (capital per head). Kuznets's data for western countries show the 'long-term proportion of net domestic capital formation to net national product ranges from about 5 to about 15 per cent', and 'the long-term proportion of gross domestic capital formation to gross national product ranges from about 10 to about 25 per cent'.[20]

An industrializing élite starting with a net investment no higher than 5 per cent per year of net national income is confronted with the basic problem of how to raise this figure substantially if a cumulative increase in output is to be achieved. The minimum necessary level will depend upon the rate of population increase and the (marginal) capital-output ratio. Thus, if population increases 1·5 per cent a year and the (marginal) capital-output ratio is 3:1, which may be said to approximate conditions in India, then 13·5 per cent of net national income is required as savings to increase net income 3 per cent per year. This rate of increase in real output would require 25 years to double national income and could scarcely be regarded as fast enough to narrow substantially the gap between India and the more advanced countries. A rate of 22·5 per cent of net national income allocated to capital formation would increase net income 5 per cent per year and result in some appreciable narrowing of the gap between a newly industrializing country and the most advanced, under the specified conditions.

But a more rapid rate of increase in population than 1·5 per cent a year (and rates of 3·0 per cent a year occur in some underdeveloped countries) would depress the rate of capital formation and the rate of increase of net national income. How is capital formation to be increased from 5 per cent of net income to a higher level such as 13·5 per cent or 22·5 per cent? What are the alternative methods among which an élite must choose?

In general terms the savings for capital formation may be derived from the following sources or achieved through the following mechanisms: (1) domestic savings from a given national income; (2) domestic savings from a larger national income; and (3) international transactions. Domestic savings from a given national income may arise from voluntary reduction of consumption, a change in the distribution of income favourable to high income recipients who save a higher proportion of their income, higher taxes, enterprise savings, reduced imports of consumption goods, and an inflationary process which transfers incomes to savers and restricts consumption among some groups. In addition, savings for capital formation may arise from the higher levels of income created in the course of economic growth such as from the profits of new industries and the development of resources, such as oil. Particular mention should also be made of increases in real output arising from the use of resources previously only partially employed or subject to disguised unemployment as in agriculture. The use of rural populations for road building and irrigation projects which do not require large outlays of capital is also illustrative. International transactions may result in private or public loans or grants. Changes in the terms of trade, which result in relatively more favourable movements in export prices than import prices, may be used for capital formation.

Industrializing élites have differed quite widely in their policies regarding sources of capital and their choices among the possibilities. The sources of capital may also vary in the course of economic growth. Some élites are fortunate in being able to secure capital for economic growth from the development of a few key resources sold in the world markets, such as oil in Iraq and oil and minerals in Venezuela. In other cases, the élites have had to rely almost entirely upon domestic savings, as in the case of the Soviet Union.

The sources of capital are closely related to other decisions in the strategy of industrialization adopted by an élite. The more rapid the rate of industrialization, the greater the reliance upon domestic savings and particularly upon various forms of forced reduction in consumption by taxation and inflation. When an élite seeks as much as 25 per cent of net national income for capital formation, voluntary savings cannot be expected to supply such amounts. The larger the amount of capital expected above the levels of voluntary savings, in general, the more stringent the system of controls required to secure the requisite reduction in consumption. The pace of industrialization and the sources of capital are thus related to the means chosen to secure the requisite savings. The more rapid the pace and the greater the reliance on the constriction of domestic consumption, in general, the greater the scope and depth of governmental controls, including the control over the relations of workers and managers.

Among the different ideal types of élites with internally consistent strategies of industrialization, there are distinctive patterns of the sources of capital formation.

The industrializing middle class tends to rely upon domestic and foreign capital markets for capital formation. The voluntary choices of individual households between present consumption and a future stream of income, plus private business profits and savings, all supplemented to some degree by taxation, constitute the domestic sources of capital. The foreign sources are determined in relatively free capital markets by the decisions of business leaders seeking private profits. The amounts of capital available from these sources may be expected to vary from period to period, depending on economic conditions.

The dynastic élite tends to make governmental grants and subsidies for the establishment of new industries which are frequently protected by continuing high tariffs. Taxation and inflation, in which wages lag, are characteristic sources of capital. Agricultural rents may be channelled systematically into industrialization, as in Japan. The system of direct controls is not so rigid as in the case of some other élites since the required rate of capital formation is not large unless the nationalists and military are in the ascendancy. The amount of capital available from period to period depends largely upon the fluctuating favours of a paternalistic government.

The transitory élite of colonial administrators secures capital largely from the home country for major projects of development, designed to fit into the needs of the home country and for the defence and administration of the colony; other isolated capital formation is secured from the natives by taxation, but no rounded or balanced programme of economic development is contemplated. The amount of capital formation from period to period depends on the competing needs and urgencies in the governmental and private budgets of the home country and in the sharp variations in the terms of trade, and there is apt to be a high degree of variability in capital formation under these circumstances. British India, the Dutch East Indies, and colonial Africa are well-known examples.

The revolutionary intellectuals secure capital almost exclusively from the strict control over consumption by an elaborate system of governmental controls. Even when gross product rises with industrialization, consumption tends to be kept at previous levels or increased only slightly in order to use the surplus value of economic growth for further expansion. Foreign sources of capital do not play a role except as governmental grants or loans may be made from other sympathetic élites, as in the case of Russia's assistance to China. The amount of capital available from period to period tends to be relatively less liable to short-term variations as the revolutionary élite seeks to devote a relatively constant percentage (and growing absolute amount of national product) to capital formation under a series of long-term plans.

The nationalist leaders in the early stages of industrializing are likely to be in a particularly difficult position with regard to securing capital. The drive for independence and national prestige may conflict in a variety of ways with the need for capital (and skills) from abroad. Foreign property may be expropriated or nationalized at the very time a promised increase in goods is held out to the masses as the achievement of independence (Indonesia). Foreigners may be less acceptable precisely at the time when the need for them is greatest if industry is to be established. There is a demand for quick results and for a show of national performance. It is hard to squeeze consumption tighter than did the previous colonial administrators or semi-feudal governments, particularly when production may be reduced from the dislocations arising with independence or revolution. There is a great tendency under these circumstances to seek large political and governmental loans from abroad to provide major capital formation, and to resort to inflationary fiscal policies. The amount of capital formation from period to period under these circumstances may be expected to go in spurts with loans covering a period or a series of projects, followed by a period of uncertainty and decline until new arrangements, if any, can be made.

Priorities by Sector

A decisive question for an industrializing élite is the priority to assign to the development of particular sectors or industries. What industries shall be pushed first? How broad or how concentrated a sector of development should be attempted at one time? Shall the 'classical' form be followed – attention first to light industries such as textiles, shoes, and other consumer goods – or shall the model of heavy industry first be adopted? What emphasis shall be placed upon industries which yield immediate results in greater food output, foreign exchange, prestige or popular support compared to those which provide a longer period base for broad industrialization such as transport, power, and utilities for urban growth? What priority is to be assigned to housing which can be an enormous consumer of available capital outlays? What expenditures are to go to the development of the educational system? How large an expenditure is to be made on health services, sanitation, and other means of raising efficiency and alleviating sufferings which are also likely to increase population by reducing the death rate? In more formal terms, what shall be the allocation of capital and other scarce resources at the margin?

The task of assigning priorities among sectors is the more difficult the greater the economic limitations and the less the volume of capital formation, where a little capital confronts large conflicting claims, and where there is danger that a scattering of capital resources and a change of emphasis from year to year may show few cumulative results. The larger the capital melon the easier it is to split.

The assignment of priorities must take into consideration certain technical interrelations among industries and among the skills required of managers and workers. A textile machinery plant generally awaits the growth of an extensive textile industry and an electric motor plant the development of power generating plants. An automobile factory awaits the earlier development of steel and an engineering base.

The view that an advanced industrial plant can only be built upon the base of less complicated plants does not appear to be as valid as it was once thought to be, because of the possibility of importing a limited number of technicians. There is apparently no technical reason for industrializing countries now to repeat the sequence of industrial development of the earliest countries – from cotton textiles, to light machinery, to heavy industry. The establishment of an oil refinery appears to pose, even in the least advanced countries, few more serious difficulties than the establishment of a modern textile mill in the same country. In so far as considerably less labour needs to be trained, the more advanced technology may be easier to establish. The availability of transport, power, repair, and financing facilities are the types of external economies, however, which are frequently significant to the priority for the establishment of an industry, and in this sense an industrializing economy may have to go through some of the same stages as the economies which started earlier.

All industrializing élites adopt policies about the priorities in development. Although each must confront the particular economic limitations of its country, the technical interrelations among sectors, and the facts of external economies, each of the ideal types of élites faces these issues of priorities consistent with its larger strategy of industrialization.

When the middle class directs the industrializing process, the size of the agricultural sector is determined much more by the rigours of international competition, and it tends to be a relatively smaller sector unless it constitutes an industrial agriculture of highly specialized crops. The sequence of industrial growth among sectors depends largely upon the market process and the prospects for private investment opportunities. The pattern of industrial growth tends to proceed from the relatively simple technologies to the more advanced. This sequence may be modified by military considerations. Public works are a relatively less serious claimant for capital resources, and the extent of housing expenditures depends upon the market and the incomes and preferences of households.

The dynastic élite tends to preserve the traditional prestige and position of agriculture, and it is likely to be highly protected by tariffs. Industrial development which is particularly significant for a military base tends to receive encouragement, subsidy, and protection. Public works, monuments and shrines, and paternalistic projects including housing receive relatively liberal allocations of capital.

The colonial administrators seek to develop first those industries which are expected to be most essential to the mother country for direct consumption or for raw materials, or which furnish needed foreign exchange in the world market. 'Foreign capital continues to be strongly attracted to extractive industries . . .'[21] The range of development tends to be constricted.

The revolutionary intellectual élite stresses a programme of intensive capital outlays on basic industries essential for long-term growth and a military base. Agricultural manpower is sharply constricted to speed the forced-draft industrialization in rural or urban areas, and agricultural produce is procured from farmers at the least favourable terms consistent with requisite production. In keeping with the constriction of consumption, housing receives a very low priority except where absolutely necessary to recruit labour supply. The Russian experience is a clear example of these points.

The nationalist leaders are primarily concerned with broadening the economic development of the prior colonial or quasi-feudal administration to achieve a full scale and full range of industries.

Many industries, such as basic steel, shipbuilding, or air transportation are developed for reasons of prestige as well as economic growth. Industries of military significance emerge and capital expenditures for military installations are made where facilities are not taken over from the colonial or feudal administrators.

Pressures on Enterprises

An industrializing élite, in arranging its broad policies, has a variety of alternatives concerning the pressures to place on industrial enterprises and their managers. Shall they operate under great and immediate pressure for output, or shall they feel little direct compulsion to perform? Shall the pressure come predominantly from the product market or from governmental bureaucracy? Shall the labour market be used to place pressures on enterprise managers, or shall they be substantially freed, to the extent possible, from such direct pressures? These questions are closely interrelated with the other decisions considered in this chapter. The decision on pace of industrialization is again decisive. The general strategies of the various ideal types of élites create quite different pressures on enterprise managers (Chapters 4 and 5).

The middle-class élite relies on competitive markets to generate pressures on enterprise managers. The tendency to cartels is curbed, and the test of profits is used to generate pressures on enterprise managers to become more efficient, to expand output and to develop technical change. Labour organizations are designed to regulate management narrowly at the work place; they press for wage increases and rules at the work place which constrict enterprise managers. This type of society believes that managers squeezed between competitive product markets and labour markets with plant-oriented labour organizations will generate under profit incentives the highest standards of performance, as in the United States. Managers produce when placed in a market sweat-box. The planned direction of a centralized bureaucracy in this view is unwise and violates the general middle-class strategy of industrialization.

The dynastic élite places enterprise managers under little pressure from any source; the pace of industrialization except when directed by strong nationalist drives makes no strong demands. The enterprises are organized into cartels, and the domestic product markets transmit no strong demand for efficiency or for production. International competition is often limited by tariffs and quotas, although the quest for international markets may be a pressure making for efficiency in certain enterprises. The labour organizations are not interested or designed to place pressures on enterprise managers for efficiency and productivity. The governmental bureaucracy does not provide quotas or detailed plans, although a patriotic and military-minded élite can generate considerable pressure on enterprise management for modernization and industrial output, as in pre-war Japan.

The colonial system by and large places relatively little pressure on enterprise managers. The enterprise confronts little domestic or international competition; its markets tend to be highly protected. The administrators of the home country are at great distance, and do not closely supervise the enterprise. Local 'managing agents' may develop, as in British India. No labour organization places significant pressure on managers, although labour shortages and labour turnover may compel attention to labour efficiency if other measures, including forced labour, cannot be found to secure a labour force at low wages.

The revolutionary intellectuals seeking rapid industrialization are compelled to place enterprise managers under very heavy pressure. They use the carrot of premiums and money rewards, but they also rely heavily on the bureaucratic stick. The enterprise is under great pressure to achieve the production plan targets established by the centralized state. The career aspirations of the manager, the party apparatus, the labour organizations, and the ideology all focus upon this objective. Managers produce when placed in this bureaucratic squeeze. The market, domestic or international, plays a relatively little role in placing pressure on enterprise managers. Labour organizations are directed towards increasing the productivity of workers rather than regulating the managers, as is true of Russian trade unions.

The nationalist élite faces perplexing problems in organizing the environment of the enterprise manager. The independence movement may have affected the production and efficiency of enterprises under foreign managers. Domestic product markets are not well established, and the nationalist leaders may wish to insulate the new enterprises from the rigours of international markets. Labour organizations arising in the independence movement are not particularly concerned with plant level issues. Moreover, they have high aspirations for rewards. This élite struggles with the problem of how to organize the environment of enterprise managers, and it tends to attempt to regulate private entrepreneurs and encourage the formation of public enterprises. This has happened, for example, in India and in Egypt.

The Educational System

An industrializing élite confronts a variety of questions concerning the educational arrangements it shall encourage. More issues are involved than the priority to be given to the development of educational institutions. Shall the education be generally available, or shall it be restricted to the few? Shall education be general and liberal or narrowly related and specialized to the technical needs of industrialization? An élite comes to develop an educational policy consistent with its general strategy of industrialization and its other policy decisions.

The middle-class élite believes in widespread public education. The faculty and students are free to pursue their interests and lines of training and careers suggested by individual tastes, the culture, and the market. Education is general and is not uniquely related to the technical needs of industrialization, though increasing attention comes to be given to the sciences and to professions and skills required for industrial growth, as in Great Britain and the United States. The educational arrangements constitute one of the principal means of vertical mobility in the community. Widespread education is essential to the political processes.

The dynastic élite, in the preservation of tradition, provides education for the relative few and for select élite groups. Education stresses the humanities and law and provides only the amount of scientific education required for its rate of growth. Traditional values and religion are stressed in the educational system at all levels. The universities have little role in the industrialization process. There is little interest in the formal training of workers at the work place or community beyond elementary education and apprenticeship; the family managers receive little specialized education. When the dynastic élite is determined to industrialize quickly, as in Japan after the Meiji reformation, however, the emphasis on technical and engineering training and university development is much greater.

The colonial administrator largely adopts the educational system of the mother country, except that higher education is often confined to only a small number of indigenous people, and they are often educated in the mother country. Education is limited to the number required to perpetuate and administer the colony. This was certainly true in British India.

The revolutionary intellectuals develop an educational system narrowly specialized to the imperative needs of rapid industrialization. Scientific education receives a high priority, and specialized training is developed for rapid growth. Mass education at the level of workers is pushed to eliminate illiteracy and to make a more functional and productive work force. The Russian educational system is a prime example.[22]

The nationalist leader seeks to free the educational system from its ties with the previous power group and to develop educational forms which reflect prestige on the newly industrializing nation. The choice between using limited resources for mass education or for the development of universities and research organizations for the training of high level manpower is a major dilemma, as nearly every developing country today is discovering.[23]

Self-sufficiency or Economic Integration

An industrializing élite must decide the extent to which a country seeks economic self-sufficiency and the extent it shall partake in the world economy through capital and commodity markets and, to a lesser extent, through labour migration. The same range of alternatives is not open to all élites since the economic limitations, including the size of countries, vary so widely. But at the margin each élite decides on a greater or a lesser degree of a self-sufficient economy.[24]

Before the Second World War, countries at the early stages of industrialization tended to specialize in the production of primary and raw materials which were exported to the industrially more advanced countries in exchange for finished products for consumption and investment goods. The less developed countries brought three major complaints against this arrangement: (1) in periods of depression the terms of trade moved sharply against the raw materials producers, but in prosperity, as terms of trade reversed, they were frequently unable to secure deliveries of finished goods without great delays, and these delays were accentuated by war-time and periods of crises; (2) the instability of income and the high degree of uncertainty added significantly to the difficulties of economic development and left public and private planning to the mercy of exterior events; and (3) the concentration on raw materials production in accordance with the economic law of comparative advantage hindered economic and political development.

There has developed since the end of the Second World War a considerable tendency towards a higher degree of self-sufficiency in raw materials among economically advanced countries and a lesser degree of specialization in raw materials by many of the former exporters of raw materials. (This condition is not, of course, incompatible with an expansion of international trade in manufactured goods among industrializing countries.) This development is the consequence of synthetic raw materials and the drive for industrialization among producers of raw materials.

The general strategy of the ideal types of élites with regard to self-sufficiency or economic integration may be characterized as follows:

The middle-class-directed industrialization relies heavily on the market for economic decisions; it tends to create an economy relatively highly integrated with the rest of the world through private commodity and capital transactions. Protectionism is applied on military and 'infant industry' grounds, and international competition is seldom allowed quickly to destroy an industry. But the integrated economic world and the common market are the ideals for countries at all stages along this road.

The dynastic élite tends to develop a relatively high degree of self-sufficiency; tariff and subsidy policies are designed to reduce the dependence upon the rest of the world. However, a strong drive towards military strength may lead towards a development of manufacturing export industries with which to procure the foreign exchange to build up an industrial base for the military establishment. Generous loans from allies may accomplish the same purpose without increasing integration to the same degree with the rest of the world.

The colonial administrators seek to integrate fully with the mother country, rather than with the rest of the world, as suppliers of raw materials and as a protected market for exports. The range of exports and imports to the rest of the world will be determined largely in relation to the needs of the home country for foreign exchange in world markets.

The revolutionary intellectual élite tends to create a highly self-sufficient economic system with a strong military base. Even among allies exchange tends to be sporadic and irregular, unless it is the concomitant of political decisions. Trade and exchange are a sign of weakness, and self-sufficiency proof of strength and economic development. Imports are concentrated upon strategic materials, equipment and technical items, and exports are only those requisite to purchase strategic imports or to implement political activities.

The nationalist leaders are torn between continuing and expanding specialization in raw materials exports, particularly if terms of trade are favourable to raw materials producers, in order to increase foreign exchange for later economic development, and the need to show prompt signs of industrial development by devoting capital resources directly to industry and to an industrial base. A larger stream of resources over time for foreign markets may be sacrificed to immediate self-sufficiency in industrial production. The nationalist leaders are particularly ambivalent to world markets as they balance economic integration with national prestige.

The Response of Population

The decisions of an élite in the area of population policy are not independent of other major questions, although an élite may be less able to affect population than other constraints to industrialization. It may be observed again that the pace of industrialization and the source of capital are particularly dependent upon the response of the population. In considering the strategy of any élite, a distinction should be drawn between policies which are specifically designed to affect the response of population and the indirect effects of a variety of other policies upon the response of population. Within a given framework of economic limitations, the different types of élite seek to influence the response of population to industrialization in the following ways:

The middle class tends to regard population as largely beyond the range of direct public policy, except for immigration. The natural change in population is the consequence of market forces and incomes, including public expenditures on health and sanitation, on birth rates and death rates. An 'empty' country is likely to permit widespread immigration, possibly restricted to particular ethnic groups.

The dynastic élite tends to adopt a variety of policies which stimulate population growth, except in the face of gross overpopulation, as in Japan. The family is given a high value; compensation often includes family allowance payments, and paternalism is the dominant philosophy towards workers. A strong military policy may also seek to encourage the expansion in population. There is little, if any, encouragement of immigration.

The colonial administrators are unconcerned with population responses as long as there is a liberal supply of labour at the work place. When there are shortages, various means are adopted, including forced labour, to encourage internal migration or immigration. The different policies of recruitment of males from villages by contract for limited periods, as compared with recruitment by families and the establishment of company towns and urban communities, may have important consequences for the birth rate.

The revolutionary intellectuals approach population responses more explicitly, with their longer view of the industrialization process, than do other élites. They seek in different ways to hold down the birth rate through less attention to housing, recruitment of women to industry, the rapid contraction of agriculture where birth rates tend to be higher, and with lesser expenditures on public health and social overheads except as they affect directly the efficiency of the work force at the work place. The industrializing process is admittedly more harsh. Immigration is not encouraged and internal movement of the work force is frequently subject to rigid controls.

The nationalist leaders, particularly in 'crowded' countries, are likely to find that the response of population to the beginnings of industrialization constitutes one of the most difficult and perplexing questions, about which very little can apparently be done. Industrialization in such a country drops the death rate; the population increases rapidly for a period until birth rates are reduced. But the rise in population in the 'crowded' country tends to make the task of industrialization vastly more complex. It is difficult for this élite to encourage emigration. Population responses pose the sternest of problems to the nationalist leader in the 'crowded' country, as in India and Egypt.

Implications of Decisions for Workers and Managers

Every industrializing élite must confront the group of seven decisions outlined in the preceding section, although the choices are not always conscious. How fast? How to finance? What priorities? What pressures on managers? What educational system? Self-sufficient or integrated? What population? Each of the ideal types of industrializing élites develops a body of more or less internally consistent policies incorporating these decisions. The decision on the pace of industrialization is the most fundamental, but the decisions as a group must be internally consistent. These decisions and policies have decisive implications for workers and managers. The set of seven decisions as a group predisposes a distinctive pattern of labour-management-state relations (Chapters 4–7). They narrowly determine, for instance, the extent to which consumption need be curtailed, which groups shall have their consumption constricted and by what methods, how workers shall be made to work harder and faster, the severity of the rules of the work place, how a work force is recruited and moved about, what forms labour organizations take and the functions they exercise, and other features of industrial relations.

The middle-class élite is characterized by reliance upon the markets and elected governments to determine the pace of industrialization. Domestic savings reflected in the domestic capital markets and international transactions largely establish the pace, although it may vary a good deal among countries with different economic limitations and with different individual choices reflected in the markets. The reduction of resources in agriculture is a gradual process, largely based on the decisions of individuals (landlords, farmers, tenants or labourers) to seek higher incomes in urban employment. Inflation is not an approved method of restricting consumption, except in war-time or in moderate degree. The labour market is relied upon to reallocate the labour force by occupation, industry, and regions. Considerable emphasis is placed upon the pace of work; discipline is highly developed; the principal means of motivating the labour force is resort to monetary incentives and to individualistic ethical values. Original recruitment to the industrial work force is by individuals or families seeking their best opportunities; the population response is left to individual choices without public policy. The reliance upon the market means that the effective web of rules is established at decentralized points between enterprise managers and independent workers.

The dynastic élite is generally content (except under strong nationalist drives) with a less strenuous and a slower pace. Less consumption need be diverted to investment out of a given national income, and the prestige position of traditional farmers and landlords means that agricultural arrangements are seldom drastically reorganized to release resources, although technical improvements to increase agricultural output may be stimulated. The requisite constriction of consumption, above voluntary savings, is frequently achieved by price inflation and unbalanced budgets. There is less pressure on workers to develop discipline and a rapid pace of work or to disturb traditional values; there is less need for geographical mobility, particularly in a community exalting family and tradition. Recruitment of the work force to industrial activity from the native reservation or rural areas is by families rather than by bachelors. Population increases are viewed favourably without regard to narrow economic considerations, except in cases of extreme overpopulation, in line with traditional values and a lesser concern with a rapid pace of industrialization. The slower pace and the views of the dynastic élite tend to create a general body of minimum rules which has little direct impact upon most workers and managers at actual work places. The paternalistic enterprise managers largely establish the rules for the dependent workers.

The colonial administrators determine an industrialization pace according to the needs and interests of the home country. This pace may be rapid or slow, and hence workers and enterprise managers confront problems and develop characteristics indicated by the three major élites discussed above. The colonial administrators' concentration upon extractive industries, such as plantation agriculture and mining, tends to create a limited group of occupations in the work force rather than the full range which arises under broader-scale industrialization. The organization of the labour market is a major preoccupation, to provide a surplus of unskilled labour by force if necessary. The colonial administrator reserves certain occupations, particularly in the managerial and supervisory categories, to citizens of the home country. The wage and salary structures reflect accordingly very wide differentials among occupations.

The revolutionary intellectuals are devoted to the most rapid possible pace of industrialization consistent with continued control. Traditional agriculture is rapidly and drastically reorganized to release resources to urban areas and to industry. The rapid pace also may require constriction of incomes of industrial workers for an extended period. The accumulation of savings from industry is put back into heavy goods expansion rather than to raise current living standards. The use of stringent direct controls means that inflation is a less essential and generally less effective device to constrict consumption. Labour is recruited and allocated

Chart 5. (a) Summary of Policies of Élites Shaping Industrialization

Basic decisions	Middle-class	Dynastic
Pace of industrialization	Pace set by prospects of private gain, individual choices and limited actions of government. Moderate pace.	No faster than necessary to preserve the traditional élite and its values. Military needs may dictate a more rapid pace.
Sources of funds	Market decisions by voluntary household and business savings, bank credit and international capital market. Continuity depends on uncertainty and variations of the market. International sources sometimes significant.	Paternalistic grants and protection. Agricultural rents may be significant. Continuity of funds depends upon government favours which vary. International sources rarely significant.
Priorities in development	Agriculture compressed by international competition. Sequence depends on market, and traditional pattern is from consumers to basic industry. Housing depends on market.	Preserves and protects agriculture; public works, monuments and paternalistic projects including housing.

Revolutionary intellectuals	Colonial administrators	Nationalist leaders
The fastest possible pace under an extensive set of controls.	Dependent solely upon the advantage of the mother country.	High aspiration and promises but uncertain rate.
Forced restriction of consumption by taxation and other means to secure very large proportion of net national income for capital formation. Continuity stable. Largely domestic supply.	Funds from budget of mother country; continuity depends on budget pressures.	Tend to seek large sums from abroad to supplement domestic savings but difficulties great, supply variable and short-term.
Agriculture compressed by draining manpower and preventing individual agricultural enterprises. Priority to basic industry with a vengeance. Housing compressed.	Industries developed which furnish materials or consumption goods to mother country or supply foreign exchange.	Aspire to a broad industrial base, expand on the range of the previous colonial administrator. Prestige items.

Basic decisions	Middle-class	Dynastic
Pressures on enterprise managers	Strong pressure: competitive product markets domestically and internationally. Labour organizations oriented towards the plant level generate pressure on managers.	Weak pressure: cartelized product markets and tariffs restrict international competition. Labour organizations have little interest in the plant level.
The educational system	Liberal education; mass education; educational system a major instrument in vertical mobility for workers and their families.	Preserves traditional values; higher education limited to élitists; universities have little role in industrialization; workers have only elementary education.
Self-sufficiency or economic integration	The financial and commodity markets tend to create a high degree of international interdependence.	A relatively high degree of self-sufficiency particularly where military considerations are important.
The response of population	Population a response to few public policies; largely depends upon market forces, incomes and public expenditures on health which may be indirectly encouraging. Permit immigration.	A variety of policies tend indirectly to stimulate growth. No encouragement to immigration.

Revolutionary intellectuals	Colonial administrators	Nationalist leaders
Strong pressure: bureaucratically determined production plan targets are supported by party, labour organizations and career interests.	Weak pressure: domestic and international product markets have little impact, and labour organizations are oriented to nationalist interests. Labour shortages may generate some pressure in some cases, but other methods of recruiting cheap labour are likely to be emphasized.	Complex and difficult problem of organizing the environment of the enterprise manager. Little pressure on the whole.
Education bound to revolutionary ideology; high priority to science and specialized fields; workers receive specialized training.	Education adapted from mother country; higher education limited to few natives and training often only in mother country.	Educational system designed to be independent and to seek prestige. Dilemma of general education versus training of high-level manpower.
A high degree of self-sufficiency.	Integrate with the mother country.	Conflict between the aspirations for self-sufficiency and the need for integration for development.
A variety of policies are designed to constrict the tendency of population to increase in response to industrialization. No immigration.	No concern with population if labour supply adequate. Otherwise recruit labour in the colony or abroad.	Conflict between means to decrease death rate and the impediment of population increases in 'crowded' countries.

to new occupations, industries, and regions by a combination of monetary incentives and compulsion. The great emphasis upon the pace of work and discipline is stimulated by universal incentives, methods of pay, and devotion to a rigorous ideology. Where population increases are viewed as an impediment to the pace of industrialization, public policies are adopted to constrict the population response to industrialization. The web of rules is centrally determined by the élite for the dependent class of workers and administered at the work place by managerial, party, and labour organization representatives of the élite.

The nationalist leaders confront most serious problems in setting the pace of industrialization. The aspirations of the masses have

Chart 5. (b) Implications of Policies for Workers and Managers

Implications for workers and managers	Middle-class	Dynastic
Pressure to constrict consumption	Savings arise from voluntary savings and taxes of democratic government.	Relatively little pressure since slow pace.
Methods of restricting consumption	Private savings.	Inflation.
Policies towards agriculture	Contraction by market forces alone.	Minor structural dislocation except to increase efficiency for export surplus to cities.
Methods of allocation of labour	Reliance upon the labour market and public training.	Family and community ties limit mobility of labour and make for greater need for mobility of capital.
Methods of motivating labour force	The personal ethic of hard work and money rewards.	Loyalty to tradition, family and church.

been stimulated to expect immediate and large results with national independence, while the political uncertainties of a new state and often the loss of confidence by foreign sources of capital make only a much slower pace possible. The nationalist leaders are concerned to expand the scope of industrial activity beyond the extractive industries of the colonial administrators and to open up new occupations to nationals, particularly in technical, administrative, and managerial posts. The wide wage and salary differentials of the colonial administrators are narrowed. The nationalist leaders find it necessary to control in a variety of ways the organizations of strategic industrial workers in the interest of the national effort to industrialize.

The implications of the policies of each ideal type of industrial-

Revolutionary intellectuals	Colonial administrators	Nationalist leaders
Stringent constriction of consumption for rapid pace.	Depends on needs of mother country.	High aspirations but pressure difficult to apply.
Direct controls on a broad front.	Direct controls on a few items, particularly imports.	Inflation.
Sweeping reorganization to release resources and increase output.	Develop in specialized directions for mother country.	Tendency to neglect in programme for industrial development.
Direct allocation and training with emphasis upon monetary incentives.	Direct allocation of native labour and importation of high-level skills.	Training of nationals to replace foreigners.
An ideological compulsion and money rewards.	Limited compulsion, limited acceptance into ruling group in a few cases.	Nationalism as an ideal.

izing élite for workers and managers are summarized in Chart 5.

Conclusion

Each of the industrializing élites confronts a specific set of cultural factors and economic constraints which shape the industrialization process. These tend to impart a unique character in a particular country to the more universal aspects of the industrialization process.

For example, the nationalist leaders in India since independence in 1947, in their pursuit of rapid industrialization, have emphasized cultural and religious values which stressed saving and hard work; preserved a legal system which protects individual and property rights; strengthened the role of the central government in economic planning and development; borrowed modern technology and imported technicians from abroad; emphasized heavy industry; stressed the importance of advanced training in science, engineering, and industrial management; encouraged family planning to limit population growth; sought foreign capital (both private and government) to help finance the industrialization effort; and (because of difficulties with earlier forms of private enterprise) put pressure on private and public enterprise management to produce more efficiently and with a greater sense of social responsibility.

Even though many of these same developments would be found in other countries seeking to industrialize, the Indian effort is distinctive because of the special cultural and economic factors peculiar to India. The divisive forces present in the caste system and the linguistic and regional groups have made the central government's task more difficult, as has the heritage of an educational system more appropriate for a colonial country than for an industrializing nation. The support for cottage and handicraft industries traditional to Indian villages has sometimes been in conflict with modern technology.

These forces make India's industrialization effort different from that in Japan, or Egypt, or Brazil, or Ghana. These special features resulting from cultural and economic constraints need emphasis as we turn to the impact of the industrialization process and the strategies of the industrializing élites on managers and workers and on their relations with each other and with government.

4   Managers of Enterprises: Their Power, Position, and Policies

In the preceding chapters, a central theme has been presented: industrialization is spearheaded by a minority group. This group comprises particular types of élites or combinations of élites. These élites are confronted with certain historic and economic facts, and they operate within identifiable cultural contexts. The uniformity and diversity which are observable among industrializing societies are thus explained by the nature of the élites and the decisions which they make in the light of environmental forces which press upon them.

In this and the following three chapters, attention is directed more specifically to the position, attitudes, policies, and actions of managers, workers, and governments. Here the principal objective will be to explain in more concrete terms the structure and organization of the industrial labour force and the factors which determine relationships between the managers and the managed in industrializing societies.

The managers of enterprises, public and private, obviously play a pivotal role in any industrialization effort. Together with their technical and professional associates, they are part of every industrializing élite. And their policies and practices have far-flung influence in shaping the structure and organization of the industrial working forces. The managers in this context include entrepreneurs, administrators, engineers, and specialists who hold top positions in public or private enterprises.[1] Collectively, they form a hierarchy of functions and people which is called management.

Management may be analysed from different perspectives. First, it may be looked upon as an economic resource or factor of production. In this respect it is analogous to capital, labour, or natural resources, and it is combined with them in varying factor proportions in productive processes. Second, management is a class into which access is limited. In any industrializing society, the members of management are a small but active minority, and they enjoy a measure of prestige, privilege, and power as part of the élite. Third, and finally, management can be viewed as a rule-making authority over the workers. In this role, it seeks to establish, to bolster, and to make legitimate its prerogatives to determine the conditions under which the industrial working forces labour.

Management as an Economic Resource

As an economic resource, management is similar in many respects to capital. A growing economy must be able to accumulate capital and invest it in productive activity. It must likewise accumulate managerial resources and utilize them effectively in public or private enterprises. Management, indeed, is a form of human capital which is indispensable for successful industrial development.

As a country industrializes, it uses management more intensively – the proportion of managerial resources in the labour force increases with economic growth. There are several reasons for this development.

First, as enterprises become larger and more complex, they require greater numbers of highly trained people. Pre-industrial societies are characterized by small handicraft and trading shops or small loan enterprises run by individuals or by families. Although they may require an 'enterprising spirit' and a good deal of shrewdness, they do not call for much integrative or managerial skill. But, as a country industrializes, it begins to develop sizeable wholesale trading organizations, financial institutions, railways, ports, public utilities, and factories. These require much larger and more complex managerial hierarchies that ordinarily cannot be drawn from single families. Here a great many more managers, professional specialists, and administrators are required.

Second, as markets grow wider, enterprises become more complicated. The local market, which is characteristic of the less developed economies, is a relatively simple institution. Buyers and sellers all congregate in a single location and clear the market through direct dealings. But nationwide and international markets, which are characteristic of advanced industrialization, require a wide range of detailed information at frequent intervals. The price and quality of products have many dimensions and often require technical specification. The costs of wrong judgements may be very high. Thus, enterprises tend to make large investments in market research departments, sales forces, and economic analysis, as well as in accounting, costing, and budgeting. Such activities call for considerable expansion of specialized personnel in the managerial hierarchy.

Third, as product processes become more capital-intensive, they also tend to become more management-intensive. Large investments in machinery and processes in themselves require more and better trained managerial resources. If, as is usually the case, the machinery and processes are complicated, engineers, chemists, or other technical staff specialists are required. Labour-saving machinery usually requires greater investment in personnel who specialize in planning, production scheduling, engineering, and 'control' of all kinds. When a business organization employs technicians to supervise and control more complicated processes, there is also need for more experienced top management to co-ordinate their activities and to plan for future developments. The technological revolution requires more management, not less.

Fourth, as the external political and social environment of enterprises becomes more complex, staffs of specialists are necessary to deal with external problems. The large-scale enterprise must have tax experts, lawyers, management association representatives, labour relations specialists, and those with political and governmental contacts.

Fifth, and finally, as the pace of innovation increases, the utilization of high-level manpower resources expands. The classic individual inventor, who developed a new process or product in his isolated workshop or laboratory, is increasingly being replaced in advanced industrial countries by the industrial research laboratory, which represents a substantial investment in highly trained chemists, physicists, engineers, and other technically trained manpower. As industrialization reaches an advanced state, the enterprise emerges as an organization of high-talent managerial resources, with product development specialists, production engineers, and planning departments, all coordinated and directed by divisional and top managers.

There is clear evidence of the relationship between investment in high-level human resources and innovation in the United States. An examination of the changing employment structure in fifty American companies since the Second World War showed very clearly that the greatest proportional increase in technical, professional, administrative, and managerial personnel took place in the firms which were investing most heavily in changes in processes, machinery, products, and methods of distribution.[2] The same relationship between innovation and the utilization of high-level manpower is evident in other industrial countries.

Thus relatively advanced economies demand larger investments in management. Industrialization entails a substitution of both capital and management for labour. And the productivity of labour in an industrializing society is dependent upon management as well as upon the capital invested in machinery and processes.

The skills and qualities of the working force are often affected as much by what management does as they are by any innate characteristics of the workers themselves. Most, though not all, skills of manual labour and even clerical employees are acquired on the job. Management develops the incentives for work. It is also responsible for proper layout of machinery and processes, work-study, breakdown of jobs in order to economize on use of critical skills, safety programmes, systems for appraising performance and discovering talent, and many other related policies. These techniques are not easily applied. They require the employment of specialized personnel and investment of time on the part of members of the line organization. Even more important, they require relatively high levels of education, experience, and training among the members of the managerial organization; and they require a high degree of coordination.

In some respects, of course, the efficiency of labour resources may be independent of management. The more important factors here may be levels of education, conditions of health and nutrition, ideological orientation, and general experience and attitudes towards work. Management, however, is able to influence some of these factors at least in part. Attitudes towards work can be moulded by supervision; enterprises can provide medical services and adequate diets for employees; and some firms in under-developed countries even provide facilities for general education of members of the labour force. In the industrially advanced countries, of course, the labouring population may be generally more efficient because of long tradition and previous experience with industrial enterprises. The development of high labour productivity in an economically underdeveloped society may be particularly dependent upon managerial initiative and skill.

As the skills of the working force are increased, moreover, the need for management of higher quality becomes greater. This reinforces the general conclusion that, as societies move from earlier to later stages of industrialization, they must invest ever more heavily in the building of managerial resources, private or public or both.

The Generation of Managerial Resources

In all industrializing societies, the accumulation of managerial resources is of critical importance. Dams, power plants, and factories can be built in a few years, but it may take decades to develop domestically the engineers, scientists, administrators, and managers to operate them. Managerial resources, in short, require a long period of gestation, and in all industrializing societies substantial investments must be made to develop them.

Management manpower may be accumulated in different ways. In some cases the first industrialists may be drawn from the ranks of the handicraftsmen; small traders and money-lenders have often been a recruiting ground for management; and the wealthy merchant capitalists may take the initiative in establishing industrial enterprises. In other cases, as, for example, in Japan, an oligarchic clique may be induced by the state to build the nation's basic industries. In some countries the government civil service is a source of technical and administrative manpower. And in many of the newly industrializing countries, such as Egypt, army officers with technical and organizational training have been assigned to the management of the larger and more complicated enterprises.

Most industrializing countries have at one time or another imported managerial talent from the more advanced countries. For example, the United States drew upon British and European managerial resources during the nineteenth century. And today, the newly industrializing countries make extensive use of managers, engineers, and technicians from the United States, Britain, the western European countries, and the Soviet Union. They are often the 'seedcorn' for development of indigenous managerial talent, for they help train the latter.

The latecomers to industrialization may also send persons to the more advanced countries for general education, technical training, and industrial experience. For example, in 1958 and 1959, India alone sent several hundred engineers to the Soviet Union, Germany, and the United States for technical and managerial training in steel mill operations. Indeed, in modern times far more than in earlier periods, the training of managerial resources in foreign countries is a widely accepted method of developing high-talent manpower. The role of the foreign-trained national is reflected in one passage from the South African novelist Peter Abraham's book about Udomo, a fictional prototype of the African nationalist leader. Udomo in an impassioned dialogue with some of his adversaries says:

As I say, our country has three enemies. First there is the white man. Then there is poverty. And then there is the past. Those are the three enemies.

When I first came back I recognized only one of the three: the white man. But the moment I defeated him I saw the others, and they were greater and more dangerous than the white man. Beside these two the white man was easy, almost an ally. Well, I turned him into an ally against poverty. He works for us now, builds for us so that those who come after us will have bread and homes. There are schools and hospitals in the land. The young men and women are waking up. Why do you think I spent so much money sending them abroad? I'll tell you. Because I need them as allies to fight our third enemy, the worst enemy we have: the past. I've paid lip-service to the ritual of ju-ju and blood ceremonies and worshipping at the shrines of our ancestors. Now I don't have to any more. There are enough liberated young people now for me to defy all that is ugly and evil in our past. We can defeat it now. And you, Selina, and you, Ade, whom I once loved as a brother: you are the past. I'm going to defeat you! It is you who now stand in the way of Africa's greatness. Go on: fight me at the party conference and see who wins! You're too late, my friends. You're too late . . .[3]

Yet, no country is likely to progress very far industrially by exclusive reliance on joint ventures with foreign interests, the temporary hiring of foreign managers, or sending its own nationals abroad for training. The modern industrializing nation requires engineering universities and technological institutes; it needs specialized programmes for development of administrators for its governmental services and managers for its industrial enterprises. This means heavy investment in institutions of higher learning and a priority for education which is functionally oriented to the needs of the industrial process. And the institutions of higher learning must be built upon a base of extensive primary and secondary education, which in turn requires orientation to the needs of an industrializing society.*

Access to the Managerial Class

Only a few gain access to the ranks of management. Some families or family groups may control important segments of industry, as in Japan in the late nineteenth century or in India at the present time. In the Soviet Union, the government, and more particularly the Communist Party, may designate the factory manager, although

* This discussion does not consider the relative priorities at the margin. Should more resources be put into expanding technological institutes, medical schools, or centres for training of elementary school teachers? Manpower planning and manpower budgeting are complex problems, related to the stage and pace of industrialization. We intend to devote attention to these problems in a number of countries during the next few years. The observations above, therefore, should be considered as an interim report.

technical training is also usually a prerequisite. Education is increasingly an important entrance requirement in many societies, and a degree from one of the status universities, such as Tokyo Imperial University in Japan and similar universities in other countries, may be the best assurance of entry. Professional training and experience in management becomes an avenue to higher managerial positions.

Incumbents in the managerial hierarchy seek as new recruits those they can rely upon and trust. They demand that the newcomers be loyal, that they accept authority (of the family, the government, or the professional superior, as the case may be), and that they conform to a prescribed pattern of behaviour. And, of course, the orientation and outlook of the managerial group in an enterprise and also within an industrializing society as a whole usually reflect the criteria which govern admittance to it.

For analytical purposes, it is useful to consider three ideal types of management: patrimonial, political, and professional.*

Patrimonial Management is management in which ownership, major policy-making positions, and a significant proportion of other top jobs in the hierarchy are held by members of an extended family. The effective decision-making authority is centred in the family, and the goals of the enterprise are oriented towards the interests and aspirations of the family.

Patrimonial management is a common first stage in a country's economic development. The early merchant-capitalists in England were heads of family enterprises. In the early stages of industrialization the family enterprise is a simple and logical instrument of business activity. Loyalty and trust within the hierarchy are assured. Often the forces of tradition and religion support the essential integrity of the family dynasty. The enterprise provides the means for safeguarding the security and the reputation of the family.

* It is important to stress that these are points on a spectrum or a continuum rather than discrete instances of managerial philosophies and approaches. Some mixture of each of these ideal types may be present in the managerial philosophy of a particular enterprise and in the managerial philosophies found in an industrial society at any one time.

In a society where trained skills are scarce and the sons of the wealthy have much of the training, nepotism may be relatively cost-less. And, if the key members of the family dynasty are competent, well-educated, and diligent, patrimonial management can be quite dynamic. This is well illustrated in Germany where the typical family-type industrialist is usually himself a man with extensive technical or professional education. He frequently exerts great pressure upon his sons or sons-in-law to prepare themselves for the responsibilities they will be 'called' to assume. Thus, when moti-vated by a creed of hard work and determination to acquire or maintain a position of power, the family enterprise can be an effective agent of industrialization.

However, the key members of the family dynasties are often in-capable, either by training or psychological inclination, of sustain-ing the progress towards industrialization. The typical French family firm has been described as placing '. . . inordinate stress on safety and security. It fears change and is unwilling to borrow for fear that the lender, whether individual or bank, will gain a foot-hold in the enterprise. As a result, the firm prefers to enjoy its own little market . . .'[4] Traditionally, Italian capitalism remained family-capitalist for many years, and this was a major factor re-tarding industrial growth; only in very recent times has Italian industry begun to break away from this patrimonial management pattern.

The family enterprise is usually most effective in small and relatively simple organizations such as retail and wholesale trade, craft industries, and small or medium-sized industrial plants. In such cases it is relatively easy for the family, particularly in the ex-tended form, to recruit and generate from within most of the capital and managerial resources it needs.

When the family enterprise expands, its patrimonial form is undermined. To find technicians, engineers, and administrators with the requisite knowledge, training, and skill, it must go beyond blood relatives. As the number of professionals in the patrimonial enterprise expands, the members of the family find it increasingly difficult to maintain their control. There comes a point where the interests of the family are better promoted by turning over the operation of the enterprise to competent professional managerial careerists. This is what happened in the case of hundreds of family enterprises in the United States, and the same trend is apparent in the larger enterprises in England, Germany, and even France and Italy today. In the most advanced economies, therefore, the family enterprise, though still important in petty trade or small-scale industry, no longer plays a widespread role in large industrial establishments. The proprietary capitalist, who used to own and control the large business houses, tends to disappear as a power in industrializing societies.

Political Management is less common, and like patrimonial management, its chances for survival are slim in modern industrializing societies. Political management exists where ownership, major policy-making positions, and key administrative posts are held by persons on the basis of political affiliation and loyalties. Access is thus dominated by political considerations, and the orientation and interests of management are coloured throughout by political goals. However, just as patrimonial management may hire professionals to work under its direction, so political management may enlist the services of professionally trained managers and technicians.

Sometimes, as in the case of postmasters in principal cities in the United States, political managerial appointments are regarded as a reward for the politically faithful. Some of the nationalized enterprises in India were at first headed by managing directors whose principal qualifications appeared to be their government connections rather than their proven ability as managers. The Egyptian National Railways had for many years managements which were essentially political in nature. Indeed, a danger in all socialized industries is that managerial appointments may be made at the outset on the basis of political connections rather than professional competence.

As in the case of patrimonial management, however, there may be an element of loyalty and trust involved in managerial appointments to public enterprises. When a new revolutionary élite seizes power, as it did in Russia, for example, it may have good reason to doubt the loyalty of the old managerial cadre. In the Soviet Union, warnings about the necessity for political loyalty in state-enterprise management appeared in the late 1920s, and there were official notices of reprimand and discipline in the early 1930s. The 'kill the Kulaks in management' period occurred approximately five years after its application to agriculture. The general purges of 1937–8 coincided with the more specific elimination of the politically questionable from managerial authority. Caught between pressures for maximum output and the fear of sedition, therefore, the Kremlin demonstrated an extreme example of political management. Not only were party members appointed to managerial positions, but in many cases, these managers and others were checked by political commissars or representatives with power equal to that of the technical managers in each enterprise. Some of these managers, sharing the commitment to revolutionary goals, accomplished remarkable feats of production. Eventually, however, the inefficiency of this system resulted in the establishment of 'one-man management' in the factories, although party membership and loyalty was still an important criterion.[5] This coincided with political stability of the régime, and in post-Stalin Russia, professional competence clearly is the primary standard for managerial appointments among party members.

Political management, however, is simply incapable of coping successfully with the intricate tasks which must be performed in modern, large-scale industry. In this respect, it is even less viable than patrimonial management. But this does not imply that management is likely to be free of political influence even in the most advanced societies. For example, when the protection of the enterprise is dependent upon receiving favours or special treatment from the government or from the political party in power, it may be important to have someone in the managerial ranks who is close to the seat of power and who can 'get things done'. In most countries, 'political connections' are indispensable both to patrimonial and professional management.

As industrialization proceeds, it becomes increasingly evident that reliance on competence rather than merely on connections must become the standard for access to managerial positions.

Moreover, the test of loyalty may be less decisive when the society has developed a high degree of consensus.

Professional Management is enterprise management in which major policy-making positions and nearly all other positions in the hierarchy are held by persons on the basis of claimed or demonstrated technical qualifications. In professional management, technical ability, experience, education, knowledge of the organization, and ability to impress people who make decisions are more important than relationships to a family or a political régime.

Professional management is most common in advanced industrializing societies. The need for professional management is as great in a state-enterprise economy as it is in a capitalistic society. In both the United States and the Soviet Union, for example, professional management holds the reins of power within large and strategic enterprises. The professionals are likewise now dominant in the industrial empires of Japan and Germany, in the state-owned enterprises of France and Italy, and even in many of the emerging large-scale enterprises in the newly developing countries.

The professionals, however, do not take over without a struggle. In the intermediate stages of industrialization, they are only the hired subordinates of the proprietary capitalists, the family patriarchs, or the political commissars. In this capacity they may feel indignant at taking orders from persons they deem to be technically incompetent, and they may resent the ceilings which arbitrarily restrict their upward movement into the top echelons of the managerial hierarchy. But as industrialization advances, they gain access to the top command posts and become the organization builders.

Although professional management is destined to sweep aside its political or patrimonial predecessors, the class of business managers *alone* seldom becomes a ruling élite in any society. In other words, the state does not become the property of the professional managers, as James Burnham envisioned in his 'managerial revolution'.[6] Rather the managers may be as much servants as masters of the state, as much subordinates as controllers of the market. The managers are a *part* of the ruling élite, but they are not alone *the* élite. In the Soviet Union, for example, the industrial managers are clearly subservient to the political and governmental élite. In Japan the heads of the great *zaibatsu* were always conscious of their prior obligation to serve nationalist objectives and the interests of the state. The German industrialists became the willing instruments of Hitler. In the United States, the professional managers argue that the market is really the supreme master of their destiny. Some markets are an exacting task-master while others contain such extensive monopoly elements that they are a lenient and even lax governor. If management were to claim to be the dominant élite in the United States, it would be rebuffed, investigated, and shackled with further legislation designed to protect the public interest. In the modern industrializing society, it appears, management can be supreme only within the orbit of the enterprise, and even here it must share its authority with others who demand and obtain a share in the making of the web of rules which governs industrializing man.

The process of industrialization universally tends to change management from patrimonial and political to professional, but the patterns of change in management vary with the ideal types of élites. In the dynastic and middle-class-led societies, the change is from patrimonial to professional; under the revolutionary intellectuals and nationalist leaders, the change is from political to professional. The colonial administrators are pressed to move from foreign managers of various types through native political managers to native professional managers.

Rule-making Authority over the Managed

A primary concern of management, in its relationship to workers, is to establish, to make legitimate, and to maintain its authority. The specialization of functions which industrialization demands also requires that the work force accept tasks whose nature, time, and method of accomplishment are to be determined by management in its role as planner and order-giver.

Acceptance by workers of this role for management typically means a substitution of one authority for another in the transition to industrialization. Management of the enterprise tends to displace the head of the village family, the tribal chief, or the communal leader as the authority which prescribes the duties, obligations, rewards, and punishments of workers at the work place. If management is completely free to make the rules at the industrial work place, without interference from other contenders such as labour organizations or government, its philosophy or approach towards workers may be either (1) dictatorial, or (2) paternalistic. But if various pressures, including labour organizations and governments, force management to share its authority and modify its philosophies and approaches, the new managerial approaches may be characterized as (3) constitutional, or (4) consultative and participative.

Dictatorial or Authoritarian Management

This characterizes the manager who arbitrarily and often ruthlessly compels workers to accept his unquestioned authority, with very little concern for their dignity as human beings and with virtually no feeling of responsibility for their welfare on or off the job. According to this philosophy, the worker must never question the authority of the manager; indeed, to do so is cause for immediate discharge. In the manager's eyes, the worker should have no recourse if for any reason his services are no longer required.

At some point early in the industrialization process, the imperatives of rapid capital formation may result in ruthless exploitation of industrial workers. This was the case in nineteenth-century Russia,[7] and in England in the early nineteenth century the rising entrepreneurial class refused to accept the earlier notion that its claim to authority over the workers created reciprocal responsibility to look after their welfare. Although there were striking exceptions to this attitude, the common conviction was that a person could do well in the world by hard work and diligence, and that in any case the employer's responsibility was filled by buying labour services and providing employment.

While there are still instances among management of dictatorial or authoritarian treatment of workers, this approach is seldom a stable one over time in the absence of police or military support. It may be able to achieve subordination of labour, but it usually fails to develop loyalty and productivity. Industrial workers everywhere sooner or later rebel against or resist such unmitigated exercise of authority.

Paternalistic Management

This philosophy carries forward the traditions of responsibility and subordination of the master-servant relationship; it often serves to smooth the major dislocations which an industrial way of life forces on the newly recruited workers. Paternalism reflects the tradition in which the lord of the manor has some responsibility for the welfare of his subordinates in return for faithful service. The manager may provide housing, food, medical care, and social services for the worker. In turn he is expected to be grateful, and also productive. The worker is regarded as dependent on the manager for security and welfare. Here the image of the industrial *pater* takes the place of the head of the family, tribe, or primary group in pre-industrial society.

In the early stages of industrial development in many societies, the paternalistic approach is quite consistent with the prevailing social order. In small establishments, where the proprietor may hire his relatives as workers, it affords an ideal rationale for maintaining the security and integrity of the family. It is a logical first step in some countries, Germany and Japan, for example, where the members of the pre-existing dynastic élites became the agents of industrialization. Thus:

Patriarchal management in Japan retained the socially responsible characteristics of the traditional kinship system. Although it gave little encouragement to individualists and indeed individualism was frowned upon if not actually punished, each member of the organization was regarded as an integral and important cog in the functioning of the whole enterprise. Conformity to the purpose of the unit rested upon fostering and structuring the situation to achieve complete identification between superior and subordinate. The reward was life-long security within the group and full acceptance of one's functional role.[8]

In India today there are examples of this 'benevolent paternalism', based on an apparent willingness of the employee to accept a

157

dependent status and of the manager to play the role of a wise father. An indication of this is suggested by the words of the founder of an important family group of Indian enterprises:

At first . . . I found that if workers got a few annas more, they were absent more often; they didn't know how to live properly. So I had to show them how to live better, to keep their houses clean. I started various games and recreation centres. I had to provide these outside interests to soothe the workers' minds.[9]

Managerial paternalism, moreover, has not been confined to the early stages of industrial development. In the United States the present personnel policies of International Business Machines, Eastman Kodak, and the Hershey Chocolate Corporation, for example, seem to reflect a considerable paternal concern for the employees' welfare which is bound up with management's expressed conviction that such programmes are sound investments in long-run employee productivity.

Managements may also find it necessary to provide many services for employees for reasons which have little connection with a sense of moral obligation. Malnutrition may force managements to provide free lunches in the interest of higher productivity. Other services or payments in kind may be required in enterprises which operate in areas remote from centres of population. The oil-producing companies in Saudi Arabia, Iraq, and Kuwait are good examples, as are the sugar plantations and mills in the sparsely inhabited coastal deserts of Peru or the copper mines of Rhodesia.

Paternalistic management, with all its overtones and variations, tends to be most stable (1) when the pre-existing culture and social structure are congenial to this type of superior-subordinate relationship, as in Japan, India, France, and Italy; (2) when strong labour organizations do not challenge management's decisions at the work place concerning what should be done for employees; and (3) when the community does not provide housing, schools, medical, and other services.

Pressures on Management for a Different Approach

In the advanced industrializing societies such as the United States,

Great Britain, Sweden, and Germany, managers are forced increasingly to abandon many of their authoritarian and paternalistic practices. They do this reluctantly because of their natural desire to be the rule-maker and dispenser of favours in the work place, in exchange for gratitude, loyalty, and good work. The more important of the pressures forcing managers to change with advancing industrialization are the following:

First, there are the social values of a society, and they are not static. If the society places increasingly high value, through its educational system or its religious ethic, on the freedom of the individual to have a voice in determining his own present and future, it will be increasingly difficult to maintain autocracy or even paternalism in industry.

Second, there are pressures from individual workers. A worker may protest against managerial authority by being absent from work, restricting output, rebelling against discipline, or quitting. Pressure of this kind, of course, is greatest where some types of labour are relatively scarce. In the course of industrialization, workers tend to acquire more skill, higher education, and more knowledge of alternative conditions which influence their relations to management.

Third, there is the pressure of government legislation, often influenced by international comparisons and conventions of the International Labour Organization. Increasingly, the unilateral authority of the manager is restricted by government intervention in the labour-management relationship. In many industrial countries, the government restricts the right of the manager to discharge or lay off workers and sets minimum wages; in some it prescribes mandatory benefits in the form of housing, medical care, vacations, or sickness allowances. In nearly all countries the government prescribes minimum working conditions and safety standards. Thus, in the area subject to government regulation, the manager exercises his rights only within legally determined limits.

Fourth, there is pressure from labour organizations. The growth of strong labour organizations in advanced industrializing countries and their emergence in various forms and under various auspices in the less-developed economies likewise brings varying pressure on management to share rule-making authority.

Fifth, there is pressure from other managements. The individual manager may be significantly influenced by the actions and policies of other enterprises, and particularly by management associations, business schools, 'staff colleges', and other institutions which tend to disseminate less paternal and less authoritarian concepts of managerial organization and managerial policies.

Sixth, in some economies the pressure of competition from other enterprises forces managers to become more efficient. Greater efficiency is achieved, in part, through improving relationships with employees, motivating them to work more effectively, and increasing their pace of work in conjunction with better methods and equipment.

Of course, the pace of economic development itself puts pressures on management to change its policies. A faster pace generated by governments under economic planning may temporarily enhance the authority of enterprise managers over workers by instituting controls over labour which protect managerial power. But often the other pressures discussed above work in the direction of limiting managerial authority over workers, possibly at the expense of a faster pace of economic growth.

Thus, in industrializing societies managers must often share their authority over workers with other contenders. Their policies are the result of accommodations, and their philosophy at any one period is likely to be a rationalization of the cumulative impact of the pressures on management. As these pressures mount in the modern world, the managerial approach tends to become 'constitutional' rather than dictatorial or paternalistic.

Constitutional Management

This term is used to characterize management which governs its working forces according to procedures and policies which have evolved from the intervention of other forces in the rule-making process. Here the rule-making power of managers is shared in a constitutional manner with other agencies. Wages and working conditions may become subject to determination by collective bargaining or various forms of governmental determination, and jointly negotiated agreements or governmental regulations may establish a constitutional framework within which management exercises its functions. In some countries, such as the United States, these agreements are more frequently company-wide in scope; in others, such as Sweden, national agreements between industry-wide unions and employers' federations establish the constitutional limits within which the manager deals with his workers.

In some cases, labour organizations and their political allies may be the driving force behind passage of labour legislation to regulate managerial authority. This pattern is more typical in the newly industrializing countries today, where the labour organizations are so weak at the level of the enterprise that they exert little direct pressure for 'constitutional' management, and, as a consequence, government is the principal contender for sharing rule-making authority with enterprise management.

Democratic or Participative Management

Finally, pressures can lead under some circumstances to a fourth type of philosophy and approach, which may be called democratic or participative.

The democratic-participative philosophy grows out of the conclusion that people respond best in an organization when they can participate in the process of decision-making on matters that directly affect them. Here, management is not leaderless. It takes the initiative in enlisting genuine participation, as in advance consultation on proposed courses of action. The organizational structure itself may be changed by enlarging the jobs of people at subordinate levels to give them more responsibility and the information to act on that responsibility. At the shop level, it may involve something like the 'Scanlon Plan' of labour-management cooperation or, as in Great Britain and Sweden, some forms of joint consultation on production problems, with production committees to act upon suggestions submitted directly and not through suggestion boxes.[10] The works councils of Yugoslavia and other countries are in some respects another illustration. The essence of democratic-participative management is the assumption that people are not lazy, do not have to be pushed to do a good day's work, and are not simply interested in more money. Instead, they are eager to work 'for the good of the order' if they are given a real chance to share at all levels in formulating the conditions under which they shall labour and the criteria by which they will be rewarded. The managers who hold to this philosophy are indeed true believers in industrial democracy.

Using the typology outlined above, it is possible to characterize the prevailing managerial philosophy of relations with workers in many countries today, recognizing that there are variations within each country and that no country conforms fully to any ideal type. In Japan, for example, the leading industrialists follow a policy of paternalism. Because industrialization was originally sparked by a dynastic élite, the idea of paternalistic concern for the welfare of subordinates is strongly rooted in Japanese management. Although the government has intervened to regulate the manager in the field of labour relations, it has nevertheless given strong encouragement to the paternalistic approach. Until recently, the labour organizations have been fairly weak at the enterprise level, and they have made only minor inroads into the area of managerial authority. The paternalistic tradition is strong also in France and Italy, but here the inroads by both the government and labour organizations upon management's monopoly of rule-making power have been greater.

In Sweden and England, on the other hand, the middle-class tradition provides a less fertile soil for paternalism. The manager who once might have been an advocate of authoritarian policies has been forced to share the rule-making authority in the enterprise with strong unions. Management accepts unionization as a permanent and even a desirable institution in a society where all kinds of rule-making are jointly shared by many groups in a pluralistic arrangement and where every manager is to some extent a rather confident politician, adjusting to the pressures around him. In the United States, managers are constrained by constitutional limitations established by labour organizations and the government. The high cost of labour, the emergence of strong unions, and the lessons of the Great Depression have made American management aware of both the rights and the aspirations of workers, who have a strong sense of independence. The American employer simply cannot afford to be indifferent to the welfare of the labour force, and he recognizes that wages and working conditions must be established with consultation or consent of the workers.

In the Soviet Union, the authority of industrial management is rigorously circumscribed by the party, the government, and to a lesser degree by the trade unions. In some respects, the workers may circumvent the manager by appealing directly to the party functionaries. As in other societies, the workers are subordinated to management, but their ultimate master is the state. Soviet enterprise management, therefore, has reason to be cautious in its handling of workers, but as industrialization becomes more dominant in the society, the managers apparently have been able to increase the areas of authority over their working forces. The Soviet manager can never be indifferent to labour's welfare, and there is little reason for him to be paternalistic. Indeed, within the limits of his authority, he is much more likely to operate as a kind of 'constitutional' manager, although the checks to his authority in the plant are quite different from those in other societies, and he may be able to be authoritarian in some areas. The position of the Soviet manager thus reflects the broader power and authority of the country's rulers. On the surface, at least, the role of management in Yugoslavia is different from that in the Soviet Union. Here, apparently in very wide areas within the enterprise, management shares decision-making authority with representatives of the workers through the workers' councils.

Finally, in the industrializing countries with nationalist leaders, there are many varieties of managerial approaches to labour problems. There are instances of callous indifference to, as well as paternalistic concern for, labour's welfare. Labour organizations for the most part are weak, and labour is often plentiful. The only strong pressure on management's rule-making authority is the government. In Egypt and India, the government has moved with deliberation and force into the field of labour relations, thus compelling rather drastic accommodations by management.

Industrialism and Industrial Man

The logic of industrialization is particularly powerful in its impact on the rule-making authority of management. Management evolves from authoritarian and paternalistic types to constitutional management. The resistances to this development vary among the ideal types of élites. In the dynastic-led society the resistance is from the paternalistic tradition; among the revolutionary intellectuals it is from the dominant role of the state and the necessities of the rapid pace of industrialization; in the middle-class society, from the problems of individual adjustment; the nationalist leaders find resistances in the state and the older culture; the colonial administrators find a deep contradiction in the pressures for constitutional management as against their own alien character.

Elements of Unity in Management Development

In looking at management as an economic resource, as a class, and as a rule-making authority over workers, various tendencies have been described and analysed. These may now be summarized and designated as the elements of unity in the development of management in the course of economic growth.

As industrialization proceeds, the number of persons in management increases both absolutely and relatively in the economy. This is the inevitable consequence of larger capital outlay, the pace of innovation, the use of more modern machinery and processes, the growth of markets, and the increasing complexity of the advancing industrial societies. In this process, enterprise organizations become more complicated as they grow larger, and the effectiveness of management becomes increasingly dependent upon administrative skill in reducing the inherent frictions and inefficiencies of complicated human organizations.

In the early stages of industrialization, the management class may be drawn from family dynasties, from a new middle class, from political parties or the government service. But in the march towards industrialism, technical and organizational forces tend to favour careerist rather than political or patrimonial management. Increasingly larger numbers of trained engineers, technologists, and administrators are required. And, as the managerial class becomes larger, it also becomes less exclusive since of necessity the avenues of access to its ranks must become broader. In its logical development, therefore, management at all levels becomes more of a profession than a pre-ordained calling. As an industrializing society continues to lay stress upon scientific discovery, technological innovation, and economic growth, patrimonial and political managers tend to be displaced by the professionals.

Industrial growth forces enterprise managements to develop means of delegating administrative authority within a framework of centralized controls. Management by sovereign rule is not viable except in small-scale operations, and thus it tends to disappear in large-scale enterprises, in the more advanced countries. At the other extreme, management-by-participation is such a radical departure from traditional systems of authority that it is seldom realized in practice. Between these extremes is a broad range of possible combinations of decentralized administration with centralized policy control. Large and even medium-sized enterprises in all industrial societies, through conscious planning or trial and error, are continuously searching for some kind of balance in this area. Almost never do they find a perfect or permanent solution, but some are more successful than others in finding arrangements which substantially reduce organizational frictions.

As all industrial societies advance, management becomes less authoritarian in its attitude and policy towards workers. Management, of course, tries to preserve its prerogatives as the rule-maker over the workers. But others also seek and gain a voice in the rule-making and rule-enforcing process. Among the principal contenders are the state and labour organizations. They tend to limit, to regulate, or sometimes to displace the unilateral authority of management. As industrialization proceeds, management is forced to share its rule-making power with one or more of these contenders. Governments by legislation or labour organizations by collective action limit or circumscribe management's freedom to exercise its prerogatives unilaterally. As a consequence, dictatorial or paternalistic direction usually gives way to a kind of 'constitutional' management in which wages and conditions of employment are based upon laws, regulations, decisions of government, collective contracts, or procedural agreements. And in rare cases, a system of industrial relations may be established in which management and labour not only share in the rule-making process but also cooperate in improving efficiency and increasing output.

The outlays for technical and managerial education become enormous as industrialization follows its inherent logic. The advanced industrializing economy must have a fully developed system of general education, and at the same time its basic educational institutions must become more functionally oriented to the training of skilled technicians, engineers, scientists, and administrators. But it also requires the lowering of arbitrary non-educational barriers to entry into the managerial hierarchy as well as some vertical and horizontal mobility within the managerial class itself. In some societies the processes of generation of managerial manpower have been spearheaded by the state, in others by private initiative. As industrialization advances and even as it is being started in the presently underdeveloped countries, however, the means of generating and accumulating managerial resources is increasingly a matter for careful planning, judicious investment, and conscious effort. High-talent manpower does not grow wild in profusion; it requires careful seeding and meticulous cultivation.

Finally, although the professional management class is destined to grow in size in all industrializing societies, it has neither the capacity nor the will alone to become the dominant ruling élite. Being preoccupied with the internal affairs of the enterprise, which become even more complex, the members of the managerial class are prone to become conformists rather than leaders in the larger affairs of society. Modern organization builders, unlike the old-style proprietary capitalists who are being swept aside in the march towards industrialism, do not own the means of production. In an increasing number of cases, they are more characteristically the agents of stock-holders, state bureaucracies, or in some cases, workers' councils. In the logic of industrialization, management plays a vital and indispensable role. But it serves and influences rather than dominates the society of which it is a part.

Diversities in the Development of Management

Although management develops in a common direction, it does so from quite different initial positions. Particularly in the early stages of industrialization, the orientation of management in various societies may be quite diverse, reflecting the influence of the different initiating élites. The following diversities among the ideal types of élites are to be noted.

Under the leadership of a dynastic élite, family connections tend to control access to the managerial class. Careerist managers and technicians are employed, but they are kept subordinate to the members of the owner families. Patrimonial management is most likely to be paternalistic in its relationship with the industrial working classes. Owner-managers of enterprises legitimize their position on the basis of a predestination or 'calling' for industrial leadership. Their authority is rationalized more by divine or historic right than by the specific functions performed in enterprises. The dynastic élite favours the idea of education of a chosen minority, often in a status university, which by virtue of its position in society has both the opportunity and the obligation to be trained to direct the affairs of business enterprises. Since the members of this minority are 'born to manage', they scorn tasks which might dirty their hands, and they resist as long as possible the introduction of rational or impersonal procedures to govern relationships within the managerial hierarchy.

The middle class tends to favour access to the ranks of management on the basis of individual initiative and competence. This facilitates an earlier and more rapid development of a professional managerial class. Imbued with the idea that workers should be self-reliant rather than dependent upon the manager for their well-being, management is quicker to move towards the 'constitutional' approach in agreeing to rules and procedures for the governing of the working forces. Managerial authority is rationalized by the functional positions which persons hold rather than by family connections or by calling. A society in which the middle class is the leading élite emphasizes education for the masses rather than for a chosen few alone. Without centralized design, institutions of higher learning may adapt themselves to the needs of the society for engineers, technicians, and managers. In this kind of society, management moves more easily and painlessly along its evolutionary course.

The colonial administrators reserve for themselves the controlling positions in the managerial hierarchies both in government

Chart 6. Management and the Industrializing Élites

Industrializing élite	Middle-class	Dynastic
Access to management	Access to management on basis of initiative and competence – early development of professional management.	Access based upon the family with professionals subordinated to the authority of the family.
Character of managerial authority over workers	Constitutional or occasionally democratic.	Paternalistic concern for the 'dependent' workers.
Basis for managerial authority	Authority of managers based upon functions they perform.	Concept that certain families are 'called' to manage. Personal rather than functional organization.
The education and development of managerial resources	Education of the masses, and functional education in technology and management.	Education of a small, élitist minority.

and in industry. They train the local nationals to perform the lesser jobs in management, but place ceilings on their upward advancement. The authority of management is rationalized on the basis of the technological, educational and cultural position of the people of the home country. Management is likely to be either dictatorial, or, if it is relatively progressive, paternalistic in its relations with the workers. The colonial administrators favour an educational system which trains a relatively small number of nationals to assume minor positions in government, and they are reluctant to

Revolutionary intellectuals	Colonial administrators	Nationalist leaders
At first, access on basis of political affiliations, later on professional standards.	Top positions reserved for nationals of the home country.	Various, with emphasis on political and professional qualifications.
Dictatorial and authoritarian, later becoming constitutional to a limited degree.	Dictatorial or paternalistic.	Various, depending on nature of managerial class.
Managers as servants of party and state.	Superiority of nationals of the home country.	Managerial resources looked upon as necessary instruments for industrial development.
High priority to functional education at all levels.	Very limited educational development of the nationals of the colony.	Education of the masses, and priority given to higher education.

establish institutions of higher learning to develop engineers, managers, or highly skilled technicians. Advanced education is largely reserved to the home country. Indeed, the colonial administrator attempts to prevent rather than promote the emergence of an indigenous class of top-level industrial managers.

The revolutionary intellectuals try at the outset to promote political management, and to make party loyalty and service the gateway to the managerial hierarchy. Managers perform a legitimate role only as the servants of the party and the state. The revolutionary intellectuals press for a functionally oriented system of education giving the highest priority to development of technical skills required in an industrializing society as well as to the ideological indoctrination according to the prescribed dialectic. In this society, however, change also takes place towards professionalization of management. And in the relations with workers, subsequently, the authority of management is usually circumscribed by party functionaries, plans prescribed by a central bureaucracy, and also by pressures brought to bear by labour organizations or workers' councils. In this society, management also is likely to become slowly more 'constitutional'.

The nationalist leaders, in their rush to embark upon industrialization, tend to encourage use of both political and professional management, and they may also rely temporarily on foreign management. A managerial class is accepted as an indispensable instrument for industrial development and economic growth. The relationship with the working masses will be rather paternal. Nationalist leaders usually press for universal general education and also for functionally oriented institutions of higher learning, and they lean heavily on the more advanced countries for assistance and capital to develop technical colleges and industrial management training programmes. In most cases, they follow in various intermediate combinations the routes taken by the middle class in the market economies and the revolutionary intellectuals in the totalitarian states.

Chart 6 summarizes the approaches of each of the ideal types of industrializing élites to the development of management. The different approaches are most distinguishable in the early stages of industrialization. In practice the hybrid character of the élites in an evolving society imparts a blended colouration to its managerial class at any intermediate stage of development. As the society reaches the more advanced stages of industrialization, management is likely to have the universal common markings which have already been described. As industrialization proceeds, the elements of unity tend to over-shadow the elements of diversity in the development of management.

The industrial world has witnessed the increasing acceptance of the managerial function in enterprises, private or public. Industrializing countries today are demanding more competent management; the role of management is no longer on the defensive as it was in an earlier stage of industrial history. Modern management is no longer the 'alien minority' which it was in the more traditional societies resisting industrialization.

One of the universals of the industrialization process is that management of enterprises becomes professionalized rather quickly. But the characteristics and strategies of the different industrializing élites relate to the early development of management by influencing the access to managerial positions and the authority system of management. Cultural factors, and particularly family, class, and race, also have an early impact, but eventually the universal imperative – the need for competent, professionalized management – prevails. While both the stage and pace of industrialization affect the position and policies of enterprise management, the similarities of enterprise management in all advanced industrializing societies are far greater than their differences.

5   Developing the Industrial Labour Force

Industrializing élites, and more specifically the managers of enterprises, are required to recruit, to build, to maintain, and to direct a large and diversified industrial labour force. The members of this working force must learn to accept the authority of managers in place of the family, tribe, or village. They must conform to a pace of work established by the dictates of new masters rather than by their own inclinations or traditional standards. Industrialization involves the setting up of a new body of rules governing relationships between those who give and those who take orders; and this requires a new system of rewards and punishments to mobilize and to direct the brawn and brains utilized in the new productive process. Industrializing society also requires the development of labour market mechanisms to recruit, sort out, distribute, and redistribute workers into a myriad of occupations and jobs requiring varying degrees of skill, and rewarded at different rates of compensation.

There is, of course, no precise dividing line between the managerial group and the industrial labour force. Those in the lower echelons of the managerial hierarchy may differ in only minor respects from the more highly skilled members of the working forces. In some cases foremen are members of management; in others they are the highest ranking members of the labouring class. The demarcation between the managers and the managed is more like a gradient than a cliff. With this qualification, the working force may be said to include the following: manual labour of all skill levels, clerical workers, group leaders and straw bosses; first-line supervisors and the lower grades of technicians who constitute a middle group which for some purposes and in some countries may be classified as management and for others as workers;

administrators, professional employees, engineers, and scientists who are clearly in the managerial category.

This chapter is concerned with the processes of development of an industrial labour force as well as with the broader problems of the general supply of human resources for development. At various stages of industrialization, the problems encountered by the industrializing élites with similar resource constraints may be fairly similar, but their policies and approaches to the common task of developing an industrial labour force are likely to be quite diverse. These similar problems as well as the diverse policies and approaches are treated in the final two sections of this chapter.

Building the Industrial Labour Force

Most countries have human resources which are available for industrial employment, but no country is endowed with a full-blown industrial labour force. Industrial man is a product not of a particular climate or ancestry but rather of persistent development and specific policies. In the development of an industrial labour force, there are four interrelated processes: (1) recruitment, (2) commitment, (3) advancement, and (4) maintenance. These processes may overlap each other in the course of time.

The Recruitment Process

In the history of industrialization, compulsory as well as voluntary means of recruitment have been used separately and in combination. Among the more common methods of compulsion are the following: outright enslavement, various kinds of indenture, the imposition of 'labour dues', the levying of taxes payable only in money, or simply forcing people to move from the land and to seek other means of earning a living. The agents of such recruitment may be tribal chiefs, colonial administrators, labour contractors, or private or public industrial enterprises.

Slavery as a formal institution of labour force recruitment is practically extinct today, although it once played an important role, particularly in the initial development of extractive industries[1] and industrial agriculture. Indentured servants were common in the colonial United States, and slavery was a prominent aspect of development of plantation agriculture in the southern part of the United States in pre-Civil War days. Common peonage and long-term indenture systems with penal sanctions still exist today, but these are generally found only in industrialized agriculture where it is necessary to recruit workers in distant places and transport them at considerable expense to their place of employment.

The use of forced labour by some of the early colonial rulers in Africa followed the form of tribal practices, where it was customary for each able-bodied male to contribute a certain number of days of work per year for such community tasks as clearing bush, making new paths, or assisting the chief. The colonial administrators, working through the tribal chiefs, attempted to use the same device, but without the traditional safeguards which were inherent in the native systems.[2] The French system of labour dues, or *prestations*, used in Equatorial Africa (imported from metropolitan France) obliged all able-bodied males to work a certain number of days each year (theoretically about 15) on public works. These workers were sometimes assigned to the operators of mines and factories, or conscripted for temporary projects such as road repair and porterage.[3]

In modern times, forced labour has been used in the Soviet Union, but for reasons quite different from those in Africa. In part it grew out of a need to make productive use of large numbers of political prisoners, but in the main it stemmed from an attempt to stabilize the labour force and allocate it to high-priority users.[4]

But in all societies compulsory methods generally have proved to be unreliable as a permanent means of building an industrial labour force. The Africans quickly developed a desire for things which only money could buy, and thus wage employment has supplanted the older systems of forced labour; and in the Soviet Union positive incentives have proved to be superior to coercion as a means of allocating the labour force. It is true that 'labour contractors' in countries such as Egypt and India have often used methods of exploitation which at times have approached forced labour, but abuses of this kind are on their way to being eliminated by protective legislation and changes in the labour market.

In some countries labour has been 'pushed' into industrial employment by being forced out of agriculture. The enclosure of common meadows and pastures in England created a body of transient workers without land, who generally migrated to the then developing urban areas and were available for industrial employment. Similarly drastic measures were taken in the Soviet Union in modern times. For example, from 1928 to 1932 about eight and a half million workers entered the labour force, the majority of whom had been evicted from their lands or refused to work on the collective farms.[5]

For the most part, however, labour is attracted into industrial employment largely because of the opportunities afforded. People seek jobs in factories because of relatively high wages, availability of housing, aspirations for a higher standard of living, greater social prestige, challenge of the new, or simply because they prefer the kind of work offered. Workers may appear at the plant gates seeking employment. They may learn about jobs from friends or relatives. They may emigrate to 'empty countries' seeking a new life and new employment opportunities, as occurred in the United States, Canada, and Australia. Employers may send recruiters about the country to find workers. Or, in some cases, recruitment may be channelled through public or private employment exchanges or through labour contractors.

The managers of enterprise normally have some choice in recruitment. Selection may be based purely on whim or fancy, on physical fitness and health, on aptitude, or on the basis of nepotism and favouritism. In some cases, certain categories of persons are excluded from particular kinds of employment. Thus, in the Union of South Africa, the Mines and Works Act of 1926 excluded black Africans from specified skilled and semi-skilled occupations in the mines, and subsequent attempts have been made to reserve certain jobs in other industries 'for whites only'. In some parts of the United States, by custom, Negroes have been excluded from 'white' occupations. In India and Ceylon it is virtually impossible to employ members of particular castes for certain kinds of work. In the Middle East the oil companies, in accordance with their concession agreements, are required to give preference to nationals

175

in all types and levels of work for which they are qualified. And in the more advanced countries there are legislative restrictions on the employment of women, children, handicapped workers, aliens, and other specialized categories of people.

Of all the processes of labour force development, recruitment is the easiest to handle. Managers generally are able by one means or another to recruit the number of bodies they need. As industrialization advances, compulsory methods of recruitment are abandoned in favour of measures designed to make industrial employment more attractive. And along with the greater emphasis on voluntary recruitment, managers are prone to become much more selective in hiring new recruits. From a social standpoint, therefore, discrimination in recruitment is more likely to cause trouble than is the inability to get recruits.

Of course, in some countries or areas there may be an initial scarcity of human resources for industrial development. In the Middle East, petroleum was discovered in unpopulated areas, and consequently the oil companies had to import labour from distant areas. The same problem has confronted mining companies in many parts of the world, rubber plantations in Liberia, and the sugar haciendas and factories in Peru. At times, moreover, entire countries have been short of labour. The United States for many years had to import workers from Europe to man its steel mills, mines, and fast-growing manufacturing enterprises. More recently, Belgium has tried to staff its collieries with workers from Italy and other southern European countries. The Soviet Union was short of industrial labour in the 1920s until it was able to draw people from the rural areas into the industrial centres.

Yet, even in sparsely populated areas or regions, the general shortage of human resources for industrial development is likely to be mitigated in a relatively short time. Enterprises located in isolated areas can induce workers to move long distances if appropriate wages, housing, and community facilities are provided. Where living accommodations are provided for families as well as for workers, local labour supplies can be generated within a few decades. Likewise, when workers and their families are transplanted from agricultural to urban areas or from one country to another, they sink their roots in the new environment and soon generate a supply of labour. Where labour is scarce at the outset of industrialization, moreover, wages are higher and enterprise managers are forced to invest more time and resources in the proper recruitment, commitment, and advancement of human resources. As a consequence, labour may become more productive in a shorter period of time. Likewise, measures are adopted earlier to replace men with machines.[6] Thus, even in sparsely populated areas, industrialization tends in one way or another to generate the labour resources it requires.

Commitment

Hiring workers may be relatively easy, but keeping them consistently at work tends to be more difficult. A committed worker is one who stays on the job, and who has severed his major connections with the land. He is a permanent member of the industrial working force, receiving wages and being dependent for making a living on enterprise managements which offer him work and direct his activities at the work place.

It is useful to distinguish four stages or points on the continuum of behavioural change which mark the transition of the worker from traditional society to an industrial way of life. These stages are: the uncommitted worker, the semi-committed worker, the generally committed worker, and the specifically committed worker.

The uncommitted worker has no intention of entering industrial employment on any continuing basis. His is a temporary sojourn for an immediate purpose – perhaps to get a needed sum of money to liquidate tax obligations, or to buy a bride, or to tide over his family during a period of famine, price decline, or other emergency. Although the length of the initial sojourn may be determined by the immediate need for income from industrial employment, it does constitute a break with the rural tribal background, and it may be a first step towards further migrations to industrial work and to more permanent commitment as time goes on. The 'target worker' in the South African gold mine is a good example. He may accept work in the mines for a specified period of a year or two, return to the land for a time, and then seek different industrial employment again. In a number of the newly industrializing countries uncommitted workers constitute a major proportion of the industrial labour force.

The semi-committed worker is a man at the margin of two ways of life. He works more or less regularly in industry but maintains his connections with the land, the tribe, or the village. His periods of industrial employment may be no longer than those of the un-committed worker; the primary difference is that he contemplates spending a major part of his adult life shifting between agricultural and industrial employment, while the uncommitted worker re-gards industrial employment as only temporary. In many cases, the wife and family remain on the tribal land where she supports herself and the children. The industrial 'bachelor', as in Kenya, will send her small amounts of money and return home period-ically. Thus the semi-committed worker gets cash and perhaps a more interesting life from his industrial employment without giving up the security connected with the land or the tribe. For example, in some areas of Africa, about half of the national work force may alternate between tribal and industrial areas. The semi-committed workers generally show high turnover rates; they belong fully neither to the tribe nor to industrial life.[7]

The generally committed worker is one who has completely severed his connection with the village to become a permanent member of an urban or industrial work force. This requires an adjustment to all the institutional aspects of urban living and in-dustrial employment. The security of the generally committed worker is geared to the availability of industrial employment, for he no longer has strong ties to the rural or tribal society. He may have tried his hand at different occupations in a variety of in-dustries. But whatever his occupation, he must sell his labour to maintain himself and his family. All advanced economies depend mainly on this kind of committed labour, or on the more specifi-cally committed worker described below.

The specifically committed worker is one who is permanently attached not only to the industrial way of life, but to a particular employer or to a particular occupation or profession. He is a member not just of the industrial labour force but rather of a small and closely prescribed segment of it. He is committed to a particular enterprise by virtue of work experience, specific training, seniority rules, welfare programmes, pension rights, or personal obligation. In Japan, for example, industrial employment commonly has involved a life commitment to a single firm. Indeed, the non-temporary Japanese worker has been as bound by custom to his employer as if he were in the closed circle of a pre-industrial tribe. He would not think of seeking alternate employment, nor would his employer ever try to dismiss him. He has permanent membership in the enterprise. This relationship has been expressed as follows in a speech by a Japanese executive to his workers:

Not only is there the fact that our life's work is our employment in our company, but I feel that as people in this situation we have two occasions that can be called 'a birth'. The first is when we are born into the world as mewling infants. The second is when we all receive our commission of adoption into the company. This is an event that has the same importance as our crying birth.[8]

Specific commitment exists also in Germany, Italy, France, and England, and it is becoming increasingly prevalent in the United States as a result of greater occupational specialization and the growth of seniority and pension systems without vesting provisions.[9] In some countries, moreover, legislative restrictions on the enterprise manager's freedom to discharge or lay off have tied the worker to particular establishments almost as tightly as his Japanese counterpart.

In general, the degree of commitment is related to the stage of industrial development. In the very early stages of industrialization, the working forces may consist largely of uncommitted and semi-committed workers. Labour turnover and absenteeism are usually high. The managers make very little effort to build a settled labour force. Indeed, in some cases, as in parts of South Africa, the large enterprises may prefer an uncommitted or a semi-committed labour force which expects to receive only part of its subsistence from industrial employment. This preference often occurs where community facilities are inadequate, where the demand for labour is seasonal, where the managers seek to employ large numbers of unskilled labourers at low wages, where the managers wish an 'unspoiled' labour force, or where the better jobs are reserved for a class or race.

As industrialization proceeds, the enterprise managers become more interested in permanently committed working forces. High rates of turnover, absenteeism, and low levels of skill become burdensome. Efforts are made to move the families along with the breadwinners to the industrial areas. Or, if the factories are located in urban areas where there are adequate supplies of labour, attempts are made to select and retain the more stable workers. The managers devise systems of rewards and punishments to reduce turnover and absenteeism. And in the more remote areas, enterprises provide housing and other amenities for workers and their families. Managers are most likely to make an investment in building a committed labour-force where expensive machinery and processes are utilized, where the skill requirements of labour are relatively high, where quality as well as quantity of production is important, and where the work load is distributed fairly evenly throughout the year. These conditions are likely to prevail in newly industrializing countries which are placing heavy emphasis on new factories with modern technology.

A characteristic feature of all advanced industrializing societies is the existence of a fully committed industrial work force. Workers are permanently attached not only to industrial employment, but often specifically committed to particular enterprises and occupations as well. Absenteeism, except for unavoidable reasons such as illness, ceases to be a problem, and turnover is reduced to the minimum. Managers are characteristically as much concerned with the problem of discharging or laying off the workers they find undesirable or unnecessary as with attracting and holding new recruits. Tied to particular occupations because of specialized skills and to particular enterprises because of seniority, pensions, or sheer tradition, the worker's chance to change his employment is closely circumscribed. Being thus 'over-committed' to his enterprise and his occupation, the industrial worker in the advanced economies tends to demand shorter hours of work and a greater opportunity to seek fulfilment in activities unconnected with his job.

Environmental factors, of course, may speed or retard the process of commitment. In large urban areas, commitment is more easily achieved than in more isolated communities. Cultural factors, such as religious and ethical valuations, the family system, class and race, all have a bearing on commitment. But, in one way or another, workers are uprooted from the old order and relatively soon become generally or specifically committed to the new.

Advancement

Of all the processes of development of industrial working forces, the advancement of human resources is the most critical. It involves investment of time, energy, and money in the education, training, motivation, and rational utilization of labour. Commitment alone is not sufficient to create effective industrial workers. They need to have pride of workmanship, specific skills, and general industrial 'know-how', and they must be energized to do a good job.

The starting points of advancement vary from country to country. In some, for example, even the use of a long-handled broom may be a totally new experience for a manual worker; in the Middle East, bedouins employed by the oil companies may have to be shown how a door knob works. In most underdeveloped countries, new recruits can neither read nor write. In the more advanced societies, on the other hand, levels of education and experience are higher, but extensive new training or retraining may be required to develop needed skills. Cultural factors often place obstacles in the way of effective advancement. The desire for security of employment sometimes stifles the incentive for personal advancement. Or there may be a preference in the society for commercial positions which makes training for mechanized jobs less attractive. Advancement may also be hindered by negative attitudes towards heavy or dirty work.

Human resources may be upgraded for industrial employment in three ways. Workers may advance themselves. They may be provided with education by the community or the state. And they may be trained by enterprise managers. In most cases, advancement is the result of all three processes. For purposes of analysis, however, each can be scrutinized separately.

In some cases, the worker advances himself by his own efforts without much help either from management or from formal education. In many situations, the young worker is simply assigned to an older worker who is supposed to teach him the required skills. But the older worker himself may be apathetic and poorly trained; and he may be unwilling to teach the new recruit for fear that the youth will replace him. Managers who expect workers to train themselves invariably complain about the lack of understanding and motivation on the part of the workers, and use this as a justification for low wages, arguing that workers are not very productive. On their own initiative, workers can do a lot to develop skills and 'an industrial consciousness'. But industrialization in modern times can no longer rely primarily on this kind of self-upgrading.

A more prevalent notion is that the community, the state, or society is responsible for the advancement of human resources. Here the assumption is that the lack of industrial aptitude may be overcome by the proper investment in compulsory general education and enlarged vocational training programmes. This is particularly true in most western countries, and it is given great emphasis in communist societies such as the Soviet Union, Yugoslavia, and China. Certainly the elimination of mass illiteracy makes a contribution to the development of higher-capacity workers, and trade schools are helpful in 'breaking in' potential recruits for the industrial labour force.

The larger part of a worker's advancement usually takes place on the job, and thus the really critical factor in development of human resources for industry is management. Managers can provide the organization of work, the training on the job, and the incentives which make the difference between a mediocre and a highly efficient work force. Within limits, good managers are able to build a well-adjusted and reasonably contented force instead of an unadjusted and unskilled one. And poor managers may create an inefficient labour force even in countries with high levels of general and vocational education.

In the initial stages of industrialization, it is typical for the state and the managers to pay little attention to the building of an efficient labour force. School systems are designed primarily to turn out civil servants for the government bureaucracies. The universities, if they exist at all, concentrate attention on philosophy, the arts, religion, the law, and medicine. The managerial resources for incipient industries are drawn largely from the more advanced industrial countries. And the managers are interested primarily in hiring docile rather than educated manpower. At this stage workers are largely responsible for their own advancement, and as a consequence the working forces consist largely of poorly trained, partially committed, and mostly apathetic workers who have very little incentive to produce efficiently.

As the drive towards industrialism becomes more serious, the state invests more heavily in vocational and technical schools. As an attempt is made to eliminate illiteracy, the younger members of the work force have had at least some formal education. Scientific, engineering, and other technical faculties are added to the universities. The enterprise managers become interested in building stable and loyal rather than merely docile working forces. They want workers who can understand as well as take orders. More determined efforts are made to give workers systematic training on the job. The managers become convinced that a smaller, higher paid, and better directed work force is cheaper than a larger mass of illiterate labourers living on a bare subsistence wage. In this stage of industrialization, workers are advanced as much by their managers and by society as by themselves.

In the more advanced stages of industrialization, all workers have considerable formal education. Vocational schools and technical institutions are extensively developed. The universities are equipped to turn out not only scientists and engineers, but persons with some knowledge of administration and management as well. The enterprise managers concentrate primarily on building efficient working forces. They rely upon more carefully designed incentives to energize the workers; they invest more heavily in selection and development of competent supervision; they institute formal programmes for skill training at all levels; and, through attitude surveys and other forms of personnel research, they seek to discover the means for motivating men to produce at high efficiency. At this stage, society and the industrial managers are perhaps more responsible for advancement than the workers. As the productivity of workers becomes as important as the productivity of machines, there is widespread recognition of the value of conscious investment in the development of enterprise managers and workers.

In modern times, a newly industrializing society, if it so chooses, may speed up the industrialization process by making the required investments in the advancement of human resources at a comparatively early stage of its development. By studying the course of industrialization in more advanced countries, it can anticipate its requirements for trained manpower. It can purchase the latest equipment and machinery for its factories in the advanced countries. And it can likewise adapt the appropriate parts of educational systems, on-the-job training techniques, and modern methods of manpower management.

The foreign oil companies in the Middle East have demonstrated strikingly the applicability of modern methods of education and management to primitive working groups. They have taught illiterate bedouins to weld pipe and drive trucks in a matter of months, developed all-round craftsmen in a few years, trained numbers of clerical workers and technicians, and promoted local nationals into the lower supervisory positions. Within the past decade, starting from higher levels, the Egyptians have succeeded in upgrading workers to perform practically all the tasks involved in the operation of oil refineries, textile mills and steel-processing factories, chemical plants, and the Suez Canal. The same holds true for many other newly industrializing countries.

The advancement of the labour force depends, in part, upon where the line is drawn in determining eligibility for positions in the industrial hierarchy. Thus, for example, in the Union of South Africa, most skilled jobs are reserved for whites, and this is conveniently rationalized into a widely held conviction that the blacks do not have the innate capacity for development beyond unskilled or semi-skilled labour. In Kenya and Natal, the Indians form a layer of craftsmen and merchants into which the Africans find it difficult to penetrate. In the Belgian Congo prior to independence there was less of a colour bar in occupations within the industrial labour category, but executive positions were reserved for the experienced and the educated, who were mostly Europeans.

Maintenance

The final step in building the industrial labour force is the maintenance of the general welfare and security of its members. Unemployment insurance, accident compensation, old-age annuities, and other forms of social security, as well as schemes of sickness benefits, dismissal compensation and pensions, are instruments for the maintenance of working forces. And included also in this category are measures designed to regulate the lay-off and discharge of workers.

In the very early stages of industrialization the state and the managers typically make little or no provision for the maintenance of the working forces. The worker is thrown back upon his family if he becomes injured, ill, unemployed, or too old to work. In effect, therefore, the family is his only available system of social security. In Egypt, the father of the family is traditionally cared for in his old age by his sons, and thus it behoves him to have large numbers of children to ensure his support. In India, the members of the extended family expect to be supported by the family unit. The family system of 'social security', of course, is consistent with and perhaps a cause for the lack of permanent commitment of many workers to industrial employment and to urban life.

As industrialization progresses, however, wider family ties tend to be broken. Committed workers demand that the state and the enterprise share some responsibility for their maintenance. The scarcity of jobs in industry in relation to the number of persons seeking to get and hold them leads workers to attach tremendous importance to tenure of employment. Their interest centres naturally on rights to jobs, restriction of discharge, control over labour-saving improvements, unemployment compensation, dismissal pay, and other measures designed to promote employee security. In Japan, the forces of tradition and chronic under-employment have induced employers and workers alike to

185

perpetuate a system of life membership for permanent employees in industrial establishments. In newly industrializing countries such as Egypt, Brazil, Chile, Argentina, and Peru, there are networks of laws designed to protect the specific commitment of workers to their establishments and to restrict the freedom of management to discharge or lay off labour which has been engaged beyond a probationary period. Social, legislative, and trade-union pressures operate towards the same end in India, France, and Italy. And even the sheiks in the deserts of the Middle East are demanding that the foreign oil companies provide more jobs for Arab labour as well as guarantees of employment for those already in the working forces.

Advanced industrializing societies characteristically have formal programmes of accident compensation, sickness benefits, unemployment insurance, and old-age pensions for industrial workers. There is general agreement that neither the individual nor his family should assume the major responsibility for the hazards involved in being a permanent member of the industrial working force. The society is called upon to maintain persons who cannot work for reasons beyond their control as well as those who are engaged in productive activity. The responsibility for guaranteeing the minimum welfare and security of industrial man rests in large measure upon his managers and his government. This completes the severance of his dependence, both materially and emotionally, on kinship and family ties.

The transition from family to industrial systems of maintenance can be quite rapid in the newly industrializing countries. These latecomers borrow modern technology, educational methods, and systems of management from the advanced countries. In like manner, as a result of the conventions and resolutions of the I.L.O. and the demonstration effect of highly industrialized societies, they adopt elaborate systems of social security for their industrial working forces. In some cases, however, as in Chile, they move too far and too fast in this direction by instituting measures which are too costly for their stage of development and too difficult for their governments to administer. Indeed, they often are induced to give priority to maintenance before completing the more fundamental processes of recruitment, commitment, and advancement of their human resources. A major explanation for this, as explained in the next section, is the surplus of available labour for industrial employment in many of the newly developing countries.

The Problem of Labour Surpluses

Today, many of the economically underdeveloped countries have rapidly increasing populations, and characteristically they are plagued with an overabundance rather than a scarcity of labour resources. India, Egypt, Indonesia, Pakistan, and Ceylon, for example, have surplus unskilled labour in nearly every sector of their economies. Except in isolated areas, the South American countries appear to have more than enough recruits for industry. The same holds true even in Nigeria, which is not overpopulated as a country but which is experiencing large-scale migration from rural to urban areas. Industrial labour redundancy is, or will become, a persistent problem in many of these countries. The major reasons are:

First, industry by itself employs a relatively small number of workers. In countries such as India, Egypt, China, and Indonesia, for example, the proportion of the total labour force employed in the modern industrial sector probably does not exceed 5 per cent, and in the less developed countries it is much lower. Since the compensation of industrial labour is nearly always higher than that in agriculture, handicraft shops, or petty trade, the small numbers of workers needed are easily attracted to the larger factories.

Second, in most of the newly industrializing countries, a population explosion usually precedes rather than follows large-scale industrial development.[10] In modern times economically underdeveloped countries are able to reduce death rates far below birth rates long before any substantial industrialization occurs. India, Egypt, and China are prime examples, and it appears that the same trend may be starting in the presently pre-industrial economies of Africa.

Third, the bulk of industrial growth takes place in urban areas, and large urban populations are likely to build up prior to extensive industrialization in those areas.[11] As a consequence, cities such as Cairo, Bombay, Calcutta, Baghdad, and Lima all have a mass of unemployed or underemployed workers, and similar tendencies in this direction are already evident in Accra, Ibadan, and other growing African cities.

Finally, as industrialization gains momentum, the productivity of factory labour tends to rise sharply, and this limits the expansion of demand for general industrial labour. As the skill levels associated with more modern technology increase, the need for masses of manual and clerical workers declines.

For all these reasons, the development of new industries and modern factories is likely to afford employment for only a fraction of the labour resources which are available. In Egypt, for example, there are large surpluses of unemployed or underemployed agricultural labour located fairly close to most of the factories. In addition, there is a vast and expanding pool of unemployed persons in the major cities. The number of persons entering the labour market each year greatly exceeds any conceivable requirement over the next few decades for new workers in the expanding industrial sector. Yet despite the existence of abundant and cheap labour, the large Egyptian factories continue to introduce new labour-saving machinery and processes wherever possible. If this trend continues, it is likely that industrial production may be doubled in five years with little, if any, corresponding increase in factory employment. In India, the same problem is illustrated by the 'rationalization' of the textile and jute mills. India's jute mills in recent years have increased their production and reduced total employment from 300,000 to 220,000 workers.

The large sugar haciendas in Peru have done the same thing. Here in recent years production of sugar and related products has been increasing sharply, while the number of agricultural and factory workers needed on the haciendas continues to decline. In this case the problem is even more serious because the original workers and their families were imported from distant locations and housed in company communities. As the children of these workers have grown up, the labour force has greatly expanded in the face of an ever-shrinking number of available opportunities in the area.

Surplus labour is a problem which industrialization of relatively empty countries such as the United States, Canada, or Australia never faced. How, then, may the industrializing élites cope with the social and economic consequences of the under-utilization of human resources?

One means is to make the industrialization process as labour-intensive as possible. Logically, this would suggest relatively heavy reliance on handicraft or cottage industries, together with the use of comparatively simple and inexpensive machinery in industrial plants. But for a number of reasons most of the newly industrializing countries are likely to reject this approach in favour of reliance on factories using the most modern technology. Countries such as Egypt, India, and Indonesia cannot be persuaded to invest in antiquated steel mills, fertilizer plants, textile mills, and metal-processing factories. In terms of both quality and long-run costs of production, the modern technology is deemed to be more efficient. And aside from considerations of efficiency, many of the under-developed countries are tempted to favour modern factories purely for reasons of prestige. If modern plants are built, of course, measures may be taken to force enterprise managers to use more labour than they need. This can be achieved by restricting discharges and preventing managers from reducing working forces. Logically, it is shortsighted to employ unneeded persons to do little or no work in modern factories, but this policy has been widely used.

If the surplus workers cannot be used within the plants, they then become a charge on the community. Some may find employment in petty trade, in local government services, in construction, or as domestic servants. Here, however, opportunities are likely to be limited unless incomes and services in the community are expanding fairly rapidly. As already indicated, however, the migration of persons from rural to urban areas is likely to precede rather than follow the expansion of economic opportunities in the cities. The maintenance of such persons on public relief is usually beyond the means of the community. Quite rightly, therefore, the governments of these countries are alarmed about the social and political consequences of 'storing' unneeded labour in already overcrowded and overburdened areas.

Another alternative may be to hold the surplus human resources on the land. Theoretically, excess labour may best be kept in the agricultural areas. But, in many countries, the rural areas are already overcrowded and there is considerable disguised unemployment. Indeed, in some countries, it is conceivable that total agricultural export to urban areas could be increased if fewer people were living on the land and the size of agricultural units was increased.

A further alternative is to utilize surplus labour in massive programmes of public works. Of all the alternatives, this is perhaps the most promising. The community development projects in India have utilized labour on a limited scale in the villages for building schools, digging irrigation canals, and improving roads. The mainland Chinese mobilized masses of people for work on dams, roads, irrigation systems, and other large construction projects in many parts of the country. The employment of labour on public works however, takes a considerable amount of capital and a great deal of organization, requiring in many cases the diversion of scarce financial resources and high-level manpower from other development projects.

Clearly, therefore, industrialization by itself is not likely soon to solve the problem of surplus labour in most of today's underdeveloped countries. Birth rates may decline if standards of living can be raised substantially, but increases in the standard of living require greatly increased levels of capital formation and investment over long periods of time. The problem of surplus population and surplus labour is likely to persist for many years in most of the underdeveloped countries. Table 3 illustrates the differential rates of population increase among countries.

Some Common Themes of Labour Force Development

It may be argued that the more rapid the process of industrialization, the more painful it is likely to be. Certainly, rapid industrial development normally requires high rates of savings which must be achieved in most cases largely by holding down levels of consumption. If people must be uprooted from rural backgrounds, a rapid transition may result in greater stress and tension than a slow one. And, if compulsory measures are to be used to recruit workers, the adjustment can be extremely painful. In addition, poor living conditions, ineffective upgrading, and arbitrary use of managerial authority may add to the strains of workers entering the industrial labour force. Any kind of shift from one culture to another is apt to cause distress and dissatisfaction, and the problems of adjustment in some cases may well be aggravated by rapid change.

On the other hand, there is also reason to believe that in modern times rapid industrialization may be less painful in some respects than gradual industrialization. In overpopulated countries with disguised unemployment on the land and overcrowded conditions in the urban areas, rapid industrialization coupled with rapid development in other sectors of the economy may alleviate the miseries of unemployment. In modern times, moreover, the managers of enterprises may use enlightened measures to recruit, commit, and advance workers. Education, in itself, may make the transition easier. Indeed, education raises the expectations of people, makes them less satisfied with traditional ways of life, and thus creates a desire for almost immediate change to the industrial way of life. At the same time, of course, there is the possibility that failure to realize these expectations may accentuate the transition difficulties. The central problem in too many countries already is too many people with expectations too high relative to prevailing possibilities.

The underlying problem in the transition from a traditional to an industrial society is not the adaptability of man. His capacity and eagerness for change is infinitely greater than is commonly recognized. The more fundamental factors are the endowment and availability of resources and the suitability and adaptability of institutions. The transition from the old to the new order can be managed well or managed poorly. Newly industrializing societies need not repeat the mistakes made by the presently advanced countries. Population pressures, which are building up now in advance of economic growth, put industrialization in a new and different light. The underdeveloped countries do not by tradition

Table 3. POPULATION GROWTH

Country	Annual Rate, 1953–7
United Kingdom	0·4
Italy	0·5
Sweden	0·7
France	0·8
Luxembourg	1·0
W. Germany	1·2
Netherlands	1·2
Japan	1·2
India	1·3
Uruguay	1·4
Yugoslavia	1·4
Ghana	1·6
Kenya	1·7
U.S.S.R.	1·7
United States	1·8
Egypt	2·2
Brazil	2·4
Peru	2·4
Chile	2·6
Mexico	2·9
Jordan	2·9
Venezuela	3·0
Malaya	3·2
Sudan	3·3
Dominican Republic	3·4
Nicaragua	3·4
Iran	3·4
Taiwan	3·6
Laos	3·7
Swaziland	4·9

Source: United Nations, *Demographic Yearbook, 1958*, New York, 1958.

resist industrialization but instead seek to achieve it. In so far as the development of industrial working forces is concerned, a speedy rather than a gradual transition may well turn out to be less painful and most acceptable for most of the peoples of the modern world.

Diverse Approaches of the Industrializing Élites

The common problems of development of the industrial working forces have been set forth above, and the general approaches associated with the various stages of industrialization have been suggested. Within limits, however, the various ideal types of industrializing élites may be inclined to emphasize different tactics in effecting labour force development. These may now be traced briefly.

The middle class is likely to rely on the labour market for workers. It is primarily interested in the productivity of the workers. It assumes that there will always be a relatively large supply of workers committed to industrial employment who will be seeking jobs in the labour market. For this reason, the middle class is not so much concerned as the dynastic élite with paternalistic measures to tie workers to a particular establishment, although it may favour limited private benefit plans. The middle class tends to emphasize skill development within the plant, and supports the idea of public responsibility for general education of the masses. It relies on incentives of various kinds to quicken the pace of work and to increase productivity. At the same time, this type of society thinks that self-reliant workers should be responsible for their own maintenance, with a minimum of assistance by the community, and thus it accepts somewhat reluctantly government social security measures. The middle class has typically assumed no direct managerial responsibility for unemployment, since it argues that a free market and a free economy can be relied upon to provide jobs in the long run. Indeed, it accepts some unemployment as both normal and necessary in a market economy, although it may advocate limited programmes of unemployment compensation, accident insurance, and old-age pensions. In the United States, however, some large business enterprises have recently undertaken a share of responsibility for unemployment in

Chart 7. Diverse Emphases in Building the Industrial Working Forces

Industrializing élite	Middle-class	Dynastic
Recruitment	Relies on the labour market. More interested in productivity of labour than in its loyalty.	Relies for longest period on family or tribal recruitment. Insists on hiring docile workers.
Commitment	Assumes large supply of generally committed workers. Sometimes develops enterprise pension and welfare plans.	Relies on paternalistic devices (housing, company communities, etc.) to command the loyalty of working forces.
Advancement	Provides extensive training on the job. Supports idea of public responsibility for general and vocational education. Uses incentives to motivate workers.	Least concerned with skill development and with general educational policy – accepts slow pace of work.
Maintenance	Tends to disregard problem of maintenance, or develops enterprise benefit schemes. Reluctant acceptance of government social security.	Requires enterprises to accept obligation to maintain permanent workers for life as they remain loyal. Takes no responsibility for temporary workers.

Revolutionary intellectuals	Colonial administrators	Nationalist leaders
Direct flow of labour to priority employment by both compulsion and positive incentives.	Try to recruit docile workers. Occasional use of forced labour. Rely on family or tribal recruitment.	Use all means of recruitment to speed industrial development. Inclined to develop mechanisms for central direction of recruitment.
Use combination of ideological appeal, direction of employment, and differential incentives to get effective commitment.	Sometimes use paternalistic devices to tie workers to the enterprise. Least interested in permanent commitment, particularly of unskilled and semi-skilled labour.	Use combinations of nationalist appeal, differential incentives, and occasionally direction of employment.
Emphasize training on job, and also vocational training in schools. Encourage workers to be productive through ideological education, differential rewards and compulsion.	Some emphasis on training within the enterprise; little interest in general education. Put ceilings on levels of jobs for which 'natives' are trained. More interested in control than in productivity.	Emphasize training within the enterprise, and rapid expansion of general and vocational education. Interested in increasing productivity of workers and pace of work.
Establish formal systems of social security, administered by the state and controlled labour organizations.	Either disregard problem, or follow policy similar to dynastic élite. Depend upon tribes or villages as the traditional social security mechanism.	Attempt to introduce social security systems similar to those in advanced countries.

Industrializing élite	Middle-class	Dynastic
Unemployment	Accepts little responsibility for redundancy. Assumes that free market will in long run provide jobs. Considers some degree of unemployment as normal and necessary, and advocates limited social security measures.	Accepts obligation to maintain employment for those with jobs. Less interest in providing or creating jobs.

their immediate sectors of the economy, through such programmes as supplementary unemployment benefits and special assistance for workers displaced by technical change and automation.

The dynastic élite is likely to rely as long as possible on recruitment of labour through family and tribal connections. The dynastic élite holds in high esteem paternalistic devices to tie the worker to the enterprise, and at the same time it expects the manager to assume responsibility for the well-being of his dependent workers. Unless under pressure, it is the least concerned with skill development, and it shows comparatively little interest in general education for the masses. At the same time, it is most likely to tolerate a slow pace of work so long as labour remains loyal. The dynastic élite is most likely to place the obligation of maintenance of workers on the paternalistic manager. The manager, moreover, is expected to provide jobs for all permanent members of the working force, but is not to concern himself with employment problems beyond the factory gates or with jobs for the temporary work force.

The colonial administrators, like the dynastic élite, are more likely to favour docile workers. At the early stages they may resort

Revolutionary intellectuals	Colonial administrators	Nationalist leaders
Either refuse to admit existence of unemployment, or mobilize entire work force on labour-intensive projects such as road building, irrigation projects, and other forms of public works.	Little concerned with problems of unemployment or with creation of jobs for the natives.	See in industrialization a 'solution' to problems of unemployment and surplus population. May overburden factories with surplus labour.

to forced labour of one kind or another, and they often rely heavily on tribal and family recruitment. For the managerial and high level positions, they usually bring in nationals of the home country. They often use paternalistic measures to get skilled workers committed to an industrial work force, but they are of all the élites the least interested in getting permanent commitment of unskilled and semi-skilled labour. The colonial administrators are apt to provide only a minimum of training on the job, and show relatively little interest in general education. They are prone to accept a slow pace of work as unavoidable. For the most part, the colonial administrators are opposed to government-sponsored social security measures, since they rely upon the native economy, through tribal, village, or family organizations, to maintain those who for one reason or another are displaced from industry.

The revolutionary intellectuals are likely to direct the flow of labour to priority employment, using both compulsion and positive incentives. They are also more likely to favour recruitment of women for industrial as well as for agricultural work. They get commitment of workers by ideological appeals, direction of employment, and differential incentives. The revolutionary intellectuals stress training on the job, and give high priority to education, particularly along vocational lines. Thus, the revolutionary intellectuals favour broad systems of social security, usually administered by the state and by labour organizations. Finally, they can readily utilize what might otherwise be a redundant labour force on labour-intensive projects such as road building, irrigation ditches, dams, and other large-scale public works.

The nationalist leaders, in their drive to press rapid industrialization, may use any and all means of labour recruitment. And they will resort to nationalist appeals, differential incentives, and even compulsion to build a committed labour force. They are interested also in a highly productive labour force, and they emphasize skill development within the enterprise and press for rapid expansion of general and vocational education. All these things they do in a hurried and often spotty manner. They are also prone to introduce at an early stage ambitious social security schemes patterned after those in the very advanced industrializing societies. Finally, the nationalist leaders see in industrialization a solution to problems of unemployment and expanding population, and for this reason they may attempt to overburden the new factories with surplus labour and resort to other questionable measures for maximizing employment.

The dynastic élite and the colonial administrators are most likely to favour those approaches which are characteristic of the early stages of industrialization. For this reason, they usually tend to retard rather than to accelerate the effective development of industrial working forces. The revolutionary intellectuals are likely to adopt earlier those measures which are consistent with rapid industrialization. The middle class uses the market and those measures which are most consistent with gradual rather than rapid transformation. And the nationalist leaders may adopt almost any approach which economic and political pressures are likely to dictate. The approaches likely to be emphasized by these ideal types of élites are summarized in Chart 7.

6   The Workers: Impact and Response

Industrialization, whatever the source, characteristically re-designs and reshapes its human raw materials. The drastic changes in human beings and their relationships required to achieve a settled industrial work force have been made only with significant reactions from the workers-in-process. In the end, the work force has adapted to many of these changes, and has in turn exerted pressures to force management and government to adapt to others. This complex pattern of interaction has often involved consider-able stress and tension and even violence.

The impact of industrialization on the work force and its response has been a persistent theme of study since the early days of the classic British case which so concerned economists, social historians, legislative investigators, novelists, and reformers. The following excerpts refer to the early British experience:

A new sense of time was one of the outstanding psychological features of the industrial revolution . . .[1]

The discipline of the early factories was like the discipline of a prison. Small children were often cruelly treated to keep them awake during the long hours, which shortened their lives or undermined their health . . .[2]

But to all the evils from which the domestic worker had suffered, the Industrial Revolution added discipline, and the discipline of a power driven by a competition that seemed as inhuman as the machine that thundered in factory and shed . . . if he broke one of a long series of minute regulations he was fined . . .[3]

All I wish to prove is that the discovery and use of machinery may be . . . injurious to the labouring class, as some of their numbers will be thrown out of employment . . .[4]

The operative is condemned to let his physical and mental powers decay in this utter monotony, it is his mission to be bored every day and all day long from his eighth year.[5]

The work force in process of industrialization is not passive or inert and responds in a variety of ways to the impacts of the new civilization. A few references also from the early British experience are illustrative:

There were others who – whether from inertia, conservatism, or an understandable wish to control their own lives – refused to conform to the new order . . .[6]

There is actual evidence of the rise of one of the oldest of the existing Trade Unions out of a gathering of journeymen to take a social pint of porter together. More often it is a tumultuous strike, out of which grows a permanent organization. Elsewhere . . . the workers meet to petition the House of Commons, and reassemble from time to time to carry on their agitation for the enactment of some new regulation, or the enforcement of an existing law. In other instances we shall find the journeymen of a particular trade frequenting certain public-houses, at which they hear of situations vacant, and the 'house of call' becomes thus the nucleus of an organization . . .[7]

The framebreakers called themselves Luddites, and signed their proclamations Ned Ludd, sometimes adding Sherwood Forest. The original Ned Ludd . . . was a boy apprenticed to learn frame-work knitting . . . Being averse to confinement or work, he refused to exert himself, whereupon his master complained to a magistrate, who ordered a whipping. Ned in answer took a hammer and demolished the hated frame.[8]

The response of the new workers may be a covert withdrawal of effort or overt action by isolated individuals or groups; and concerted action may be a temporary flurry or involve continuing organization. The total of these negative reactions and responses to the impact of industrialization on the work force is drawn together under the term 'worker protest'.

Continuing industrialization and its spread throughout the world might suggest that worker protest is on the increase, confirming the predictions of Marx. But the dominant finding about protest disclosed by this present study is in fact its secular decline.

The Workers: Impact and Response

The present chapter will consider first the universal impacts of industrialization on workers, the universal responses of workers, and the diverse characteristics of protest arising from different policies of the various élites and their different speeds of industrialization. It will then turn to an analysis of the secular trend of worker protest, the reasons for its early peak and subsequent decline, and the long-run effects of worker protest as an historical force.

Universal Impacts of Industrialization on the Labour Force

The industrialization process has certain uniformities in its impacts on the labour force. These universals are operative at the immediate work place, in the community and home, and in the larger national community.

Destruction of Old Trades and Creation of New Skills

The skilled occupations of agrarian or traditional societies are typically broken down by industrialization into a series of separate operations, often performed by many semi-skilled workers and a few highly skilled workers. The experience of the cordwainers, tailors, and the skilled tradesmen in glass-making are classic illustrations. Generally the old skills facilitate the learning of new jobs, although on occasion the old habits are an impediment:

> The problem of security arises especially with the loss of skills involved in the shifting of handicraft workers into the factory . . . little effort has been made in recruitment and initial placement to utilize these skills already developed in the pre-industrial economy . . . it may be guessed that this circumstance has led to considerable frustration and loss of confidence on the part of the worker . . .[9]

> To begin with, these are people whose skills relate to old technologies or demands, and who cannot adjust to changing conditions . . . Since each of us is likely to suffer from change, in our capacity as producers, economic growth makes as many enemies as friends.[10]

The industrial order requires many new skills and ever-changing skills. There is a chronic shortage of skilled labour, or at least a relative scarcity. The levels of skill are gradually rising. The ever-shifting demands of skill – eliminating traditional occupations and

201

creating higher-skilled and more specialized workers – constitute a universal impact on the labour force. The uncertainty and the real costs of these changes, particularly for older workers, are sources of tension.

The Web of Rules

There is a popular image of primitive society pervaded by customs, rites, and rituals for the workaday world of agriculture and the household arts which is sharply contrasted with the *laissez faire* of modern society. But industrializing societies at the work place and work community are in fact characterized by a vast network of detailed rules, regulations, and norms. The web of rules is a universal of industrialization. The content of many rules at the work place is closely related to technology and market or budget restraints and, accordingly, many rules are similar in different countries, despite wide differences in political and economic institutions.

The complexity of the rules in early New England textile towns has been described as follows: 'The factory and boardinghouse regulations were innumerable, and covered every smallest corner of the operatives' lives ... The operatives were told when, where, how, and how much they must work; when and where they were to eat and sleep. They were ordered to attend church, for which they had to pay pew rent. They were discharged for immoral conduct, for bad language, for disrespect, for attending dancing classes, or for any cause that the agent or overseers thought sufficient.'[11] The factory system was depicted by Engels in these terms: 'Here ends all freedom in law and fact. The operative must be in the mill at half-past five in the morning; if he comes a couple of minutes too late, he is fined; if he comes ten minutes too late, he is not let in until breakfast is over, and a quarter of the day's wages is withheld, though he loses only two and one-half hour's work out of twelve.'[12]

The web of rules becomes more explicit and formally constituted in the course of industrialization. At the very early stages, individual incidents are confronted without regard to their more general implications. The continuing experience of the same work place tends to result in customs and traditions which begin to codify past practices. Eventually these may be reduced to writing in general form. Some rules may later emerge which anticipate problems rather than merely summarize past decisions. The statement of the rules then becomes more formal and elegant, particularly as specialists are developed in rule-making and administration. The process of industrialization thus brings more and more detailed rules and a larger body of explicit rules. Changing technology and markets produce new situations; higher compensation takes new forms; organizations of workers and managers develop new interests; a general rule invites loopholes and exceptions. While there may be periodic codification and simplification, the dominant tendency is towards a larger complex of rules.

Two of the most significant groups of rules or norms in their impact upon an emerging industrial work force are those relating to discipline and to the pace or tempo of work operations. Chapter 5 noted that all managers require a disciplined work force. It was also observed that as industrialization proceeds, managers become increasingly concerned beyond subordination with the efficiency, skill, and pace of the work force.

Levasseur observed of employers and workers in the United States in the 1890s: 'As an employer he expects his men to work, and he rids himself without hesitation of those who are unsatisfactory in this particular; as a workman he is exacting in many respects, but realizes that he should work hard during working hours . . .'[13] In reference to Meiji Japan, an economist notes, 'Two supplements to *Shokko Jijyo* give details of these brutal punishments, which were meted out not only to runaways but also to girls whose work was not up to required standards of efficiency . . .'[14] 'An extreme type of labour indiscipline is illustrated by physical assaults on managerial staff by workers. In eight months during 1946, for example, 75 assaults were reported in Bombay cotton textile mills, on managers and other higher staff, clerks and timekeepers.'[15]

Discipline and pace are embodied not only in a complex of formal rules of the work place, but in a set of values or an ideology to reinforce these rules. Even though industrialization is seen as an affirmative good by workers in economically underdeveloped areas today, the universal impact of the rules, in particular relating to discipline and pace, is so potentially disruptive in the first instance that a basis for these rules is always sought in an ethic, national ideal, or ideology.

The Industrial Community

The urbanization process has a variety of impacts on the emerging industrial community. The urban slums are a symptom of a society in transition towards industrialism, as any tourist in Bombay, Osaka, Kirkuk, or Brazzaville can report. Capital cities in industrializing countries reflect the same features even more vividly as rural population flocks to old capitals. The worker is uprooted from the larger family and the village. The immediate family, at least for a period, has been left in the village. These dislocations are accompanied frequently by a new position and status for women, many of whom may also come to be wage workers in factories or service employment. New relationships based upon employment or occupation come to replace the larger family and village attachments. New methods of communication among city dwellers – newspapers and radio – replace those of the village. As noted in an earlier chapter, the role of the extended family as a source of security and an object of loyalty is weakened and its place is taken in some measure by the governments of the city and nationalist state. The simple response to the immediate need, to nature, and to impulse in the village gives way to the variety, perplexity, and indecision of the industrial community.

The new industrial towns in the early nineteenth century in Great Britain have been described as follows: 'They were not so much towns as barracks: not the refuge of a civilization but the barracks of an industry . . . They were settlements of great masses of people collected in a particular place because their fingers or their muscles were needed on the brink of a stream here or at the mouth of a furnace there . . .'[16] In the contemporary world, 'It is not the noise or soot in the city which corrodes the nerve of the worker . . . but rather the "absence of neighbourhood" – the anonymity and impersonality of life in a big city. These factors go far to explain the high absentee rate, the high rate of turnover, and the low standard of performance of many industrial workers in underdeveloped countries.'[17]

The industrializing cities are comprised of populations with great diversity. They magnify contrasts. There are rich and poor; employed and unemployed; the settled city dweller and the newcomer; racial, language, and tribal mixtures; the isolated individual and the established system; the literate and the illiterate. The city shows the mass of have-nots what they might have. The diversity and contrasts of the industrializing city excite discontent and stimulate unrest and reform. The constraints and authority of established religion are weakened, and the eternal battle between the generations is sharpened as contrasts and frictions between father and son are magnified. The city has often been the locus of revolt, even prior to industrialization. 'In the rise and fall of societies, the urban mob has always played its part, impelled partly by instinct, and partly by instigation.'[18]

The emphasis upon the creation of new skills, the web of rules, and the turmoil of the emerging industrial community is not intended to detail the full range of the universal impacts of industrialization on the labour force. There are effects upon health, literacy and education, and standards of living. But the features here stressed are those decisive to the responses of the labour force which constitute worker protest.

Universal Responses of Workers

The wrenching from the old and the groping for the new in the industrializing community create a variety of frustrations, fears, uncertainties, resentments, aggressions, pressures, new threats and risks, new problems, demands and expectations upon workers-in-process, their families, and work groups. The emerging industrial work community, locality, or nation is no less in ferment. The surface may be quiet by virtue of strong controls, dedication to a national dream or an ideology, a sense of futility or resignation, or on account of hopes spurred by small tangible evidences of improvements. But beneath the exterior is always latent protest, seething and simmering, to erupt in violence or to overflow in indolence in times of crisis or tension.

One of the classic analyses of labour protest, that of the Wheatland, California, riots of 1913, states: 'Resistance by the worker to an employer's labour policy takes one of two forms: either an open and formal revolt such as a strike; or an instinctive and often unconscious exercise of the "strike in detail" – simply drifting off the job.'[19] The distinction between the spontaneous responses of individual workers or small groups and the planned and coordinated reactions of workers, particularly in large-scale organizations, continues to be insightful.

Individual or Small Group Responses

The response of workers to industrialization typically reflects the extent of their attachment or the stage of their commitment (see Chapter 5) to the industrial work place and community. Recruits secured by labour contractors or a push off the land, and the recent arrivals in urban areas in the early stages of industrialization, all reflect a high degree of absenteeism in industrial employment. Thus, 71 per cent of Bombay textile workers in 1953–4 visited their villages at least once a year. They went to escape the city and factory routine, on account of homesickness, to visit kinfolk, for religious festivals, to help with the harvest, and to attend to personal business.[20] It is probably impossible to separate the relative roles of the dissatisfactions arising from the new industrial work place and the ties to the old village and extended family. The high absenteeism of the uncommitted and the semi-committed worker often reflects both. The accommodation to the new work place and work community is evidenced by a significant drop in absentee rates as industrialization proceeds, although wide differences may remain among industries and types of workers.

The 'strike in detail' may take the form of turnover rather than irregular attendance at one job. Turnover is apt to be lower where there is a substantial labour surplus relative to available jobs and where enterprises are more lenient with absenteeism, as in India. Turnover rates tend to be higher when recruitment involves single workers rather than married workers, when it involves a transfer of residence for workers-in-process from their villages, and when it envisages temporary periods of industrial work rather than a permanent commitment to urban and industrial life.

As an example, in the plantation region of Gagnoa in the Ivory Coast during the years 1949–50, 'it was necessary to recruit 1,000 workers to maintain a labour force of 100 on European plantations, and in other regions of the Ivory Coast, quit rates of 80 per cent are not rare. In towns, the problem is less acute, but nonetheless real. In 1953, a new textile mill in the Dakar area attempted to "train its own work force" by hiring young workers, but found it necessary to take on 908 different youths in a seven-month period in trying to fill its labour needs of 170 men.'[21]

'High labour turnover is ... endemic wherever modern economic enterprise relies on the native social structure to provide the worker's security, or has at least not offered sufficient inducement to capture the worker's whole loyalty.'[22]

The 'strike in detail' also takes the form of withdrawal of effort on the job and lack of attention, application, cooperation, and morale compared to workers in more advanced industrial communities. It may take more violent expression in fighting, spontaneous flare-ups, and work stoppage by small groups, and even machine or parts breakage and sabotage to the production process. The chafing of the rules of discipline and pace, the lack of industrial experience, the absence of motivations geared to the industrial community, and poor physical health may combine to produce lethargy, poor workmanship, indiscipline, theft, vice, and violence. 'Indeed opium smoking, the use of other narcotics, and alcoholism are commonly associated with the worker's sense of frustration and dissatisfaction.'[23] The outward forms of indiscipline tend to disappear as the work force becomes fully committed to industrialization, but morale and its effects upon productivity and output remain a major problem even in advanced industrial communities.[24] The large gap between the potential and the actual performance of workers in modern industry is the basis for continuing experiments in many countries with incentive pay and worker participation in management processes.

Organized Responses

The responses of workers to industrialization are not confined to isolated individual or spontaneous small group reactions. These responses tend to become formally organized, although the evolution, forms, and programmes of these organizations may vary widely among societies and although organizations may in time develop functions remote from their origins in protest. (Worker organizations will be considered in detail in Chapter 7.)

The following account describes the evolution of labour organizations over the course of a decade in the Northern Rhodesian copper mines:

As a result of the recommendations by the Foster Commission the system of consultation between the mine managements and African tribal elders, established at some of the mines prior to 1940, was developed in 1942 and 1943 into a general system of Tribal Representatives. In 1943 'Boss Boys' Committees' were formed at individual mines. The Tribal Representative system continued to deal with domestic matters, living conditions, etc., exclusive of industrial matters, until it was terminated in 1953. In 1947 and 1948, from the 'Boss Boys' Committees' were evolved 'Work Committees' representative of African workers in all departments, and during the year 1948 those committees were finally replaced by four African Mineworkers' Unions established at the four major mines with the assistance of a Labour Officer with trade union experience. In May 1949, those four separate Unions were amalgamated to form the Northern Rhodesian African Mineworkers' Trade Union . . .[25]

This experience illustrates both the waning influence of the traditional society in the form of the tribal representatives and the gradual adoption of the organizational form of labour unions from western industrial societies.

Workers organized into groups may have strategic economic power to affect vital production in the short period and the rate of economic development over the long term. Industrial workers constitute an urban group; they are relatively better off and more literate than villagers; and they may seek to transfer strategic economic power into the political arena as well. Thus, in a community with competing elements seeking to direct the industrialization process, there is keen competition for control over or alliances with workers' organizations. Among the contenders are managements, rival labour organizations, political parties, and nationalist movements. The resort to strikes and riots in the independence movements in India and Indonesia illustrates the control and manipulation of tensions and frustrations of workers by a nationalist movement. A disturbance or violence in a foreign-owned plant may be part of the same pattern. The general strikes and demonstrations in Egypt in 1954 in support of Nasser and against Naguib and in 1956 in support of the government's position in the Suez crisis illustrate the use of protest for wider political purposes. The Peronista strikes in Argentina were of the same sort. 'Often the protest tends to become generalized, starting as a demonstration against a decision of the employers or the Administration and ending as a protest against the Administration proper. In the Conakry strike of September–November 1953, for example, the union leaders asked all Africans to avoid the Armistice Day ceremonies and festivities, a request that was remarkably effective.'[26]

The response of organization among industrial workers is associated with the development of explicit and distinctive ideologies defining the role of workers in industrialization and the relations of their organizations to the rest of the society in transition. The Marxian ideas, either in their pristine form or in various revised or watered-down versions, have afforded the most widely influential body of doctrine. Appeals to this ideology have been made by a variety of labour organizations ranging from revolutionary to mildly reformist in their approaches to the political, social, and economic structure of society. The labour organization in the orthodox Marxian view should be subservient to the guiding discipline of the Communist Party. 'The spontaneous labour movement is able to create (and inevitably will create) only trade unionism . . .'[27] Underlying Marxian themes of class consciousness and class conflict and of nationalization of major industries have had their historic appeal in circumstances where the trade-union movement long dominated the political party established by labour to implement its demands, as in Great Britain, and in the close alliance of social-democratic political parties and trade unions in Scandinavia and Germany before the Second World War. At the national level in Japan after the Second World War, the political protest of one of the major labour federations finds its base in a version of the Marxian ideas. And in many of the less developed countries today, labour organizations propelled, at least in their rhetoric, by these ideas may be found in large numbers.

A competing body of ideas is represented by the Papal encyclicals as developed by Catholic labour organizations, particularly in France, Belgium, Italy, and the Netherlands. The body of ideas developed by Gompers and the American Federation of Labor with the rejection of socialization of the means of production in the 1880s is distinctive to the industrial scene of the United States. In the newly industrializing countries the nationalist ideas have pervaded the emerging labour movements.

The response of workers in groups also consists of various forms of conflict, centred about various causes. In the early stages the provocation for conflict, or the centre of protest, as frequently concerns complaints in the community as at the work places. Issues of transportation, housing, return to the village and extended family, and racial, nationalist, and religious diversity within the work force, and protests against the racial and nationalist character of supervision tend to ignite and precipitate conflict.

In a major work stoppage in Basrah, Iraq, in December 1953, for instance, the initial demands of oil workers included a requirement for the company to provide a school, transport for shopping, and a dispensary for workers compelled to live in company houses in Subair, and to cease discharges on unsupported complaints of American engineers.[28] In Qatar the following are among the incidents reported in 1955: a deputation purporting to represent all Qatari mooring launch crews at Umm Said demanded the removal of a mooring master. A two-day strike developed over the dislike of two Pakistani traffic clerks; in the strike roaming gangs at Dukhan and Umm Said took very threatening attitudes. Forty employees from Umm Bab camp commandeered two trucks and drove to Dukhan for lunch (thereby missing most of their afternoon's work) on the grounds that they had been served cauliflower on the previous day which they did not like. The May 1958 strike at Jamshedpur, India, has been described as follows: 'The ensuing week of violence saw police firings, mob destruction of property, looting, arson, prohibition of all meetings, scores of arrests, and the imposition of a curfew, and the movement of federal troops into the city . . .'[29] These episodes from newly industrializing communities have their counterparts in the earlier history of the United States and other more advanced industrial countries: the looting and riots in July 1877 which destroyed the Pittsburgh round house and shops of the Pennsylvania railroad and killed scores; the Molly Maguires in mining communities; the bitter and violent strikes in mining at Broken Hill, Australia, in 1892 and 1909; the Swedish general strike of 1909; and the clashes and violence in Italy in the first decade of this century.

In the course of economic development a sharper division tends to arise in industrial conflict between the issues of the work place and those of the larger community. The forms of organized protest tend to divide between those directed towards enterprise management and the industry, and those directed towards the community and political authority. As noted earlier, the 'political party' protest in contemporary England or pre-war Germany was distinguished from the more work-oriented trade union protest. In post-war Japan, the distinction between 'enterprise union' activities at the plant level and 'national union' activities (largely political and almost entirely separated from plant problems) is particularly discernible.

There is a tendency for industrial conflict at the early stages of industrialization to consist of short-lived incidents and to involve spontaneous fights, riots, demonstrations, violence, and mob action. As organizations of workers develop, the forms of conflict tend to become more disciplined. But instances of spontaneous outbreaks, wildcat strikes and emotional mob action may persist into the more advanced stages of industrialization in some communities and under special provocation, or they may on occasion break through strong repressive measures, as in the case of coal stoppages in Spain and Yugoslavia.

The following list summarizes the forms of protest which are characteristically related to the stages of commitment of workers to the industrial work place and the urban industrial community. Just as the process of commitment is a gradual process and a continuum, so is the transformation of the forms of worker protest.

STAGE OF COMMITMENT	CHARACTERISTIC FORMS OF PROTEST
Uncommitted workers	Turnover Absenteeism Fighting Theft and sabotage
Semi-committed workers	Spontaneous stoppages Demonstrations and guerrilla strikes
Committed workers	Plant and industry strikes Political protests and activity
Specifically committed workers	Grievance machinery, labour courts, and disputes settlement machinery largely without stoppages Political party and organizational alliances

Worker Protest and the Élites

The facts of worker protest pose basic issues of strategy for each élite directing the development of industrialism. How do alternative policies of the élites affect the forms of worker protest? Can groups of workers be used to increase output, skill, and discipline, or must they be disruptive of the productive process? Can worker groups be used to support the power and prestige of the élite; indeed, can they constitute an element of the ruling élite, as many of the new African nationalist parties have attempted?

The policies of an élite towards worker protest must fit into and be consistent with its grand strategy of the industrialization process (see Chapter 2). These issues are the more difficult when a dominant industrializing élite is confronted by competitors. Then the groups competing for control of industrialization strategies tend to fan worker protest for their own purposes; the expression of protest may become exaggerated above its natural level for the stage of development, and the leaders of labour organizations are often split in the contest for power.

The pace of industrialization, which is a central decision facing every élite (see Chapter 3), has a significant impact on the response of the emerging industrial work force. The faster the pace, other factors being the same, the more sudden will be the transformations required of workers-in-process, the greater the impact of discipline and pace at the work place, the greater the limitations on consumption, and the greater the dislocations in the community. The faster the rate of industrialization, with comparable resources, cultural settings, and historical periods, the greater will be the degree of latent worker protest. The faster the pace of industrialization in comparable settings, and the greater the pressures upon the managements of enterprises from the market, budgets, or directly from the élite, the greater will be the derived pressures and protest from the emerging work force.

Similarly, the more drastic the methods used to structure the labour force (see Chapter 5), and the greater the adaptations required in the arrangements to recruit, hire, allocate, and train the labour force, the greater will be the latent protest in any period. Or, the greater the resistance of the traditional culture to industrialization and the more virile that pre-industrial culture (see Chapter 3), the greater will be the stresses and the latent protest involved in the industrial transformation.

These analytical propositions do not readily lend themselves to the direct test of historical experience, since two industrializing efforts are seldom, if ever, fully comparable. Moreover, historical experience provides better measures of overt protest than of merely latent or potential protest. Further, the character of protest, as was pointed out in the last section, changes significantly in the course of industrialization. But there should be general assent to the propositions that protest is distinctively shaped by the strategies of the particular élite, and further that the measures adopted to control or contain worker protest are distinctive to a particular élite and reflect its basic strategies.

The following discussion of worker protest under the different industrializing élites focuses on three interdependent features: (1) the leading principle around which protest tends to be organized, (2) the forms of group protest, and (3) the attitude of the industrializing élite towards protest.

The Middle-Class Élite

Job control has tended to be the principle around which protest is organized in the middle-class community.[30] The tensions of the work place focus attention of workers upon control over the job and job conditions. The worker is not so much against society as against specific features of the job and work community. The pluralism and social mobility of the society led by the middle-class élite preclude the concern with class consciousness of the more rigid dynastic élite. This assumes, of course, that the issue of participation by workers in the political community has been settled earlier in the society's development.

The organized economic strike is the main form for group protest in the community of the middle-class élite. The strike is essentially non-violent, disciplined, and may be of considerable duration.

The middle-class élite today treats a degree of conflict – in the form of the strike or lockout – as no more than an extension of the market and the necessary corollary of voluntary associations. If buyers and sellers are to be free to refuse to buy or sell under terms regarded as unsatisfactory, then a strike or lockout is a logical extension of the market. This is the only élite to tolerate in its strategy of the industrializing process a measure of industrial conflict and to assert for strife even a degree of positive value.

The Dynastic Élite

In the society led by the dynastic élite, protest tends to crystallize around the principle of class consciousness. The traditional élite and the new industrial workers do not arise at the same time; they do not have a common origin in the industrialization process. The élite is fundamentally bent on the preservation of the old order and upon the maintenance of its paternalistic influence over the workers. But the gulf between élite and workers is so wide, social contacts on the basis of equals so infrequent, and vertical mobility so rare that worker protest is congealed around antagonism to the old order and its representatives in the work place.

In the dynastic-led society, demonstrations of a relatively short duration and political strikes constitute the overt forms of group protest. The following description is illustrative of this general response to a sense of grievance. 'The traditional manner for the Italian people, from the Renaissance on, to express dissatisfaction with their lot is to mill around in the central squares of their cities, making and listening to fiery speeches. These demonstrations last from several hours to several days, during which time there may be no casualties. The whole affair is often quite disorganized and generally constitutes no real threat (no clear and present danger) to the government.'[31] In other cases the demonstrations have been more violent and a serious threat to the dynastic élite.

The dynastic élite considers industrial conflict and strife as inconsistent with its paternalistic view of the traditional society. In this view, managers are devoted to protecting the interests of their workers, and the workers are in turn loyal to the firm and its managers. Discord is looked upon as raising serious questions about the integrity of management or the loyalty of the work force, and thus about the basic ideals of the established order.

The Colonial Élite

In the colonial community, protest by indigenous workers is generally organized around the principle of anticolonialism and independence and turned against the mother country and her representatives. The élite, of course, regards industrial strife as inconsistent with the ideals of the relations of the colony to the mother country. As a practical matter, conflict is abhorred as a breeding ground of independence movements and a stimulus to direct action in the political area.

Protest against the colonial élite usually takes the form of the political demonstration or strike. The experiences of India, Ghana, Egypt, and Indonesia before independence and the unsuccessful Hungarian revolt are replete with the mobilization of workers for nationalist purposes and political freedom.

Industrialism and Industrial Man

The Revolutionary Intellectual Élite

This élite tolerates no overt forms of group protest in the society it leads towards industrialism. Its ideology requires that there be no division of interest between managers and managed. Only occasional and isolated instances of overt group strife are encountered, and these may be severely dealt with as incipient revolt against the régime and, on more immediate grounds, as production stoppages which are detrimental to the basic goal of rapid industrialization.

Chart 8. Worker Protest and the Élites

Industrializing élite	Middle-class	Dynastic
Organizing principle of group protest	Job control.	Class consciousness.
Forms of group protest	Organized economic strikes.	Demonstrations and political strikes.
Attitudes of élites towards conflict	Affirmative role for limited conflict.	Inconsistent with paternal society.

But latent worker protest is inevitable, and so the élite provides for a carefully controlled channel for organizing and directing this protest – the principle of self-criticism. The chafings and tensions from rapid industrialization are turned largely inward. Protest is pointed towards the workers themselves and carefully contained and absorbed within the ruling party rather than directed against the ruling class of the old order or towards control over the job and work community. Protest may also be directed against foreign enemies or rivals of the élite.

The Nationalist Leaders

Worker protest in the newly independent nation is organized around removing the vestiges of colonialism, including the elimination of control by foreigners, and it is also an expression of

216

impatient anticipation of a vaguely perceived 'good society'.

The nationalist élite encounters demonstrations which tend to be more peaceful and less violent than before independence. They are likely to be more organized and, in the early years of independence, to be constrained by nationalist fervour and to be directed against foreign scapegoats. Labour strife and demonstrations may also reflect and be used in contests for power where the élite faces serious competition.

The leaders in power abhor industrial conflict because of its potential political dangers and because it threatens the announced goal of rapid industrialization and a higher living standard. They

Revolutionary intellectuals	Colonial administrators	Nationalist leaders
Self-criticism.	Anti-colonialism.	Nationalism.
Diffused and suppressed, except for occasional outburst.	Demonstrations for independence, often violent.	Demonstrations, ordinarily peaceful.
Inconsistent with ideology and rapid industrialization.	Inconsistent with role of mother country.	Inconsistent with nationalist ideal and economic development.

attempt to constrain protest by appeals to the nationalist dream, or to turn it against enemies of the élite within and outside the country.

The discussion of worker protest and the ideal types of industrializing élites is summarized in Chart 8. It should be mentioned again that protest changes, sometimes markedly, in the course of an industrialization under whatever type of leadership. The present discussion, however, has sought to focus attention upon the character of protest inherent in the strategies of the several prime movers of industrialization.

The Natural History of Protest

The course of worker protest during the transition to the industrial society has long been a focal point in the analysis of capitalism and industrialization. Marx saw the intensity of protest and discontent rising as capitalist production expanded and skills were destroyed, with falling rates of profit, increased misery of the working class and increasingly severe crises until protest reached the crescendo of the revolution under the communists. The reconstituted society would eliminate the bases for protest; the classless communist society would confront no worker protest problem. The view that worker protest increases in the course of industrialization under capitalist direction was also held by Veblen and Schumpeter, although a violent revolution does not play the same role. Tannenbaum and Mayo appear to hold that the dislocations of status created by industrialization are gradually restored in the new industrial society and that the curve of protest reflects a gradual rise and then a gradual decline in the course of industrialization. Perlman seems to have suggested that left to themselves, without the interference of intellectuals, manual workers would show no significant variation in protest in the course of capitalist development.

The conclusion of the present study, as stated at the outset of this chapter, is that worker protest in the course of industrialization tends to peak relatively early and to decline in intensity thereafter.[32] The critical period of industrialization is during the early stages. It is the current generation which is decisive in the newly industrializing countries. At the early stages, the break with the traditional society is sharpest; the labour force is making the more basic and difficult adjustments to the discipline and pace of industry; the plant and work community are the most formative stages; nationalist and social revolutions are likely to be occurring in addition to the introduction of modern industry; the reactions of workers are more direct and violent; the appeal of utopias and grandiose schemes for transforming society is likely to be greatest in such periods.

The amount of latent protest at the early stages is related directly to the pace of industrial growth. The faster the pace, relative to resources, and the harsher and quicker the adjustments required of the work force, the greater the potential protest, and the greater the technical need for controls over the work force, labour organizations and the labour market, if latent protest is not to be explosive.

The amount of latent protest at the early stages is also directly related to the extent to which the new industrial order adapts or destroys the institutions of the traditional society. Protest in Denmark was significantly checked by the gradual growth of industry, and the legacy of the guilds early disposed both workers and employers towards organization. In Japan the role of the old order in promoting industry and in constraining manifestations of worker protest through paternalistic enterprises and the state tended to create an atypical pattern of relatively little protest.

Protest as a significant response has declined as industrialization has spread around the world primarily on account of the greater positive attractions of industrialization, despite the dislocations and readjustments for emerging workers. Industrialization has become a prime objective of nationalist movements and political parties; it is often requisite to national survival. The potential benefits to the individual worker nearly everywhere appear to transcend the negative consequences of industrialization. This is not a moral judgement, but a description of the dominance of the demands for modern goods: clothing, transport, movies, education, health, and so on. Moreover, the rewards to industrial workers in the earlier stages are often substantially greater than for other producer groups; the industrial workers are often a preferred group.

A century ago, workers opposing the rise of industrialization had a wide range of alternatives for the organization of society. These included the programmes of the anarchists, utopians, communal groups designed to escape the wages system, producer co-operatives, the socialists, and others. A century of experience has narrowed the range of practical alternatives, since programmes to escape, to avoid, or to overthrow the industrial order have lost any appeal. The choices for workers are seen to be more limited: how to accommodate, to participate in the industrial order, and to share in the gains.

The ideologies of the early period now seem dated, and the old slogans lose their meaning and their appeal. The 1959 programmes of the German Social Democratic Party now declare for 'free competition in a free economy' and denounce a 'totalitarian controlled economy'. The old socialist demand for socialization of the means of production has been changed to 'effective public controls' to prevent the 'misuse of economy by the powerful'.[33]

Beyond the positive attractions of industrialization, there are several other reasons for the decline of worker protest. Industrialization is often less harsh than a century ago. Industrializing élites and enterprise managers have more experience on which to rely and are more skilled at avoiding causes for protest. Managers may employ modern personnel practices. Governments in newly industrializing countries may copy advanced labour standards such as those of the I.L.O., either in direct legislation or by recognition as desirable norms. Where industrialization in recent times has been raw and cruel, the instruments of control or even repression of the work force by management or government have been more efficient and have constrained most of the outward signs of protest.

Another important factor is the decline in political motivation for worker protest. In earlier instances, as for example in England, worker protest was often aimed at securing some share in a viable political community – for some changes in the basic rules of the game as well as their immediate application in the work place. In most advanced industrial societies today, this issue has long since been resolved. And in many newly industrializing countries, the issue has been postponed by mutual agreement of workers and managers in their prior commitment to nationalist goals of rapid and unhampered economic development.

As time passes, formal organizations of workers emerge, and, as has been observed, the forms of overt protest become more disciplined and less spontaneous. The organizations gradually become centralized, formalized, legitimatized, and viable. The industrializing élite develops its strategies and means of controlling, limiting, or directing worker protest. An industrial relations system is developed for establishing and administering the rules of the work place. Spontaneous strikes give way in some industrial relations systems to the enlightened, orderly, and bureaucratic strike, almost chivalrous in its tactics and cold-blooded in its calculatedness.[34] Leaders of the worker organizations become concerned with survival and perpetuation, with finances, and with internal discipline and stability. These labour organizations take on new and expanded functions. (See Chapter 7.)

The secular decline in the outward signs of protest does not mean that the reactions of workers to the constraints, frustrations, and readjustments of industrialization have disappeared. The manifestations of protest operate beneath the surface in new factories and industrial communities, erupting at times into violence, riots, demonstrations, and passive resistance when the pressures can no longer be submerged or when they are ignited by national crises. But there are fewer spontaneous outbursts, chance disturbances, and impulsive melees. The industrializing societies universally come to contain, to control, and to redirect the responses of industrial workers to the transformation of society.

Worker Protest and Pressure as an Historical Force

Worker protest to Marx was not just *the* labour problem but, indeed, *the* important social force at a certain stage in history. It was the peaking of labour protest in a revolution that ushered in the new society. But Marx was not the only one who thus raised the historical import of worker protest to a dominant position. In the century from 1850 to 1950, worker protest was often as feared by the conservatives as it was worshipped by the radicals.

Theories to the contrary, however, worker protest has been a declining rather than an increasing force as the evolution of industrialization has unfolded. But this does not mean that it has been of little or no significance. Nearly everywhere it has been a social force to be reckoned with, and in a few situations it has been the critical social force.

The main effect of worker protest, however, has been its glacial impact – this is the central observation. In certain specific cases, worker protest has additionally played a large role in revolutionary transformation.

Glacial Impact

Everywhere workers have a sense of protest in the course of

221

the changes that industrialization brings. Everywhere, or nearly everywhere, they organize or are organized. Through organization, whether autonomous or controlled, they bring pressures to bear on enterprise managers and the ruling élite – pressures through grievances, negotiations, strikes, elections. These pressures work in the direction of more formal rules, more equality of treatment, more checks and balances on managers, more accumulated rights for workers and, generally, towards a sharing of power – towards the 'constitutional' approach to authority over workers. These pressures also lead towards the greater intervention of neutrals, usually through actions of the state, the greater development of formal procedures to settle controversies, the creation of experts to handle industrial relations problems. Whether faster or slower, deeper or shallower, this is the direction of the impact of worker protest.

This glacial pressure can bring substantial changes over a period of years. It can help change the strategy of a dynatic élite from unadulterated paternalism towards pluralism, as in Germany; soften the policies of a middle-class society towards labour, as in England and the United States; lead a nationalist industrialization drive in the direction of more consideration for the workers, as in Egypt; and even bring greater consideration for the wishes of the masses as against the requirements of the ideology, as in Poland and Yugoslavia. It can be an evolutionary force of real consequence.

Revolutionary Transformation

There are exceptional cases where worker protest has played a major role in a social transformation – in the rise of a new élite or the shift of power from one élite to another. Not all such social transformations, however, inherently involve a role for labour protest. The rise of a dynastic élite to control the industrialization process or the introduction of a foreign élite into control of a colony are not processes in which worker protest can normally play an affirmative role. Also, the rise of supremacy of a middle-class élite is usually achieved without the major assistance of worker protest, although the case of England shows how worker

The Workers: Impact and Response

protest may aid the new middle class in reducing the authority of the old society.

The only two élites which can count on worker protest as a key to their assumption of supremacy are the revolutionary intellectuals and the nationalist leaders. Both are likely to rely on force in taking over from an ineffective dynastic élite or from a colonial régime; and part of the force they may muster is the force of worker protest through the general strike, the urban mob, the revolution. This worker violence helped weaken and then displace the old régimes in Russia, Argentina, Iraq, Indonesia. If the old régime is not actually destroyed, as in Argentina, the organizations of workers may be held in readiness to descend again into the streets to preserve the new régime.

These revolutionary transformations with the aid of labour protest can occur only in some places (the taking over of power from a dynastic élite or a colonial régime) and also only at some times – those turning points in history when social change is made possible by the decay of an old system – and then sometimes only when such decay is made more evident by the effects of depression or of war.

The general rule is that worker protest is available as a revolutionary force only in certain situations and at certain times, and also only to certain people – the revolutionary intellectuals and the nationalist leaders.

Alliances

Worker protest, by itself, has never brought a change in the ruling élite. Workers and the middle class, with the role of the new middle class quite dominant, helped end the old régime in England. Workers and intellectuals and sometimes army officers and peasants have joined under communist or nationalist auspices to supplant a dynastic élite or a colonial power in a number of countries. Worker organizations may even be the source of the leadership of such movements, as in Kenya and Guinea.

But ruling élites may form alliances with worker organizations to direct the sense of worker protest to the purposes of the régime; and this has been one of the significant historical discoveries of the revolutionary intellectuals and the nationalist leaders in a number of countries – Russia, China, Brazil, Pakistan, Mexico. Worker protest need not be against the ruling régime; it can be turned against the defunct régime, the foreigners, backwardness, national degradation; it can be turned in favour of mutual goals of industrial progress, military power, national self-sufficiency.

The ruling élites may also form their own alliances against protesting worker organizations when these exist; alliances with the army, the middle class, the church. And they may seek to split the workers, as in Germany, into white collar versus manual, Catholic versus socialist, officials against subordinates; and to isolate them from the middle class and the peasants. Only the colonial administrators are really bereft of possible alliances with a long-term mass base, much as they may try to rely on tribal chiefs and 'tame' native leaders.

Thus protest can be 'owned' by many people, including the ruling élite as well as its opponents. Least of all is it likely to be solely owned by the workers themselves, since to be effective they must make alliances with others.

The Lessons of the Past Century

The next century of industrialization as compared with the first century of world-wide industrialization (1850–1950) may see an even less central role reserved for social protest.

1. Workers now protest more in favour of industrialization than against it. 'Machine breakers' are no longer heroes. Thus the new protest can be constructive towards industrialization and its ruling élites instead of destructive. The relations of leaders and led in the march to industrialization can be positive as well as negative.

2. Workers have proved themselves much more adjustable to the impacts of industrialization on their technical and social skills, and much more agreeable to the imposition of the web of rules, than was once suspected.

3. The élites have gained experience alike in the means of reducing protest – better housing, better personnel practices, greater social security – and in the means of controlling it – grievance pro-

cedures, incentives, development of joint goals. They appreciate more the need for consensus in society and understand better the ways to achieve it.

4. The organizations of workers and their leaders have proved quite receptive to the guidance involved in the development of consensus in an industrializing society; and even to more direct guidance by the élite through selection of goals and of men. Most labour organizations are, in fact, to one degree or another, a part of the established system. This explains, in part, the increasingly constant threat to them from 'shop steward movements'.

Earlier views on the role of worker protest reflected the facts of earlier times; periods when protest was more frequently against an authoritarian dynastic élite, a hard-pushing middle class, harsh colonial masters; periods when protest was against the new technology itself. It then seemed reasonable to suggest the universal nature of class warfare, with the possibility of a few exceptions (the Netherlands and the United States).

The conditions for class warfare still exist; but they are increasingly the exception. These exceptions are most likely to rest on the failure of an élite group – a dynastic élite that does not adapt fast enough or a colonial régime that does not transfer power fast enough. A related but separable phenomenon is where the incompetence of particular leaders among the revolutionary intellectuals or the nationalists creates the basis for violent worker protest against those leaders (Hungary and pre-Nasser Egypt).

The role of worker protest is both different and more complex than has been postulated in the past. It can affect the selection, the performance, and the survival of each of the élites, but more frequently through its steady glacial impact than through sudden exertion of massive force. It may also be a supportive feature to the élites more often than a destructive one. Thus the direction of its impact may be different as well as the force of its influence on history less decisive.

The general phenomenon now to be explained is class collaboration on the road to industrialization; the collaboration of the new dynastic élite, the new middle class, the new revolutionary

225

intellectuals, the new nationalists, with the workers and their organizations. What were thought to be the exceptions have become the rule; what was thought to be the rule has become the exception. The road to industrialization is paved less with class warfare and more with class alliances.

7   Industrial Relations Systems and the Rules of the Work Place

All industrializing societies – the last three chapters have shown – create managers and industrial workers and labour organizations. These societies also develop and define the arrangements among managements, labour organizations, and governments which in turn establish, change, and administer the growing body of rules of the work place. Industrialization requires an industrial jurisprudence at the work place and in the work community. In short, each industrializing society creates an industrial relations system.

Industrial relations systems reflect both uniformities and diversities. All industrial relations systems serve the functions of defining power and authority relationships among managements, labour organizations, and government agencies; of controlling or channelling worker protest; and of establishing the substantive rules. Uniformities are also found in the substantive rules themselves. Even under different rule-making arrangements, it is not unusual to find similar rules where common technologies and market conditions prevail.

If uniformities emerge from common challenges and problems, diversities in industrial relations systems derive from the significantly different or unique backdrops against which they are fashioned. In different societies, these systems have been started at different historical periods, each of which has left its indelible mark. They have started from different degrees of economic backwardness. They also differ at the present moment of time since they reflect different stages and speeds of economic development. They contend with quite dissimilar pre-industrial cultures. And as has been seen, the industrializing societies are under

the command of different élites with different visions, programmes, and tasks for their emerging industrial relations
systems.

This chapter describes some of these uniformities and diversities
in industrial relations systems. The first section concentrates on the
rule-making process; it examines the worker organizations that
arise under the several types of élites in the course of industrialization – their structure, functions, ideologies, and roles in establishing and administering the rules of the work place. The second
section considers briefly the substantive content of some of these
rules themselves and illustrates how these may be affected both by
the logic of industrialization itself and by the particular strategies
of the different élites.

There is great variety in the ways of arranging the actual network
of power relationships among workers, managers, and the state to
perform the common functions of establishing the web of rules and
of controlling protest. Rule-making, for example, may be largely
unilateral. Employers, or the state, or labour organizations alone
may set the rules. Rule-making power may be dominated by any
two of the three groups in the industrial relations system; in Great
Britain before the Second World War the employers and unions
shared the major responsibility. Or, management and the state
may divide authority between them, as in Nazi Germany; or the
state and the labour organizations may dominate the rule-making,
as in certain periods in the development of Israel. Finally, the three
contestants may share rule-making power in a pluralistic system.
In such a system – the United States today is an example – power is
fragmented and the state, managements, and the labour organizations are independent entities – each able to share in the making of
rules.[1]

Worker Organizations

Organizations of workers vary widely from one design of industrial
relations system to another in terms of structure, functions, leadership, and goals. Indeed, we have sought to avoid the term 'labour
union' here to escape the implications that worker organizations

generally are necessarily similar to the middle-class type of 'trade union'.

This section reviews the kinds of labour organizations which arise under each of the ideal types of élites. The labour organizations are described in terms of a list of seven features: (1) their ideology, (2) the functions of labour organizations, (3) the degree of labour organization participation in setting and administering the web of rules, (4) the extent of competition among labour organizations, (5) the structure of these organizations, (6) their sources of funds, and (7) the sources of leadership.

The Middle-class Élite

The middle-class case, typified by the United States, is characterized by a society in which labour organizations are bargaining institutions primarily; they are mildly reformist in their ideology and attitudes towards the larger community.

The labour organizations generally help regulate relationships with management at both the plant and the industry levels. There is close coordination and often direct lines of authority in these workers' organizations between the industry and the plant level; in some cases this authority extends to a single national centre, as in Sweden, at least on some questions. The political organizations of workers are less concerned with detailed regulation of managements and more preoccupied with community issues. The middle-class élite regards such organized political activity as legitimate, and the workers' political organizations are less dedicated to challenge or to displace the industrializing élite.

The web of rules is largely established jointly by management and workers in direct negotiations, within a framework of procedural rules established by government with participation by workers' organizations and management. The rules at the work place are detailed, and managerial authority to administer the rules is subject to constitutional limitations and review. Labour organizations play an active role in the administration of the rules of the work place within established limits and according to established procedures.

In the society led by the middle class there is typically supposed to be one workers' organization for each type of worker by craft or industry. The scope of labour organizations often conforms to the contour of the market. There tends to be sharp competition among contending organizations since the triumph of one means the loss of recognition to the rivals among a particular group of workers, at least for a period. A degree of competition among workers' organizations may even be regarded as an affirmative good to stimulate more responsiveness to the wishes of the workers. There is relatively little overt competition, however, between organizations over the distribution of functions at the plant and industry levels, although there is internal tension in workers' organizations over the extent of centralization and decentralization of functions.

The workers under the middle-class-led industrialization tend to build a variety of unions: craft, industrial, and general. The range of functions is broad, not constricted by other forms of worker organizations. The diversity in structure represents a response to a gradual historical development, to a lesser degree of confederation centralization, and to a greater responsiveness to the preferences of particular sectors and groups of workers. It also reflects an economy with more reliance upon the market mechanism, under which the pattern of union growth may have had to conform to market constraints to survive. The powers of the confederation often tend to be weaker than in the other ideal types; the principles of decentralization and autonomy are highly regarded values.

The country led by the middle-class élite develops labour organizations that are relatively well financed by dues regularly collected from the membership. The labour organizations seek to build strong financial positions, partly to provide more effective services to the members and partly to provide security in case of struggle with managements. The labour organizations typically receive little, if any, support or subsidy from the government (except in a few cases related to social services). Financial independence from government is a cherished value. The emphasis upon regulatory functions, in constraining management through rules at the work place, operates to create modern administrative organizations, as in the United States, which require large-scale budgets.

The leadership tends to be drawn almost exclusively from the ranks of workers. The predominant concern with the immediate work place necessarily places a premium upon leadership seasoned in the practical operating problems of enterprises. The intellectual would be out of place. The more direct organizational tie between plant and industry or confederation levels of workers' organizations creates more a ladder on which leadership starts at the bottom. Full-time officers arise who regard the labour organizations as a career; they are in a sense professionals or bureaucrats of the labour organizations with a primary concern for administering and negotiating agreements with professionals in management.

The Dynastic Élite

Under the dynastic élite the dominant labour organizations tend to be class-conscious and even revolutionary; they advocate the drastic overhaul of the traditional society. There may also be some labour organizations, particularly those organized along religious lines, which are more loyal to the traditional society.

The dynastic élite does not in principle encourage labour organizations. At the plant level, organizations of workers supplement and help to administer the paternal activities of the managers and the state, but they provide little effective constraint on the decisions of management. At the industry level they provide a broad form of minimum regulation which the enterprise managers often find congenial to the support of cartels or associations. These standards have little relevance to actual plant conditions, and there is little connection between the plant level and the industry level of workers' organizations. Political organizations of workers emerge which often have only indirect connections with the plant and industry levels of workers' organizations, and they seek detailed government regulation of compensation and working conditions to offset plant and industry-level weaknesses and divisions of workers. These political organizations also seek to challenge the established élite and conduct political demonstrations.

The web of rules is established by general regulations issued by the state applicable to an industry or sector, often under the predominant influence of management. The detailed administration of the work place is the prerogative of paternal management, and detailed rules of the work place are not generally prescribed but left to managerial discretion. The élite sets or reshapes the regulations of the work community.

In the traditional society led by the dynastic élite there are frequently deep social distinctions and religious, racial, nationalist, linguistic, and political party divisions among workers. There tends to be multiple representation of workers at the plant level, as in workers' councils; and at the industry level, as in negotiations for agreements signed by several overlapping workers' organizations. Among these organizations at the plant and industry level, and in political activities, there may be keen rivalry and competition. In the absence of exclusive jurisdiction or exclusive representation for the majority organization, the rivalry is limited since it need not end in extinction for any of the competitors. Majority rule does not apply, with the winner-take-all. Changing conditions lead to relative shifts in workers' support, but the existence of the organizations is not endangered. There may also be keen competition between organizations at the plant level and at the national level over the distribution of functions. Any competition among workers' organizations is lamented; but it is tolerated as an unavoidable consequence of historical divisions in the traditional society.

A society dominated by a dynastic élite tends to build worker organizations which provide only minimum regulation on an industry basis and have no direct line of control to the plant level. The trade union is constricted on the one hand by work-level groups, such as workers' councils, over which it has little, if any, control, and the political organs which seek regulative legislation. The trade union operates in a relatively narrow corridor between plant groups and the political parties. There is strong internal confederation control but the effectiveness of this control is limited by the existence of rival confederations.

The operations of labour organizations, as any other, are much influenced by the funds at their disposal and the source of their finances. Under the dynastic élite labour organizations tend to be relatively poorly financed. There are a variety of competitors for support by the workers – work-level organizations, national-level groups, and political parties – and their access to workers for funds is competitive. The focus of the society around the family, state, and religion is not congenial to the financial support of vigorous voluntary associations. Labour organizations do not place a high preference upon building strong financial positions in view of their major activities. At times the government, however, may provide resources in the form of buildings, a subsidy for the operation of labour exchanges, or social insurance services, or it may pay the salaries of some leaders who may fill some nominal public function in exchange for loyalty.

Leadership of labour organizations may be drawn from the ranks or from intellectuals outside the organizations or be imposed by a party or subject to government approval. The leadership of labour organizations in the country under the dynastic élite tends to be drawn from those ideologically oriented towards political activities and from intellectuals. The activities of the trade unions, as opposed to works councils and enterprise or plant bodies, are primarily at the industry and national level. The emphasis upon social policy and law places a relative premium upon learning. The absence of plant-level problems as a concern in these organizations decreases the need for leadership more familiar with the actual work processes. The income of such leaders may not always depend solely upon the labour organization, but may be based also upon political activity, legal practice, journalism, and other activities. It should not be inferred that leaders do not arise from the ranks, but the dynastic arrangements tend to favour the intellectual type for labour leadership, as is seen in the case of Japan.

The Colonial Élite

Although the colonial industrial relations system varies somewhat with the type of colonialism, generally the élite treats workers as a labour force to be used for the best interests of the home country. The colonial workers in turn develop a personal dependence upon the foreign managers.

The web of rules is established by management under the authority of the home country. The rules tend to be general, allowing wide discretion for the colonial management at the immediate work place.

Labour organizations of indigenous workers tend to be largely a part of the nationalist and independence movement. The groups are usually united on the theme of independence, but they are likely to be divided on a wide range of ideological, regional, and tactical grounds. The rivalry is one of slogans, programmes, and personal leadership rather than of representation or constraints on management. The organizations of indigenous workers are not well developed; they reflect a wide variety of structures; they have no systematic dues collection; and they are poorly supplied with funds.

Both their funds and their leadership may come largely from other nationalist groups. The leaders tend to be intellectuals with a personal following. The ideology of these labour organizations is built around independence and anticolonialism.

After a country has passed through the portals of political independence, the dilemma of the function of labour organizations arises with perplexing urgency. There is, of course, the purpose to 'consolidate independence', to 'liquidate the evil remains of colonialism', and to push for the more practical objectives, in foreign firms particularly, of training local citizens to replace foreigners in managerial, technical, and highly skilled positions. Beyond that, the organizations, however, must find a completely new orientation to replace the fight against the foreigners.

The Revolutionary Intellectual Élite

Labour organizations under the revolutionary intellectuals have no ideology apart from that of the ruling élite. They seek to preserve the true revolution envisaged by the élite.

The revolutionary intellectual élite views organizations of workers at the plant or industry level as its own preserve. The purpose of the workers' organizations is not principally to constrain managements but to educate, to stimulate production, and to lead the industrial workers on behalf of the ruling élite. Independent political organization or activity is precluded.

The web of rules both at the industry and plant levels is established by detailed regulations issued by the state with varying degrees of internal consultation by managers and labour organizations, both in turn subject to direction by the state and the party. Labour organizations have only a minor direct role in the administration of most rules affecting management at the work place.

In the society led by the revolutionary intellectuals there is no room for competition between contending labour organizations at the plant level, nor is there any contention over functions to be performed by rival workers' organizations. Since the organization of workers is an instrument of the ruling party to educate and to lead workers, discordant tones serve no purpose and are not tolerated. Labour organizations are agents of the state; and there is only one state. A degree of tension may arise between plant-level representatives and those higher in the hierarchy. Competition among workers' organizations, however, is seen only as an evil, weakening the régime.

The revolutionary intellectual élite tends to create a limited number of labour organizations, industrial in form, with a high degree of centralization over district and local groups and at the confederation level. The structure reflects the deliberate design of labour organizations by the élite rather than the more gradual evolution or conformance to the market. This structure also reflects the functions of the organizations: to serve as an organ of education and communication between the party and the industrial workers and to stimulate industrial output. This narrow range of functions reflects a design in which the party and the state fulfil the functions of regulating or constraining managers which is elsewhere performed by labour organizations and the market. This type of organizational structure may be vulnerable to the rise of plant-level worker organizations from below as illustrated by works councils in Hungary and Poland.

Labour organizations are relatively well financed by assessments levied upon all workers. The organizations are particularly well supplied with buildings appropriate to their status as an arm of the régime. Finances and resources are no problem.

The leadership tends to be drawn from reliable party leaders, many of whom have devoted a career to the work of the party in labour organizations. They are financially secure and are in a sense professionals or bureaucrats of the labour organization and the party. They are concerned with the administration and implementation of policy and ideology developed by the party.

Nationalist Leaders

Workers in the new nationalist state regard foreign managers as a lingering vestige of colonialism and indigenous managers ideally as partners in the new nation. The ideology of labour organizations under the nationalist élite is that of partners in development, as in Egypt and Ghana.

The nationalist leader seeks the support of the rising group of industrial workers and is concerned to ensure its reliability. Industrial workers are a strategic group to the nationalist élite. The élite tends to bestow favours upon reliable organizations and to assist in the opposition to rivals for worker support in exchange for subordination to the nationalist objectives.

The tendency is to adopt the organizational form of labour organizations from some more economically advanced country held in high prestige by the nationalist élite. The élite tend to promote reliable and loyal labour organizations and to encourage the collection of membership dues for them. These dues may even be required of all workers. The élite may also provide funds directly for local organizations, and it may support reliable groups by government grants to worker education and by employment on public payrolls of a number of leaders of labour organizations.

The web of general rules is largely established by authority of the nationalist government, which has a major role in their formulation. In some cases labour organizations and in other instances enterprise managers may be the more influential in affecting the rules announced by the government. Rules of the immediate work place are more likely to be the preserve of management, although labour organization influence is not unknown where labour is scarce or where the organizations of workers played a decisive role in bringing the nationalist leaders to power. But labour organizations generally have little systematic and direct impact on the administration of the rules at the work place.

The reliable leadership of labour organizations is drawn from nationalist leaders in the first generation after independence. The leadership includes many intellectuals responsive to the nationalist élite, except in cases in which leadership is specifically confined to manual workers.

The Dilemmas of Labour Organizations

Succinct and composite characterizations of labour organizations such as have just been outlined can rarely capture the multiple postures of the 'portrait-in-action'. Beyond the broad overview of the general role and nature of labour organizations in the different industrializing societies, it is important, therefore, to add several explicit comments to describe some of the choices and dilemmas, which, at some point in history, face all labour organizations and élites to some extent. These are of special significance to the contemporary nationalist élites and to the labour organizations in those societies currently at the early stages of industrialization. Four issues particularly deserve mention: (1) wages versus capital formation; (2) strikes versus production; (3) grievance-handling versus discipline; and (4) organizational prestige versus political subservience.

The policy choices inherent in these issues are difficult ones even in advanced industrialized countries led by a democratic and middle-class élite. The already mature labour organizations in these countries continue to be concerned about some of these questions – particularly the wage and strike issues – in the economic and political arenas. Recent controversies over 'wages policies' in the United States and Great Britain and the enhanced concern over industrial conflict in the United States attest to the continuing vitality of these questions. But in the middle-class countries, the essential role of labour organization is rarely in dispute and the fundamental delineation of the process of bargaining is not at issue.

By the same token, the choices have in large part already been made under the revolutionary intellectual élites; labour organizations in these countries face fewer dilemmas since there is less leeway for choice. Economic development takes first priority over wage increases; production cannot be interfered with by strikes; labour organizations are designed to increase labour productivity; and they are always subservient to the party and the government.

There is more of a problem in a country under the dynastic élite, but strikes are generally little more than demonstrations. The labour movement cannot secure many concessions from the government, although individual leaders or factions of labour organizations may secure benefits in exchange for political support. The degree to which support for or attack on the ruling class should be mustered remains, however, a troublesome question for labour organizations under the dynastic élite.

For the labour organizations in the newly industrializing countries with a new nationalist élite, all these questions, however, are of fundamental significance and deserve special discussion:

1. Wages versus Capital Formation

There are conflicting claims of economic development on the one hand and immediately improved wages and other benefits for workers on the other. The nationalist labour leaders' dedication to industrialization, which requires increased savings, conflicts with the labour organizations' declared purpose and their often promised gains from independence, to provide immediately improved wages and working conditions. Within some limits, higher wages may increase worker productivity, but this is likely to be a narrow and a difficult range of wage policy to find.[2]

2. Strikes versus Production

The nationalist labour leader must choose again on strike policy. Strike action tends to decrease production where successful and may make development investments less attractive to foreign investors, but strike action may be necessary to achieve economic objectives of the labour organization, to build a disciplined labour organization, and to retain the interest of the membership.

3. Grievance-handling versus Discipline

Individual workers and small groups in an emerging industrial work force have numerous complaints, grievances, and frustrations. The nationalist labour leader must choose in some degree between supporting the immediate reactions and grievances of workers or supporting the insistence upon higher standards of discipline, a faster pace, training, and production which are vital to economic development.

4. Organizational Prestige versus Political Subservience

The labour organization is often long on political influence and short on economic power. It must weigh the costs of faithful support and dependence on a political party or government against the benefits of governmental recognition and support in a variety of ways, including exclusive labour rights and favouritism in treating rival labour organizations and outright financial support. The immediate attractiveness of financial solvency and a strong legal position in dealing with managements, members, and rivals is to be balanced against the loss in independence of action in being subservient to the government.

It is easy to understand why many leaders of industrializing countries outside the communist orbit find the choices posed above to be very hard, and they talk of ways to develop labour organizations that will make a more affirmative contribution to the national objective of industrialization. The circumstances they confront do not make the traditional model of the 'free trade union' and 'free collective bargaining' drawn from advanced western countries a very congenial one. As Dr Nkrumah has said, 'The trade union movement has a great part to play and a far wider task to perform than merely the safeguarding of the conditions and wages of its members.'[3] The debate and the experimentation over the role of labour organizations in recently industrializing countries is one of the focal points of the competition among groups for leadership in the process of industrialization.

Chart 9 summarizes the characteristics of labour organizations arising under the various ideal types of industrializing élites.

The Substantive Rules of the Work Place

The preceding section has focused on some of the uniformities and

239

Chart 9. Worker Organizations and the Élites

Industrializing élite	Middle-class	Dynastic
Ideology	Reformist.	Class-conscious and revolutionary except for a minority.
Functions of workers' organizations	Regulates management at the local and industry level. Independent political activity accepted. Does not challenge the élite.	Social functions at plant level; little constraint upon management. Provides minimum industry conditions by legislation. Political activity challenges the élite.
Role of labour organization at work place	Active role under established procedures. Regulates management.	Little role, competitive with works councils. Cooperates with management.
Division of authority on rule making	Pluralistic with workers, management and state having an active role.	State and management dominant.
Broad or detailed systems of rules	Detailed regulation at the work place primarily through collective agreement.	General rules at the industry level with management free at the work place.
Competition among workers' organizations	Exclusive representation and keen competition. Some rivalry between plant and industry levels over allocation functions.	Limited rivalry at the plant level and the distribution of functions between the local and industry levels. No exclusive representation

Industrial Relations Systems and the Rules of the Work Place

Revolutionary intellectuals	Colonial administrators	Nationalist leaders
Preserve the true revolution.	Independence.	Nationalism.
Instrument of party to educate, lead workers and to stimulate production. No political activity except through the party.	Largely a part of the independence and nationalist movement.	Confronts the conflicting objectives of economic development and protection of workers.
Little direct role; influence through party. Increase productivity.	Little role, force for nationalism and independence.	Little direct role influence through government tribunals; increase productivity.
Party and state, with management and labour organizations as instruments.	Manager dominant with support of mother country.	Nationalist state and enterprise managers.
Detailed regulation at industry and work levels prescribed by the state.	General rules prescribed by state with management free at the work place.	General rules prescribed by state with management often free at the work place.
No rivalry or competition allowed.	Divided by ideological, tactical, regional and personal leadership factions.	Tendency for consolidation among organizations recognized as loyal by nationalistic élite. Advantage over those not so recognized.

Chart 9 continued

Industrializing élite	Middle class	Dynastic
Structure of worker organizations	A variety of structural forms. Confederations not centralized. Organizations perform a wide range of functions.	Relatively large number of industrial unions. Centralized confederation often limited by rival confederations. Unions perform narrow range of functions.
Sources of funds	Substantial resources secured by regular dues; regulatory functions require administrative organizations and large budgets.	Meagre resources from irregular dues payments and indirect government allowances. Financial success not highly regarded by workers' organizations.
Sources of leadership	The ranks through lower levels of workers' organizations. They have an established career.	Intellectuals and those ideologically oriented towards political activity. The leaders' income position is often insecure.

diversities to be found in the industrial relations rule-making process with particular attention to worker organizations. The focus here is on some of the emergent rules themselves.

Economic growth has a systematic impact upon the substantive rules of the work place, irrespective of which élite leads the industrialization process. There are many common developments in the complex of rules. But there are also significant variations in these rules because they evolve from different industrial relations systems created under different types of élites. This section will consider some of the more significant kinds of rules of the work place both as they are commonly developed by the industrialization process

Revolutionary intellectuals	Colonial administrators	Nationalist leaders
A few industrial unions. Centralized confederation. Organizations perform a narrow range of functions.	A wide variety of structures. Organizations not well developed, often personal.	Tendency towards industrial unions with one confederation acceptable to élite.
Substantial resources secured by assessment of all workers; financial resources present no problem with support of régime.	Meagre funds often raised outside workers' organizations.	Funds often secured indirectly from government in addition to meagre dues. Officers receive other salaries.
Reliable party leaders with experience in worker organizations. They have an established career.	Nationalist and independence leaders. Intellectuals with a personal following.	National leaders and intellectuals except where confined to manual workers.

itself and made distinctive in some respects by the types of industrializing élites. While a body of rules emerges in every industrial relations system to govern the recruitment, training, and redundancy of the work force, these matters have been discussed in Chapter 5 and need not be elaborated here.

Compensation and Wages

Rules regarding compensation are a central feature of the total body of rules; they often influence a variety of other rules since affecting wage costs and workers' income is often an effective method to induce action on the part of enterprise managers and workers. As an illustration, seventh-day pay for six days of work in a week (but five days' pay for five days' work) was designed in oil-producing countries of the Middle East to discourage absenteeism, a form of attendance bonus. The monthly contract in parts of Africa (Kenya) was designed to attract workers from the reserves for a stated period. Premiums for undesirable or even hazardous working conditions are in part designed to provide an incentive to managements to eliminate or to control these aspects of work operations. Compensation rules are particularly varied to meet problems of the recruitment and commitment of a labour force.[4]

Payments in Kind

In the early stages of industrialization the proportion of total compensation paid in kind, sometimes called 'hidden emoluments', may be substantial. Lodging for single men or housing for some family units, furnished by the enterprise, may be necessary to recruit a labour supply to isolated localities or from reserves as in Northern Rhodesia and Peru. The furnishing of meals or canteens as a part of compensation is quite common; the provision of food is likely to have a direct impact upon worker productivity where diet is poor and where money income would go to others in the extended family.

As development proceeds, the value of payments in kind tends to be incorporated into the money wage, and even when those services are continued by an enterprise, there is often some money charge for the services. The rise of communities around a work place and the greater role of local authorities, the heavy capital costs of tying up the funds of an enterprise in housing, the problems of housing with discharged, laid-off, or retired workers are all factors tending to curtail or to eliminate this form of payment in kind. Although some new types of payment in kind (such as medical services) arise as industrialization proceeds, they do not constitute for most workers a significant fraction of total compensation. In very highly developed communities with progressive income taxes, significant payments in kind may return, at least for very high-income individuals.

The middle-class élite regards payments in kind as temporary and exceptional departures from a market economy. The dynastic élite is most likely to adopt payments in kind and retain them longer, since such payments are consistent with the paternal attitudes of the state and management towards the work force. The colonial élite makes considerable use of payments in kind to recruit a labour supply, to offset the tendency of individuals to work less with higher money payments, to increase the calories directly available to manual workers, and to recruit and commit a labour force without relying to the same extent upon money wage-rate increases. The revolutionary intellectual élite is inclined to use these methods of compensation when essential to the direct allocation of the labour force. The nationalist leaders often seek to dismantle payment-in-kind arrangements as symbols of colonialism and as largely alien to an economically advanced country.

Components of Compensation

The money terms of compensation are customarily divided into wage rates, which may be set in terms of time or related to a measure of output or performance, and other components of compensation, such as vacations or holidays with pay, pension plans, and a wide range of supplementary-pay practices or fringe benefits.[5] In the course of economic development the total number of components tends to grow, although some components, such as family allowances, are characteristic of particular countries.[6] The proportion of supplementary pay components to total compensation varies to some degree with the industrializing élites, and the late starters have from the outset adopted many of the supplementary pay practices of the economically advanced countries. Rising incomes may be distributed in a variety of ways; inflation or a wage stabilization or a wage restraint programme has often added components to compensation. A number of the additional components to compensation can be directly related to the increasing role of government in industrial relations systems; social security programmes in their full range of components constitute the largest contribution of governments.

The middle-class élite tends to pay a much larger fraction of total compensation in basic wage rates and to look to individual workers to allocate income among competing uses rather than to predetermine the allocation. There is relatively little interest in family allowances. The separate components of compensation that arise are frequently designed to regulate enterprise management or to meet specialized industry problems rather than solely to increase income. The dynastic élite multiplies the components of compensation by placing emphasis upon family allowances, social-security benefits, and the like, so that basic wage-rates constitute a relatively smaller proportion of total compensation. The colonial élite tends to conform to the compensation components of the mother country, except that citizens of the mother country receive additional benefits such as home leave and allowances, and the indigenous workers may not receive some of the components of compensation of the mother country. The revolutionary intellectual élite usually develops a larger number of components than the middle-class élite, and these are designed to affect the direction and supply of workers rather than to circumscribe management. The nationalist leaders adopt the full range of compensation of more advanced countries. Programmes of unemployment compensation, social security, vacations and the like are imposed by regulations at an early date as a symbol of advancement.

Wage-rate Structure

In the early stages of industrial development in small enterprises only personalized wages are likely to exist; the notion of wage rates for job classifications is relatively advanced. A time rate for a job requires some degree of standardization in performance among different workers in the labour force that are grouped together in one job category. A piecework or performance method of payment is compatible with much wider variations in training, skill, and performance among members of the labour force. Piecework is predominant in many of the earliest industries to arise in the classical pattern of industrialization, such as textiles, clothing, and shoes.

During the early phases of industrialization, skill differentials tend to be relatively wide. The supply of skilled labour tends to be short compared to unskilled workers, and the requisite skilled workers must be trained or imported. In many parts of Africa and the Middle East the skilled manual jobs pay three or four times the unskilled rates, compared to 1·2 or 1·3 times in many economically advanced countries. The actual skill differentials may be further widened in the early stages by wage differentials according to race.[7] The skilled manual workers may be white and the unskilled black. In such cases some of these gross skill differentials may be often as high as ten or twelve times, or even higher.

In the course of economic development skill differentials tend to narrow. As a rough generalization, the skill wage rate among manual workers in economically advanced countries tends to be 20 to 30 per cent more than unskilled rates, compared to the two to four times that skilled manual rates exceed unskilled rates in the early stages of industrialization. The narrowing process is related to the rise of general levels of education and the spread of technical education, gradual upgrading and training on the job, the emergence of a local supply which reduces the need to import skilled labour, the rise of labour organizations which may press for more equalization in wage rates, and inflationary periods in which relatively uniform general wage increases are made on grounds of equity.[8]

The process of creating a labour market tends to eliminate many of the differentiations among workers which are a carry-over from the pre-industrial society. The assignment of manual jobs by tribe, nationality, sex, or race creates wage differentials which later tend to be narrowed or eliminated. At times the reduction of such wage-rate differentials directly reflects labour-market developments in the economically underdeveloped country, but just as often it reflects the importation of industrial values and specific legislation or international conventions from abroad.

A hierarchy of wage rates also emerges among enterprises in the same industry, among industries, and among localities and regions. In some countries there comes to be a high degree of centralization of wage-rate changes and wage-setting institutions. The arrangements in Australia, New Zealand, the Netherlands, Scandinavia, and Italy are illustrative, although the rule-making processes formally provide for quite different decision-making institutions. In other countries the interdependence of wage rates among enterprises is reflected more exclusively through the market. In the course of industrialization wage rates in an enterprise tend to become relatively more interdependent (whether or not formally recognized in wage-setting machinery) with the wage rates established in other enterprises.

Economic development tends to narrow inter-enterprise differentials in the wage-rate structure of a country. The development of the transportation system historically has affected both the movement of products and workers and hence the interdependence of wage rates in different enterprises. The interdependence of wage rates among enterprises in similar product markets, particularly in one locality or region, tends to emerge before the general interdependence among regions. As economic development proceeds further, as levels of employment rise, as capital flows more readily among regions, the wage rates among localities tend to become more interdependent and pure geographical wage-rate differentials also tend to narrow percentagewise.

The industrial wage-rate structure shows a high degree of similarity (rank correlations of industrial average hourly earnings are high) among countries at comparable levels of development. This similarity is to be explained by the fact that the same industries in different countries use roughly similar technologies with roughly similar proportions of workers in jobs of varying skills and wage-rate levels. Although the percentage differentials for skill among countries varies, as has been observed, the relative ordering of the wage rates for job classifications in an industry shows a high degree of similarity among countries. Combining a similarity in the proportion of workers at different occupations in an industry with a similarity in ranking of rates for these occupations yields industrial averages of wage rates or earnings that tend to be relatively quite similar among countries at the same stage of industrialization.[9]

As economic growth proceeds, new industries arise to be slotted into the industrial wage structure, in part determined by the proportions of workers of varying skills, by the requirements for new skills, and by the level of the rates that are required to attract workers into an expanding industry. Many of these newer industries tend to be higher-wage industries for these reasons. Industrialization thus imparts an upward drift to the average wage in the country by virtue of an increasing proportion of higher-wage industries.

In the economy of the middle-class élite, all wage-rate differentials are relatively more interdependent and more responsive to labour- and product-market competitive conditions. Skill differentials tend to be determined in the same way by relative labour scarcities.

The dynastic élite tends to establish much lower wage-rate differentials for skill. With a relatively slower pace of industrialization, this élite does not need wide differentials to recruit skilled labour. The wage structure of the country as a whole is less highly interdependent, and product market competition is a much less active factor influencing relative wage rates and the allocation of the labour force.

The wage-rate structure of the colonial élite is likely to be dominated by the differences between workers from the mother country, who receive the highly skilled and managerial and technical jobs, and local residents who are employed in semi-skilled and un-skilled jobs, at least at the outset. The gross skill differentials are accordingly very wide. Other wage rates are likely to reflect the recruitment policy of the colonial élite; thus, the wage structure may be designed for bachelors or for a family worker.

The revolutionary intellectual élite establishes relatively wide skill differentials to help attract the large amount of skilled labour needed in a short period of time. The wage structure, as the price structure, on the whole plays a less immediate and short-run role in the allocation of resources. The wage-rate structure is less respon-sive to changes in product prices, and accordingly it is less interdependent than in the middle-class-led economy.

The nationalist élite is likely to follow a policy of eliminating the extent of wage-rate differentials of the colonial period. A more egalitarian wage-rate structure is adopted.

Method of Wage Payment

The relative distribution between time and piece methods of wage payment shows little consistent pattern in the course of economic development, although there are marked differences in methods of payment among countries and in the policies of industrializing élites. At the outset there are likely to be very wide differences in the quality and performance of members of the work force; payment by time places a heavy burden on supervision which is likely to be in very short supply and relatively expensive. If turnover rates are high and labour plentiful, the enterprise can avoid substantial costs of training involved in time rates and need be less concerned about higher earnings resulting in a smaller amount of labour inputs, as is often held to characterize workers in the early stages of economic growth.

As industrialization proceeds and a more stable and committed industrial work force is established, the factors leading to the use of piece or incentive rates tend to change. Piece rates are often designed to stimulate a greater rate of effort among trained workers to get the largest utilization of expensive capital equipment; some workers are on nominal incentives to preserve wage-rate relationships and to prevent complaints arising out of comparisons with other workers on piece earnings; the selling field often leads to a compensation system which includes commission rates on account of the difficulties of supervision with changing work places and the complex salesman-customer relationship. The process of industrialization changes the problems and the opportunities for using time or piece methods of wage payment.

The middle-class élite utilizes piece rates only moderately, depending upon the characteristics of the particular industry; there are few ideological considerations involved in the choice. The dynastic élite tends to use the piece-rate method of pay least frequently. It is ideologically objectionable since it magnifies differences in earnings among workers. The colonial administrators make extensive use of piecework because of the variations in the quality of the labour force and the turnover of workers. The revolutionary intellectuals, in their drive for production, seek to use this method of wage payment as universally as possible. The nationalist élite has no distinctive policy, and in most cases tends to continue the existing method of wage payment.

Procedures for the Settlement of Disputes

Another significant group of rules developed by an industrial relations system concerns the procedures for the settlement of disputes. The distinction between procedures to resolve disputes over the application of existing rules and those concerned with disputes over a change in the rules or a new rule is a fundamental characteristic of an industrial relations system. Not all systems make this distinction. In some countries there is relatively integrated machinery for the resolution of disputes (Denmark), while in others there may be no single vertex in the procedures with a variety of autonomous bodies (England), and in still others there may be a number of procedures relatively specialized by type of issue with possible conflicts in jurisdiction among those procedures (France). The present concern is with the way economic development affects the procedures to settle disputes.

In the course of development of an industrial relations system, rules tend to limit stringently the resort to force, including the strike and lock-out.[10] The established procedures are designed as a substitute for open conflict. In some systems a limited place for open conflict (strike and lock-out) is deliberately retained, while in other systems group conflict is entirely prohibited or suppressed and forms of protest are largely by the 'strike in detail'.

In the earliest stages of industrialization, the development of dispute-settling machinery frequently utilizes the pre-existing tribal and family system among the work force. In the course of development, procedures for handling disputes create neutrals (often government representatives) who have final authority to certain disputes. The emergence of neutrals is a necessary corollary to the limitation on conflict.

There is a tendency for the neutrals to become continuing or permanent, subject often to some term of office, rather than limited to a single dispute. Industrial relations systems tend to develop specialists or professionals to administer the rules of the work place and work community and to process disputes. The rules tend to provide that all disputes must be channelled on each side through these specialists.

Industrialism and Industrial Man

Chart 10. Rules of the Work-Place

Industrializing élite	Middle-class	Dynastic
Compensation and wages		
Payments in kind	Payments in kind regarded as inherently undesirable and only temporary departure from the market.	Most likely to adopt payments in kind and to retain them longest.
Components of compensation	Basic wages a high proportion of total compensation; against family allowances. Components of compensation designed to regulate management.	Components other than basic wages a high proportion of total compensation. High family allowances and social security.
Wage-rate structure (structure varies in the course of industrialization)	Highly interdependent wage-rate structure through the labour market. Skill differentials sensitive to labour market; typically moderate.	Wage rates not highly interdependent. Relatively low skill differentials.
Methods of wage payments	Moderate piece or differential rates; no ideological influence.	Few piece rates. Ideological opposition to piece rates.

Industrial Relations Systems and the Rules of the Work Place

Revolutionary intellectuals	Colonial administrators	Nationalist leaders
Use of payments in kind when necessary to direct the labour supply to particular uses or locations.	Use of payments in kind to recruit labour supply, to offset the tendency to work less with higher wages, and to supply food to workers.	Dismantle payments in kind as backward and as symbol of colonial arrangement.
Components other than basic wages relatively large. Moderate family allowance and high social security. Components of compensation are directed to control work force rather than regulate management.	Components generally conform to home country except citizens of colonial power receive additional benefits and some components reflect colonial problems.	Components adopted to conform to full range of advanced industrial countries.
Wage-rate structure not highly interdependent. Skill differentials relatively large on account of rapid pace.	Wage-rate structure reflects differences for citizens of home country; wage differentials related to pre-existing nationality and total labour supplies; gross skill differential large.	Tendency to develop more egalitarian wage-rate structure than established by colonial power.
Extensive use of piece rates as influenced by ideology and pace of industrialization.	Extensive use of piece work for reasons of labour turnover and variations in labour force.	No distinctive policy.

Chart 10 continued

Industrializing élite	Middle-class	Dynastic
Procedures for settlement of disputes	Some disputes left to agreement making for possible conflict. Neutrals need not be government representatives or lawyers. Parties have large voice in their selection. Informal proceedings. Decisions often in the form of agreement.	Ideology permits no room for open conflict. Neutrals are government representatives. Parties have little voice in their selection. Formal proceedings. Decisions seldom a form of agreement.

Industrial relations systems also tend to develop a constantly expanding body of precedents in the settlement of disputes. These are normally in written form. Both the way in which precedents are used and the weight attached to them show a wide spectrum among systems. Systems differ depending upon whether or not decisions are accompanied by elaborate opinions and explanations. They differ in the extent to which procedures are formal and the extent to which precedents are regarded as binding on the settlement of future disputes.

The middle class establishes industrial relations systems which deliberately leave some room for conflict on some types of disputes in the event of failure to achieve an earlier agreement. Labour and management organizations play a large role in the selection of neutrals whether or not they are appointed by governments. The

Revolutionary intellectuals	Colonial administrators	Nationalist leaders
Ideology permits no room for conflict. Government and party decisions. Formal proceedings. Decisions seldom a form of agreement although worker and management representatives may play a role through the party.	Institutions modelled after the home country. Conflict tends to be associated with independence and nationalism; considerable role for colonial administrator in making decisions.	The concern for the future of the new nation tends to deprecate conflict. Workers need to be re-educated on the use of the strike, previously used against colonialists. Now government plays a decisive role in dispute settlement; often compulsory settlement. Adoption of I.L.O. conventions.

proceedings tend to be more informal, and decisions are frequently mediated and constitute real agreement between the parties. Neutrals need not always be lawyers. Precedents are more flexibly used.

The dynastic élite seeks to establish an industrial relations system which formally leaves no role for conflict. Conflict is abhorred since it would destroy the paternalistic view of the work community. The neutrals are government representatives, and labour and management organizations have little direct role in their selection or in direct shaping of the decisions. The proceedings tend to be formal, and decisions are seldom a form of agreement. The neutrals tend to be lawyers, and great weight is attached to formal precedents.

The colonial élite establishes industrial relations systems modelled after that of the mother country. Industrial conflict tends to be associated with independence and nationalism and is likely to be less tolerated than in the mother country. Labour organizations are seldom encouraged by the élite, but where disputes do arise the pattern in the mother country is adopted with an even greater role for the colonial administrators.

The revolutionary intellectuals establish industrial relations systems which provide no room for conflict which would violate the accepted ideology. The neutrals are government-appointed, and procedures tend to be formal. Neutrals are likely to be trained as lawyers. Any mediation of a dispute is likely to involve the party and governmental agencies rather than the managers and workers' organizations, although some of the same individuals may be involved.

The nationalist leaders tend to abhor conflict on the grounds that it interferes with national efforts to industrialize. Strikes which were used to harass and dislodge the colonialists are not to be used against the interests of the new nation. The forms of the conventions and resolutions of the I.L.O. have great appeal, although actual practice is likely to reflect considerable government control over labour organizations and management. The government plays a large role in the settlement of disputes, and compulsory arbitration or settlement of disputes on terms determined by the government is most common.

Chart 10 summarizes the diversity in the rules relating to compensation and wages, and procedures for dispute settlement which tend to be established by each of the ideal types of élites leading industrialization.

The last century saw the emergence of industrial relations systems in the countries first embarked on industrialization, and the years ahead will see decisions respecting the form and arrangements of industrial relations systems in the new countries. Just as ideologies and economic systems are today in conflict, so there is keen competition as the newly industrializing countries choose among alternatives and formulate their own industrial relations systems. The type of industrial relations arrangement is no less decisive of economic growth than the form of economic organization.

Industrial Relations Systems and the Rules of the Work Place

The experience of the past and the logic of industrialization teach us that each industrializing country will come sooner or later to establish a distinctive industrial relations system. The system will define the relations among management, labour organizations and the government and specify the procedures for making and administering rules of the work place. Each system will tend to establish a larger and more formal body of rules. The rules established by a particular system must have a degree of internal consistency to survive. The complex of rules tends to grow in volume and in detail. The rules tend to respond to changes in technology and competitive conditions and to be adapted to other changes associated with the stage of economic development. Some of these rules which are substantively conditioned by technology and competitive conditions will tend to be similar in different industrial relations systems, while others particularly shaped by the unique policies and strategies of the élite will be distinctive.

Pluralistic Industrialism

By the mid twentieth century, at least a third of the population of the world, or close to one billion people, lived in countries well established in the process of industrialization, and most of the other two-thirds of the world's population was in countries in the throes of starting to industrialize. Relatively few remnants of mankind were as yet untouched by this new and vital force. By the middle of the twenty-first century, industrialization will have swept away most pre-industrial forms of society, except possibly for a few odd backwaters.

This is the great transformation in the long history of mankind on this planet – more basic, more rapid, and more nearly universal than any earlier transformation.

Modern industrial civilization, with its technical evolution and intellectual drive, is, as we know, the most aggressive form of civilization that mankind has ever known. Its twin impact of science and industry is one that involves a total transformation of all aspects of life – not only of organization and technique but of fundamental habits of thought and social behaviour. You have only to consider the impact of this type of society upon people who have not yet moved beyond the simplest patterns of living and working to see that, without immense patience, understanding, and restraint, the incoming settlers will annihilate the whole social apparatus of the backward local peoples. Yet these qualities are not usually the qualities of conquerors or pioneers.[1]

Industrialization creates vast urban areas; makes possible a great explosion of population; yields a new standard of living and of leisure; draws on new skills both social and technical; requires a vast network of rules to guide and coerce men in the complex and interrelated tasks essential to its successful growth; spawns new centres of organized power and furthers the concentration of authority in old centres, particularly the state; forges new methods of attaining and retaining this power; links men together in new chains of subordination and invites frictions at each of the links in these chains; and provides a new culture based on mass tastes and mass consumption which gradually overwhelms the many and varied pre-existing cultures. It is the great transformation – successful, all-embracing, irreversible.

Central to this transformation are the relations of managers and the managed. Much of the working lives of men is spent in constant contact with the reciprocal relations of manager to managed; and these relations set the occupational roles and working behaviour of most members of the labour force. But manager and managed do not form any separate and clear-cut classes. Many of the managers are in turn managed from above, and many of the managed in turn manage someone below. Few are those who only manage, and many are those who are only managed; but there is a hierarchy of managerial relations far too complex to compress into simple class relations. Instead a society develops of the semi-managers and semi-managed.

Industrial man develops new patterns of relations different from those of tribal members and chieftain, serf and lord of the manor, craftsman and merchant prince, or even worker and capitalist. These relations are more varied and more complex than in pre-existing societies. Industrial man leads a new kind of life and, in the course of it, becomes a new kind of person. He views himself and others, society and the universe in new ways. The old ideologies and the old theories lose their meaning.

How may we interpret what is happening; what the new forms of relations really are and will be? Earlier we sought to explain the developments in part as due to the logic of industrialization itself and in part to specific cultural and environmental influences within nations. But we also related them to the strategies of the several industrializing élites, and sought to describe how the nature of these élites affected the selection and behaviour of managers, the structuring of the labour force, the response of the workers, the interweaving of management, labour, and the state.

Chapters 1–3 examined the broad implications of industrialization and the major systems and strategies under which industrialization may proceed. It also described the variety of constraints imposed by the cultural and economic heritage of a society and the manner in which these affect both the choice of general strategy and the diversity of specific policy decisions within each of the major patterns of industrialization.

Chapters 4–7 looked more closely at the evolution of labour-management-state relations as perceived in this analytical framework. Here, too, the discussions concerning the managers of enterprise, the development of an industrial work force, the responses of workers to industrialization and the structuring of industrial relations systems suggested the uniformities and the diversities that emerge over industrial time.

This final chapter draws on these earlier analytical and historical sections in an attempt to extrapolate the threads of diversity and the sources of uniformity for the road ahead.

The Road Ahead: The Threads of Diversity

Industrialization came into a most varied world; a world with many cultures, at many stages of development from the primitiveness of quasi-animal life to high levels of civilization. It was a world marked by great diversity; in terms of the contrast between the least and the most civilized societies; a world more diverse than at any other time during the history of mankind on this planet. Into the midst of this disparity of systems there intruded a new and vastly superior technique of production; a technique which by its very nature was bound to spur imitation, since the more modern was always the superior. This technique knew no geographical limits; recognized no élites or ideologies. Once unleashed on the world, the new technique kept spreading and kept advancing.

Men at first ignored or rejected or accepted this new method of production in many different reactions. Different élites undertook its sponsorship, some effectively and some ineffectively; and sought to organize society in such a way as both to use the new technique and to serve their own goals, whatever they might be.

Ideologies were formulated in an effort to understand, to control, to attack, and to defend the new arrangements.

In the intervening two centuries since the new techniques began to be a real force in parts of the world, many changes have taken place and are still taking place. This is part of the endless process of man's adaptation. The arrangements made by men are still quite various, although one might argue that with a single productive technique there should be one best way to organize its use. If there is one best way, men certainly have not yet agreed upon it. Diversity continues to mark the process of adjustment. The sources of this continued diversity are several.

The Persistence of the Strategies

To begin with, the differing élites each tend to organize the process in a different fashion. Once structured, the institutions and the ways of doing things tend to develop a life and a persistency of their own, provided the ruling élites are reasonably successful in handling the problems of industrialization and the other problems of a society. There are, after all, several possible ways of organizing an industrial society. Aside from wars and depression, the normal tests of adequacy are not too hard to meet when using a technique which, with competent direction, is capable of improving many of the aspects of the lives of men. Only the colonial system is sure to fail at some point because of its alien character.

The basic test for the middle class, the dynastic élite, and the nationalist leaders is whether they can make reasonably rapid progress. Only the middle class has fully proved that it can. The dynastic élite may be held back by tradition and the nationalists by uncertainty. The basic test for the revolutionary intellectuals is whether they can avoid going too fast, particularly in the earlier stages, for their ideology tends to draw them into pushing the population to its very limits of endurance; and, in the later stages, whether they can adjust adequately to the changing nature of the masses who in the process of industrialization have become better educated, increasingly desirous of more consumer goods and the 'good' life, and less easily roused by appeals to revolutionary ardour.

The colonial aside, each of the other élites can protect itself from sudden change, provided it pushes the new process neither too little nor too much; and the leeway between too little and too much is quite substantial. But none of the élites can insulate itself from gradual change.

As each élite maintains itself, it seeks to preserve, even though changed over time, the essential elements of its system – its role for the state, its place for the leaders, its preferred rate of development and source of capital, its place for labour organizations, and its attitude towards industrial conflict, its policies towards the pre-existing culture. Not only the élites but also the workers tend to preserve their particular institutions and their special beliefs. Each system has a degree of endurance.

This durability is strengthened by the rigidity of the ideology. Since the middle-class and the nationalist approaches have the least static ideology, they are most subject to experiment and to change, painful as experiment and change always are. Since the dynastic élite and the revolutionary intellectuals have a firmer ideological base and class identification, they are likely to be the most rigid and the most resistant to changes, and they can easily become the most 'old fashioned' and the least adaptable. But the slogans, the heroes, the vested interests that collect around an ideology and a strategy for organizing society give any system considerable tenacity and are a great source of diversity in an industrializing world.

The Imprint of Culture

The culture of a nation and the degree of its continued adherence to that culture also affect world-wide diversity in the process of industrialization. The family and the class carry on, particularly under the dynastic élite. Education often adapts quite slowly from its traditional forms, again particularly under the dynastic élite. But other national traits carry on as well – for example, the discipline and energy of the Germans, the individualism of the French, the easy-going approach of the Indonesians. France is a particularly good example of how attitudes from an earlier stage of political and economic development can survive and give a very special cast to the face of industrialization. The French are particularly conscious of their national identity and character, and intent on preserving their national traits; but they are not alone in this. Rather there seems to be a new consciousness in a number of countries of their special national heritages.

The Hour on the Clock of Evolution

The stage of development, regardless of the nature of the leadership, is another source of variation. Early industrialization, regardless of the over-all strategy, has its own special problems, its own special attitudes, its own special approaches. Mature industrialization, with its well-developed institutions and web of rules, its full complement of industries and services and trades, its settled labour force, its greater consensus, is a different phenomenon, regardless of the organizing forces. Degree of development, of course, relates both to the date of the start and the rate of change.[2]

The Culture of the Industry

The special character of the basic resources and the central industries causes variations from one country to another. Plantation agriculture, crude oil production, heavy industry, light industry, each give a tone to their society. Some industries are more prone to industrial unrest than others; some are more likely to engage in paternalistic practices; some are occupationally more highly stratified; some are more subject to a system of norms; some have more large-scale enterprises. Each industry has its own character – the waterfront, coal mining, banking – and these cast their reflections on the surrounding society. A small or a newly industrialized economy is more likely to reflect the special character of one or a few industries than is a large and mature economy. Oil gives a special flavour to Iraq, much as textiles and coal mining once did to England.

People and Performance

Finally, the demographic aspects of a nation impart to its industrialization continuing characteristics. A relatively empty country, like Australia, has quite a different course of development than does a heavily populated one, like India. Wages tend to be higher, recruitment more difficult, a significant increase in the standard of living more possible, a high evaluation of the worth of the individual worker and the attention he deserves more likely, and so forth.

Among all these forces for diversity, the two most forceful are a clear ideology held by a distinct ruling class and a persistent, recognized series of cultural traits developed in earlier times.

The Road Ahead: The Sources of Uniformity

Time moves along and, as it does, many a battle is joined between the forces perpetuating diversity and those promoting uniformity. Many of these battles are the impersonal clashes of old ways and new facts, and they are fought under many banners and in a myriad of places. But the more we look at these battles collectively, in a long distance of time and wide-ranging world perspective, the more impressed we become with the power of the forces for uniformity. What are the most striking ones?

History and Homogeneity

The passage of history itself is a force. Each industrializing nation moves farther from its introduction into the industrial world, from its pre-existing forms, from its original leadership. The early élites bring in new recruits from other strata. The élite group grows in size and becomes less identifiable, merging into each successively lower level in the new hierarchy. The second and third and fourth generations of the leaders and the led alike are different from the first.

The age of ideology fades. When man first entered the irreversible journey into industrialization, there were innumerable views about the best way to organize the society. Some of them have largely disappeared from the scene: anarchism, syndicalism, communalism, cooperativism. Others of them have been blunted and revised from their original form, particularly capitalism and socialism. The age of utopias is past. An age of realism has taken its place – an age in which there is little expectation of either utter perfection or complete doom. One of the results of the past century is the accumulation of experience about the realistic alternatives.

Industrial society conduces towards 'realism' through the elimination of certain alternatives which are unworkable, through the development of expectations by the mass of men which lie above despair but below utopian hope; and through the rise of men and institutions devoted to the compromise of differences. It requires 'realism' because an industrialized society is such a complicated mechanism, with such interdependence of its parts, that keeping it going without major disruption becomes an overriding concern. A fierce ideological battle, for example, among social democrats, communists, and Catholics, as in certain Latin American countries, can get in the way not only of economic progress but even of current production. Aspiration and attainment come closer into accord; and a leading aspiration becomes the attainment of reasonable continuity.

Thus we see the phenomenon of the one-party society which relies on a coalition of several elements, as in Egypt and Mexico; or the non-party government, as in Pakistan; or a government operated by a coalition of parties, as in Austria, Venezuela, and Colombia. Even where parties still contend, they draw close together, as in the United States, and may even drop their ideological inheritances in favour of a new pragmatism, as in England and Germany.

Solutions are negotiated among representatives of the leading interest groups rather than being fought out on the level of principle. 'Veto groups' can veto any action which threatens their survival. The negotiator takes the place of the prophet, the idealist, the demagogue.

Industrial society must be administered; and the administrators become increasingly benevolent and increasingly skilled. They learn to respond where response is required; to anticipate the inevitable. The benevolent political bureaucracy and the benevolent economic oligarchy are matched with the more tolerant mass.

The 'new realism' is essentially conservative. The *status quo* is changed only gradually. 'Balance' must be maintained. However, considerable individual liberty and social mobility are compatible with and even essential to the 'new realism'.

Parliamentary life may appear increasingly less significant and political parties merely additional bureaucracies; the great political causes of old may become little more than technical issues; and oratory may give way to committee work; but the 'new realism' conforms to the realities of industrial society.

Thus the conflict of ideologies is blunted and fades between societies. Consensus develops wherever industrialization is successful. The labour force becomes committed to and settled into industrial life. It accepts the pace of work, the web of rules, the surrounding structure. The sense of protest subsides. The enterprise managers, left to their own devices, push less hard. Society provides more of the amenities of life. Men learn from experience how to do things better, and the rough edges are evened off. Industrialization has been accepted.

Finally, as the élites become less differentiated and the ideological controversies become more barren, the cultural patterns of the world intermingle and merge. These changes are already in evidence, although the majority of nations in the world have been in the active throes of industrialization only two generations or less.

Technology and Society

Technology is also a unifying force. At one moment of time there may be several best economic combinations or social arrangements, but only one best technology. The technology can be up to date or antiquated, but there is no question which is which, and the modern is constantly replacing the ancient. The same technology calls for much the same occupational structure around the world – in steel, in textiles, in air transport. The occupational role of a man gives him a place in society and affects his behaviour in many ways. Also, there comes to be a growing diversity of occupations and of levels of management, and no really clear-cut dividing lines visible to all. The occupation takes the place of the class.

The technology is dynamic and it calls for change. Men change their locations and their occupations. A labour market must be created with substantial mobility within it. A fully paternalistic system at the plant level becomes less possible. Mobility calls at least for the semi-dependent rather than the dependent worker.

The skill level rises. Men assume responsibility for more expensive equipment and more essential processes. Their consent becomes more important. The need for their consent gives them influence. It may bring them organized power, for there is a tendency to organize around the occupation. True, only scientists may exercise this power at first, but the pressure will always exist to spread professional and occupational organization.

The Push of Progress

The thrust of progress also serves the cause of uniformity. The industry mix, country by country, becomes more balanced and thus more like that elsewhere. There is insistent pressure to obtain a rough balance of supply and demand in the labour market. The duality of economies, as in Japan with the industrial and the handicraft economies, tends to disappear in favour of the unified economy. Even agriculture becomes an industry, although this may take a very long time, as the history of France still attests.

The development of consumer goods industries and service trade requires the creation of markets – in spite of the addiction to plans (the market mentality and the planning mentality are quite different). The rising standard of living and increasing leisure create the capacity to read and travel and compare. They also encourage an aggressive materialism on the part of people. Progress brings the great metropolitan centre and the city as the natural habitat of man. Urbanization brings striking similarities in the physical environments and living arrangements of people from one society to another, even though the city has been in other ways the home of variety and freedom throughout the centuries.

Education and Equality

An industrial society must educate its people. There are at least two imperatives. First, the vast bulk of the population must be literate in order to receive instruction, follow directions, and keep

267

records. Second, managers, engineers, and civil servants must be trained to operate the new production system. Beyond that are the needs for doctors, lawyers, scientists, and university professors. Education becomes a leading activity in society.

Out of education come several results. Education is intended to reduce the scarcity of skilled persons, and this after a time reduces the wage and salary differentials they receive. It also pulls people out of the least skilled and most disagreeable occupations and raises wage levels there. It conduces to a new equality which has nothing to do with ideology; in fact, it may come faster and more fully in a middle-class society than in a society under the revolutionary intellectuals who proclaim equality as a primary goal. This equality is at first economic, but it also affects class status and political outlook. The miners and longshoremen view themselves and others differently when they become the aristocrats of labour. Middle incomes make for a middle class.

Out of education may also come a new call for freedom. This call will be most insistent at the highest levels in the educational pyramid, but it may spread down through many of the ranks of society. Education and personal independence have usually walked the road together. With an educated labour force, jobs tend to change or be changed. On the average more responsibility adheres to them; they are made more interesting; their incumbents are treated more individually and humanely.

Government and Enterprise

The state, everywhere, becomes an important instrument in society. It becomes responsible for the general rate of growth, the level of economic activity, the distribution of power, the settlement of conflicts, and the prevention of economic or other sabotage of the economy by special interest groups. It may, of course, do much more. But at least it must set the many basic rules for the economy, and it inevitably becomes a partner, but not the sole partner, in labour-management relations.

At the same time, the productive enterprise, whether public or private, becomes a large-scale organization in many industries. It comes to be run by professional managers, recruited and trained through the educational system, separated from ownership, and protected from power politics. These enterprise managers must be placed under the constraints of the market or planning budgets to assure their suitable performance, and the structuring of these pressures and controls is an essential task in society. The professional manager has great power, but it is power subject to checks and balances in all developed industrial societies.[3]

The managers are basically responsible for the web of rules within the plant and industry which relate them to the managed, although they share this responsibility with the state and the organized workers. Basically, this web of rules must spell out the authority of the managers and how far they may go, for economic enterprise is always essentially authoritarian under the necessity of getting things done, and the limits to executive authority must be specified.

The Compulsion of Comparisons

Man everywhere wants progress and participation. The two are to some extent substitutes for each other, and often progress will be accepted for a time in lieu of participation; but in the end industrial man wants both and will keep pressing for both. Progress means a higher standard of education, better health, more consumer goods and services; participation means choice of jobs, choice of consumer goods, a chance to influence the web of rules, and an opportunity to influence those who guide society itself. These same pressures develop regardless of culture and ideology.

The pressures for progress and participation are enhanced by the world-wide character of industrialization, by international trade, by travel, and by the exchange of ideas. We may never reach Sir William Beveridge's utopia where each man could pick and choose around the world the society he would like to live in; but already people are making comparisons, and these comparisons are having their impact. Generally the impact will be to bring greater uniformity in the nature of the societal product which people widely judge to be the best. People may not be willing to settle for much less in their own system than the standards and performance of competing systems.

269

Over the past few decades the threads of diversity and the sources of uniformity have been in conflict, and they will continue to be, certainly, for many decades and possibly even centuries ahead. Essentially, it is a contest between ideologies and national traits on the one hand, and technology and the changes that progress brings on the other. This opposition of forces is at work throughout the world. Our age, in particular, is witness to this titanic struggle.

The Road Ahead: Pluralistic Industrialism

Men attempt to peer ahead, to understand the structure of history, to alter the process of history, if possible, in accord with their preferences. As we have seen, the history of industrialization to date has not been a smoothly unilinear one; it has been uneven and multilinear. It is likely that in the future it will continue to be both somewhat uneven and multilinear; and there will continue to be some latitude for choice and for chance. Chance may elude man, but choice need not; and the choice of men, within fairly broad limits, can shape history. To predict the future with any accuracy, men must choose their future. The future they appear to be choosing and pressing for is what might be called 'pluralistic industrialism'.

This term is used to refer to an industrial society which is governed neither by one all-powerful élite (the monistic model) nor by the impersonal interaction of innumerable small groups with relatively equal and fractionalized power (the atomistic model in economic theory). The complexity of the fully developed industrial society requires, in the name of efficiency and initiative, a degree of decentralization of control, particularly in the consumer goods and service trades industries; but it also requires a large measure of central control by the state and conduct of many operations by large-scale organizations.

As the skill level rises and jobs become more responsible, any régime must be more interested in consent, in drawing forth relatively full cooperation. For the sake of real efficiency, this must be freely given. The discipline of the labour gang no longer suffices. With skill and responsibility goes the need for consent, and with consent goes influence and even authority. Occupational and professional groups, of necessity, achieve some prestige and authority as against both the central organs of society and the individual members of the occupation or profession.

Education brings in its wake a new economic equality and a new community of political outlook. This in turn, along with many other developments, helps bring consensus to society. The harsh use of power by the state is no longer so necessary to hold society together at the seams. Education also opens the mind to curiosity and to inquiry, and the individual seeks more freedom to think and to act. It brings a demand for liberty, and can help create conditions in which liberty can safely be assumed. It leads to comparisons among nations with respect to progress and participation.

Industrialism is so complex and subject to such contrary internal pressures that it never can assume a single uniform unchanging structure; but it *can* vary around a general central theme, and that theme is pluralism. While it will take generations before this theme will become universal in societies around the world, the direction of the movement already seems sufficiently clear.

The State that does not Wither away

The state will be powerful. It will, at the minimum, have the responsibility for the economic growth rate; the over-all distribution of income among uses and among individuals; the basic security of individuals (the family formerly was the basic security unit); the stability of the system; providing the essential public services of education, transportation, recreational areas, cultural facilities, and the like; and the responsibility of providing a favourable physical environment for urban man.

In addition, any pluralistic society is subject to three great potential internal problems, and the state is responsible for handling each. One is the conflict among the various power elements in a pluralistic society. The state must set the rules of the game within which such conflict will occur, enforce these rules, and act as mediator; conflicts between managers and the managed are the most noticeable, but by no means the only ones. Another is the control of collusion by producers against consumers, by any profession against its clients, and by labour and management against the public. Undue aggrandizement of sectional interests is always endemic if not epidemic in a pluralistic society; in fact, one of the arguments for monism and atomism alike is the avoidance of sectionalism. Additionally, the state will come generally, under pluralistic industrialism, to set the rules relating members to their organizations – who may get in, who may stay in, what rights and obligations the members have, what the boundaries are for the activities of the organization, and so on. It will, almost of necessity, be against too much conflict among, or collusion between, or domination of the members by the subsidiary organizations in society.

All these responsibilities mean the state will never 'wither away'; that Marx was more utopian than the despised utopians. The state will be the dominant organization in any industrial society. But it may itself be less than fully unitary. It may itself be subject to checks and balances, including the check of public acceptance of its current leadership and its policies.

The Crucial Role of the Enterprise – The Middle Class and the Middle Bureaucracy

The productive enterprise, whether private or public, will be in a dominant position under pluralistic industrialism. It will often be large and it must always have substantial authority in order to produce efficiently. This authority will not be complete, for it will be checked by the state, by the occupational association, by the individual employee; but it will be substantial.

The distinction between the private and the public manager will decrease just as the distinction between the private and the public enterprise will diminish; and the distinction among managers will be more according to the size, the product, and the nature of their enterprises. The controlled market and the controlled budget will bring more nearly the same pressures on them. The private enterprise, however, will usually have more freedom of action than the public enterprise; but the middle class and the middle bureaucracy will look much alike.

Associated Man

The occupational or professional association will range alongside the state and the enterprise as a locus of power in pluralistic industrialism; and there will be more occupations and particularly more professions seeking association. Group organizations around skill and position in the productive mechanism will be well-nigh universal. These organizations will affect output norms, comparative incomes, access to employment, and codes of ethics in nearly every occupational walk of life. Their containment within reasonable limits will be a continuing problem; and some of the groups will always seek to invade and infiltrate the government mechanisms which are intended to supervise them.

The Web of Rules

Uniting the state, the enterprise, and the association will be a great web of rules set by the efforts of all the elements, but particularly by the state. This web of rules will also relate the individual to each of these elements. In the contest over who should make the web of rules, the end solution will be that they will be made or influenced by more than one element; they will not be set by the state alone or by the enterprise alone or by the association alone. The web of rules will not equally cover all aspects of life.

From Class War to Bureaucratic Gamesmanship

Conflict will take place in a system of pluralistic industrialism, but it will take less the form of the open strife or the revolt and more the form of the bureaucratic contest. Groups will jockey for position over the placement of individuals, the setting of jurisdictions, the location of authority to make decisions, the forming of alliances, the establishment of formulas, the half-evident withdrawal of support and of effort, the use of precedents and arguments and statistics. Persuasion, pressure, and manipulation will take the place of the face-to-face combat of an earlier age. The battles will be in the corridors instead of the streets, and memos will flow instead of blood. The conflict also will be, by and large, over narrower issues than in earlier times when there was real disagreement over the nature of and the arrangements within industrial society. It will be less between the broad programmes of capital and labour, and of agriculture and industry; and more over budgets, rates of compensation, work norms, job assignments. The great battles over conflicting manifestoes will be replaced by a myriad of minor contests over comparative details.

From Class Movement to Special Interest Group

Labour-management relations will conform to this new context. Labour organizations will not be component parts of class movements urging programmes of total reform, for the consensus of a pluralistic society will have settled over the scene. Nor may they be very heavily identified by industry, particularly with the increasing multiplication and fractionalization of industries. Rather, they may tend to take more the craft, or perhaps better, the occupational form. With skills more diverse, at a generally higher level, and obtained more through formal education, and with geographical mobility greatly increased, professional-type interests should mean more to workers than industry or class ties.

The purpose of these occupational and professional associations will be relatively narrow, mostly the improvement of the status of the occupation in terms of income, prestige, and specification of the rights and duties that accompany it. Generally these organizations will be a conservative force in society, opposed to new ways of doing things, resistant to increased efforts by members of the occupation. The enterprise managers will be the more progressive elements in the society, although they too may become heavily weighted down by checks and balances and rules.

The techniques of the professional associations for achieving their ends will be those of the bureaucratic organization everywhere; a far cry from the individual withdrawal, or the guerrilla warfare, or the strike of the political reform movement of earlier times. They will constitute the quarrels between the semi-managed and the semi-managers.

Individuals will identify themselves more closely with their occupation, particularly if it involves a formal training period for entry, and mobility will follow more the lines of the occupation than the lines of the industry or the job possibilities of the immediate geographical area. In terms of identification, the orientation will be more nearly that of the member of a guild than of a class or of a plant community. Mayo will turn out to be as wrong as Marx. Just as the class will lose its meaning, so also will the plant community fail to become the modern counterpart of the primitive tribe. The occupational interest group will represent the employee in his occupational concerns and the occupation will draw his allegiance. Status in the tribe will not give way to status in the plant; nor will status have given way to the individual contract through the march of civilization; rather interest identification will take the place of both status and individual contract in ordering the productive arrangements of men.

Education, occupation, occupational organization will all be drawn together to structure the life-line and the economic interests of many if not most employees.

The New Bohemianism

The individual will be in a mixed situation far removed either from that of the independent farmer organizing most aspects of his own life from that of the Chinese peasant in the commune under total surveillance. In his working life he will be subject to great conformity imposed not only by the enterprise manager but also by the state and by his own occupational association. For most people, any complete scope for the independent spirit on the job will be missing. However, the skilled worker, while under rules, does get some control over his job, some chance to organize it as he sees fit, some possession of it. Within the narrow limits of this kind of 'job control', the worker will have some freedom. But the productive process tends to regiment. People must perform as expected or it breaks down. This is now and will be increasingly accepted as an immutable fact. The state, the manager, the occupational association are all disciplinary agents. But discipline is often achieved by a measure of persuasion and incentive. The worker will be semi-independent with some choice among jobs, some control of the job, and some scope for the effects of morale; but he will also be confined by labour organizations, pensions, and seniority rules, and all sorts of rules governing the conduct of the job.

Outside his working life the individual may have more freedom under pluralistic industrialism than in most earlier forms of society. Politically he can have some influence. Society has achieved consensus and the state need not exercise rigid political control. Nor in this 'Brave New World' need genetic and chemical means be employed to avoid revolt. There will not be any rebellion, anyway, except little bureaucratic revolts that can be settled piecemeal. An educated population will want political choice and can effectively use it. There will also be a reasonable amount of choice in the controlled labour market, subject to the confining limits of one's occupation, and in the controlled product market.

The great new freedom may come in the leisure-time life of individuals. Higher standards of living, more free time, and more education make this not only possible but almost inevitable. Leisure will be the happy hunting ground for the independent spirit. Along with the bureaucratic conservatism of economic and political life may well go a new bohemianism in the other aspects of life – partly as a reaction to the confining nature of the productive side of society. There may well come a new search for individuality and a new meaning to liberty. The economic system may be highly ordered and the political system barren ideologically; but the social and recreational and cultural aspects of life should be quite diverse and quite changing.

The world will be for the first time a totally literate world. It will be an organization society, but it need not be peopled by 'organization men' whose total lives are ruled by their occupational roles.

The areas closest to technology will be the most conformist; those farthest from the requirements of its service, the most free. The rule of technology need not, as Marx thought it would, reach into every corner of society. In fact, there may come a new emphasis on diversity, on the preservation of national and group traits that runs quite counter to the predictions of uniform mass consumption. The new slavery to technology may bring a new dedication to diversity and individuality. This is the two-sided face of pluralistic industrialism that makes it forever a split personality looking in two directions at the same time. The new slavery and the new freedom go hand in hand.

Utopia never arrives, but men may well settle for the benefits of a greater scope for freedom in their personal lives at the cost of considerable conformity in their working lives. If pluralistic industrialism can be said to have a split personality, then the individual in this society will lead a split life too; he will be a pluralistic individual with more than one pattern of behaviour and one dominant allegiance.

Social systems will be reasonably uniform around the world as compared with today's situation; but there may be substantial diversity within geographical and cultural areas as men and groups seek to establish and maintain their identity. The differences will be between and among individuals and groups and subcultures rather than primarily between and among the major geographical areas of the world. Society at large may become more like the great metropolitan complexes of Paris or London or New York or Tokyo, urbanized and committed to the industrial way of life, but marked by infinite variety in its details.

Pluralistic industrialism will never reach a final equilibrium. The contest between the forces for uniformity and for diversity will give it life and movement and change. This is a contest which will never reach an ultimate solution. Manager and managed also will struggle all up and down the line of hierarchies all around the world; quiet but often desperate little battles will be fought all over the social landscape.

The uniformity that draws on technology, and the diversity that draws on individuality; the authority that stems from the managers, and the rebellion, however muted, that stems from the managed – these are destined to be the everlasting threads of the future. They will continue in force when class war, and the contest over private versus public initiative, and the battle between the monistic and atomistic ideologies all have been left far behind in the sedimentary layers of history.

Postscript to
Industrialism and Industrial Man

Industrialism and Industrial Man was first published ten years ago. The intervening decade has been marked both by further rapid development of industrialization around the world and by continuing commentaries upon it by many observers. Our views of this transformation of world society have undergone some modifications as we have seen the developments of the past decade, studied the views of other contemporary observers, and the reactions of reviewers to our book. We have also had further oral discussions and seminars on our ideas in this country and abroad. This postscript will be primarily concerned with the changes in emphasis we would now make in our earlier views and with additional comments we would now add.

Major Themes Reaffirmed

Basically, however, we reaffirm the central points of our earlier analysis:

1. That 'industrialization' is a central dynamic force at work around the world. It is, of course, only a part of the modernization process which includes political and cultural developments as well. A degree of modernization can and sometimes does occur without industrialization, but industrialization is usually a basic aspect of modernization. By 'industrialization' we have meant the totality of relations involving workers, employers and society as they develop to make use of the new machines, processes and services that modern technology has made possible.[1] These relations are quite distinctive from those in a commercial and handicraft, or an agricultural, or a hunting and fishing society. Industrialization

embodies the new modes of conduct affecting men in the productive process as they shift from the 'windmill' to the 'steam-mill' – to borrow a phrase from Marx, and as they move towards a society characterized by a wide range of products and services.

2. That there is a central logic to industrialization that can be seen in every society using the new technology, regardless of its historical background or current political orientation. This is the common denominator of new and more diverse skills, larger scale productive endeavours, more large cities and much else. Industrial societies, with all their variations, are more like each other than they are like pre-industrial societies.

3. That different societies have taken and still take separate paths on the way to industrialization. To the central logic that unites all industrializing societies is added the diversity of arrangements that men fashion around this logic, the variations that men devise on the basic theme. These variations relate primarily to the approaches of the élites who organize the industrialization process – the middle class, the dynastic leaders, the revolutionary intellectuals, the colonial administrators and the nationalist leaders. We would now give greater emphasis to the mixtures of approaches within systems and would rephrase the nomenclature of one of these élites, as compared to 1960 and as will be noted below. But these remain, in our view, the five major variations on the theme of industrialization.

4. That, in addition to what is uniform to all and what is related by major approach, there are specific aspects of industrialization in each country, and even parts of each country, which are quite distinctive. However, the forces of industrialization have appeared in many countries to be stronger, and cultural factors somewhat less of a force, than we thought in 1960.

5. That management moves from a paternal or political orientation to a professional one. As we emphasized, professionals are fast becoming more highly trained technically; and the 'technostructure', as Galbraith has termed it, takes over more of the managerial function.

6. That the central problem of industrial relations around the world is not capital versus labour, but rather the structuring of

the labour force – how it gets recruited, developed, and maintained. This is the daily business of industrial relations everywhere. Here again, the similarities of actions belie the ideological conflicts.

7. That workers adapt to and accept industrialization much more readily, even avidly, than was once thought possible. Workers, we would now add, tend to become more moderate and even conservative members of the body politic than we once envisaged.

8. That systems of industrial relations, almost universally tripartite, develop with a substantial degree of compatibility among the component parts. These systems originate and administer the 'web of rules' that comes to govern daily operations within the system. The organizations of the workers become more a part of the system than an opponent against it. The system is subject more to evolutionary change than to revolutionary revision.

9. That industrial societies that start out with an atomistic approach (middle-class élites) or a monolithic approach (revolutionary intellectuals) tend to move towards pluralistic arrangements lying between full dependence on either the individual or the state; that the individual, the state and the middle-level organization all have prominent roles to play. This convergence will never be total and may take longer than we once thought, as we note below, but it remains a major tendency of industrialization. Also, we now give a greater emphasis to what we called, in 1960, the 'new bohemianism', somewhat redefined. But it still seems to us that the future of man's productive effort lies within the broad band of arrangements which we called 'pluralistic industrialism'.

As we review our analysis ten years later we should like to emphasize, once again, that we are engaged in analysis and not in prescription; that we are describing what we see and not what we consider to be a more nearly perfect solution. Industrialization places many burdens on man as well as bringing him greater benefits. We do believe that there are ways in which the burdens could be lightened and the benefits increased. This volume, however, is not concerned with our several versions of Utopia, but rather with the nature of the new society that is shaping the present and the future for so much of mankind.

A Re-examination of Critical Problems in Early Stages of Development

For the newly developing countries, particularly in their earlier stages of development, the path towards industrialization is more like an obstacle course than a paved highway. As we stressed (pp. 106–9), it may be obstructed by conflicts of cultural patterns or retarded by organizational and economic constraints. In *Industrialism and Industrial Man* we identified most of these obstacles, but some appear to have been overcome without great difficulty while others have turned out in the past decade to be much more formidable than we had anticipated.

In expanding their modern sector enclaves, for example, the developing countries have generally had less difficulty in overcoming cultural barriers than we anticipated. Constraints such as the family structure, class and race, or religious and ethical values have seldom impeded rapid development in the modern sectors. Nearly all of the less developed countries have modern office buildings, hotels, factories, airports, and highways in the urban areas. Coca-Cola, Bata shoes, Hilton Hotels, TV, and grocery supermarkets are almost as ubiquitous in Abidjan, Lagos, Addis Ababa, or Bogotá as they are in Copenhagen, Berlin, or Tokyo. The new culture of the cities acts like a magnet drawing ever larger numbers of migrants from the rural areas who quickly conform to a new culture of urban life.

The commitment of a labour force to employment in modern factories has been less difficult than expected. By paying relatively high wages and providing appropriate on-the-job training, employers have been able to minimize the problems of turnover and absenteeism and to build productive labour forces. The newcomers to modern industrial employment are quick to make a permanent attachment to it, and with rapidly expanding education in urban areas, the supply of 'trainable' workers has been constantly expanding.

Even the selection, development, and training of supervisors and managerial personnel, although not an easy task, appear to offer no insurmountable obstacles. In most countries, the replacement of expatriates with local nationals, particularly in the public service, has proceeded much more rapidly than expected, although government bureaucracies are still not very efficient. Staff training programmes in both the public and private sectors have proven to be more effective than anticipated for upgrading managerial personnel, and the time required to build experience on-the-job has in most cases been shorter than most 'colonial administrators' would have predicted. Where local talent is not available, the developing countries can 'rent' it from abroad. On the whole, the experience of the last decade indicates clearly that the newly developing countries can muster, train, rent the managerial, technical, skilled personnel to operate modern industrial complexes. Indeed, it is probable that the staffing of a steel mill is for them an easier task than the organization and training of cadres for promotion of rural development.

Finally, formal education, particularly at the secondary and higher levels, has expanded much more quickly than even the most optimistic planners ever expected. In the modern sectors of most newly developing countries, quantitative targets for educational expansion have been achieved if not over-fulfilled during the past decade. The average annual *per capita* percentage increase in expenditures on public education in many developing countries has exceeded by three or four times the average *per capita* increase in G.N.P. For some representative countries this is shown in the following table.[2]

In other significant respects, however, some problems connected with industrialization have loomed larger than we expected. Of these the most serious are: (1) rural stagnation, (2) the mushrooming growth of the urban underclass, (3) education which is poorly geared to development needs, (4) organizational 'power-failures' in government bureaucracies, and (5) excessively high rates of growth of population and the labour force. Each will be reviewed briefly.

1. A rural transformation is ordinarily an indispensable

AVERAGE ANNUAL PERCENTAGE CHANGES, 1950–65

	Per Capita Gross National Product	*Per Capita* Public Recurrent Expenditures on Education
Kenya	1·2	41·4
Mexico	3·3	35·0
Nigeria	2·8	31·1
Venezuela	3·5	29·6
Burma	4·0	28·7
Tanzania	1·4	28·7
Malaysia	4·6	27·8
Thailand	5·4	21·8
Sudan	3·1	20·9
Pakistan	1·2	17·2
India	1·4	13·3
China (Taiwan)	6·4	11·3
Guatemala	1·2	10·0
Turkey	3·8	9·2
Tunisia	1·8	8·9
Brazil	2·6	4·5

requirement for continuing industrial development in the absence of substantial exportable natural resources. Rapid development in the isolated modern sector enclaves provides no easy short cut. An increase in the quantity and particularly the quality of agricultural and livestock production is the core of any rural transformation, but along with this there must be expansion of small industries, improved education and health facilities, better housing, water supplies, sanitation, roads, and other public services. Rural transformation calls for the progressive modernization of traditional rural life, and this in turn requires investment of resources, brainpower, and human effort in programmes for raising the levels of living of rural people. During the past decade, rural development has often been neglected in favour of rapid industrialization in the urban areas.

Industrialization, of course, will provide much of the impetus for rural development. For example, modern science and technology are responsible for improved seeds, fertilizers, pesticides, and techniques which are the basis of possible 'green revolutions' in many countries. A sizeable part of the necessary resources may be generated in the rural areas themselves, for experience has shown that rural residents are willing to devote both labour and tax monies for projects from which they can clearly derive tangible benefits. But some of the profits generated in the modern sectors must also be siphoned off to help finance rural development. Yet, unfortunately, the problems of creating the organizations and developing the appropriate skills for the rural transformation are still largely unsolved. Here is perhaps the most underdeveloped area in the whole field of knowledge on modernization.

2. Unemployment and widespread underemployment of human resources in sprawling urban areas is now perhaps the central and most baffling problem facing the newly developing countries.[3] At best, employment in the modern sectors increases by three to five per cent a year, but characteristically urban labour forces are growing over twice as fast. Furthermore, an increasing proportion of job seekers are persons with considerable formal education whose expectations far exceed any chance of gaining access to work in government agencies or modern industrial and commercial enterprises. And behind those openly unemployed are growing armies of stall-holders, shoe-shiners, pedlars, beggars, casual labourers, and petty thieves who constitute a poverty-stricken, restless, and disillusioned urban underclass. In the advanced countries this underclass is usually a small minority consisting of the undereducated, discriminated-against minority groups, ghetto dwellers, migrant farm workers, and others rejected by the institutions of industrialism. But in the urban areas of the less developed countries, this underclass is in the majority even in cases where industrial growth has been most impressive.

The causes of urban unemployment in the newly industrializing countries are easy to identify: high wages and salaries compared with rural-area earnings which attract droves of hopeful job-seekers to the cities; the rise of aspirations fuelled by education oriented to the modern sector; the increase in population growth;

285

and the use of labour-saving technology in modern enterprises. In many respects, therefore, industrialization concentrates the unemployed in urban areas, even as it creates new employment. The remedies, however, are difficult to implement, e.g. wage restraint in the modern sector, greater investment in rural development, more emphasis on labour-intensive industries, and population control.

3. The remarkable expansion of education in the newly developing countries has drawbacks as well as advantages. For the most part, the underlying purpose of education is more education. In other words, the principal goal of primary schools is to prepare students for entry into secondary schools, and the purpose of secondary is to prepare the most promising students for higher and university education. This 'single-axis' orientation of the educational systems of many industrializing countries overemphasizes preparation for entry into the modern sector enclaves. It tends to produce intellectuals who are often unemployable, and it creates expectations which are inconsistent with realistic opportunities provided by developing economies. The experience of the last decade has emphasized what we stressed earlier, that irrelevant education can waste human and financial resources which otherwise might be channelled into more productive activities.[4] Now the over-investment in the wrong kinds of formal education compared with non-formal means of acquiring skills and knowledge is becoming more generally recognized, and the importance of employing organizations in providing on-the-job training and work experience is more widely understood.

4. Government ministries and bureaux, though relatively easy to man in numbers, are slower in developing efficiency. In many countries, the capacity of governments to plan, organize, manage, and implement development programmes suffers from chronic 'organizational power failure'. Even the simplest tasks are poorly performed; the most urgent policy decisions remain unimplemented; rivalries and in-fighting between ministries forestall logical decision-making; and corruption and laziness sap the resources ostensibly allocated to development programmes. All countries are subject to the danger of becoming mired in their

bureaucracies, and many of the newly developing nations appear to be particularly susceptible to this disease. In particular, the achievement of independence has not enabled the new nationalist leaders to streamline government machinery and to cleanse it of corruptive influences to the extent that we might have hoped.

5. Today nations are more aware of the population menace. Most of the developing countries now have rates of population increase in excess of 2·5 per cent a year (and these rates are still increasing) in contrast with less than half such rates in the industrialized countries. The consequent high proportion of persons in the non-working ages places almost intolerable burdens on public services, schools, health, and other programmes for improving the lot of the people. Rapidly increasing population lies at the root of mounting unemployment and underemployment. It forestalls the rapid rise of *per capita* incomes. It retards the rate of savings. In short, rapidly rising population growth may halt the march towards industrialization in many countries during the next decades.

In general, it is clear that the newly developing countries can build industrialized enclaves more quickly than they can develop their rural sectors. For this they have access to modern technology, high-level manpower, and even external financial resources. But such industrial systems produce goods and services largely for the minority of the population who are fortunate enough to be attached to the modern sector enclaves. The result is often dual economies in which the disparities between the rich and the poor are widened. And the notion that growth in the modern sector enclaves will in itself lead to transformation of entire traditional societies is now open to question. Internal markets for the outputs of modern sector enterprise are very thin, and external markets are difficult to penetrate because of ever-increasing international competition. Unless there are rising incomes for the masses in rural areas, therefore, the industrialization process can slow down once the import-substitution industries have satisfied the economic demands of the fortunate few in the modern enclaves.

In summary, industrialization in many countries has proceeded more rapidly than we anticipated. In particular, cultural restraints have been less confining, management has been more available, workers have adapted more readily, and the educational system has expanded more quickly than we had expected ten years ago. However, rural sectors have remained more stagnant, government bureaucracies have remained more lethargic and sometimes corrupt, and population increases have accelerated faster than we once anticipated, and these have proved to be great obstacles in many countries. In many African and Latin American countries industrialization has increased the disparities between the rich and the poor and between the urban and rural areas. It has meant a new and challenging life for a smaller minority but it has largely bypassed the rural masses. Particularly in countries with high rates of population increase and mounting unemployment industrialization, by itself, without appropriate measures to reduce the degree of inequality in incomes, offers no ready solution for the problem of poverty in many less developed countries.

Industrializing Élites Reconsidered

We used the term 'élites' to convey the leadership role that characterizes certain groups and individuals in any society. To some readers, this 'élitist' view has value overtones which suggest a rigid class structure, but the usage here is value-free: élites may come from all classes in contending for positions of leadership. They include political leaders, industrial managers, labour union officials, religious leaders, military officers and others making critical decisions about the direction of the society. They are assisted by civil servants and subordinate officials of all types. To those who had difficulty with our use of the term 'élites', we would say that we might just as well have used the term 'leaders'.

In distinguishing five 'generalized types of élites who may take the leadership in the industrialization process', we stressed that 'these ideal types . . . ignore much important detail in individual cases. Most actual cases are mixtures, and several societies have changed and will continue to change their essential type over time' (p. 60). [Some change gradually, others by revolutionary means.] We stress this again, because the five ideal types have sometimes been criticized as unrealistic. They are necessarily abstractions from reality, 'but by reducing complexity they can also illuminate reality' (p. 61).

With this *caveat* in mind, we have nonetheless suggested that certain countries may be characterized as having predominantly one type of élite rather than another, at a particular time. In re-examining what we said about each of the five generalized or ideal types, we would now propose to clarify two of them: 'The Revolutionary Intellectuals and the Centralized State', and 'The Nationalist Leader and the Guidance of the State'. Some students and readers have confused the two, believing that any nationalist leader in a newly-independent nation is also likely to be a 'revolutionary intellectual' in the sense that he is seeking to change a pre-existing society by radical reforms, sometimes preceded by revolutionary military means.

What we meant by 'revolutionary intellectuals' was clearly that group holding a communist (sometimes called 'socialist') ideology and who have 'full power to control society in a centralized fashion'. Once the new class is in control, the original revolutionary intellectuals 'give way increasingly to high-level political administrators and bureaucrats as leaders of the system' (p. 71). 'The society, of necessity, is monolithic – there can be no real separation of economic, political and religious institutions. Rule-making, generally, and in industrial relations, specifically, is inherently in the hands of the dominant class – the managers of this historical process' (p. 72). This is surely a *generalized* description of the communist society typified by the U.S.S.R. during most of its history, and in varying degrees by the communist states of eastern Europe. Thus, a more accurate label for this type of industrializing élite would have been 'The Communist Leaders and the Centralized State'.

Having said this, polycentrism in communist societies, which we noted in 1960, has become even more marked. The earlier emer-gence of Yugoslavian communism with its decentralization of some managerial responsibility to the enterprise level and worker self-management has been followed by other less dramatic ex-periments in economic and even political decentralization in other eastern European countries; although the Czech and Hungarian episodes indicate the political obstacles in the way of economic liberalization.

The increasing ideological conflict between the U.S.S.R. and Communist China is still another example of the breakdown of a world-wide communist ideology. Despite these divergences, which could of course be matched with specific examples in the other generalized élites, we believe that most communist societies *are* different, especially in their impact on labour-management relations, from most of the societies which tend to be characterized by the middle-class or dynastic élites.

The nationalist leader is often charismatic, and may espouse a kind of ideology illustrated by Nehru's 'socialist pattern of society', or Nyerere's type of 'African socialism'. But we reiterate that in our judgement nationalism with its chiliastic approach 'is more an opening of the gate towards industrial development than a specifically demarcated road towards industrialization' (p. 74). 'The "nationalist society" is particularly a plaything of history. Its recent past is of especial significance ... The need for clear direction is great. Yet this ... is particularly difficult to attain ... And there is no single readymade ideology for the nationalist conduct of a society. Consequently, the nationalist approach tends to be a wavering one following an unsteady course' (p. 76).

As we reflect on the nature of societies with state guidance under nationalist leaders during the past decade, we believe these characterizations remain valid. Many of the new African countries, as well as those in south and east Asia, are still on this unsteady course. Some at times were moving in the direction of the communist élites (Cuba, Guinea, Ghana under Nkrumah, and Indonesia under Sukarno), although the latter two subsequently changed course under new nationalist leaders. Other countries are characterized by a growing middle-class private industrial sector or by elements of the dynastic élite. Some are coalitions of élites, as in Brazil, with a growing middle class and a military government. In most, labour-management relations are subordinated to the broader objectives of continued modernization and economic development under state control.

While we intended no evaluation of the different industrializing élites in terms of their performance, it would be instructive to consider the record of productivity increases, as measured, for example, by relative increases in real G.N.P. *per capita*. We have not attempted to do this here, but data are available for various recent time periods,[5] and an analysis of selected countries typified by each of the five generalized élites would be helpful.

The Impact of Technology on Industrialization

A major persistent problem in all analysis of modern society concerns the role of technology. What features of the economy and the larger society does technology fully control; what features are merely influenced, and what features are relatively independent of technology? In Japan we have found a particularly insistent concern with these issues, as many Japanese are interested in the benefits of modern technology but are concerned over its impacts on the institutions of its traditional society.

For Marx, technology, or the mode of production, constituted the *Unterbau* which narrowly prescribed the whole superstructure of society, including class relationships. For a wide range of social theorists and critics, including Veblen, Schumpeter and Durkheim, change in technology constituted a critical factor producing tensions among groups and classes and providing the engine for economic and social change.

In *Industrialism and Industrial Man*, with our focus on the problems of labour and management in economic growth, we sought to be more specific as to the role of technology and technological change. To say merely that technology and technological change are important factors shaping workers and managers and the organization of the larger society is trite. The intellectual challenge is to outline the mechanisms through which technology shapes the work place and larger societal institutions, and to specify as well the limits of that influence.

Chapter 1, 'The Logic of Industrialization', summarized our views on these issues. The impact of technology and technological change is likely to be most direct in the production process itself, that is in shaping the production function, to use the language of

291

economists. The potential job activities are specified for workers, supervisors and managers, and the possible combinations of labour with capital equipment are noted at various scales of operations. The limited production possibilities – among which choices are made by managers depending on relative prices of the productive factors – narrowly specify job classifications and the occupational structure at the work place. Changes in occupational structure in turn are narrowly related at the work place to technological changes. The occupational structure in turn narrowly dictates the necessities for job training, and more generally, influences the requirements for technical and scientific education. It is for these reasons of direct determination that the work places of textile plants, oil refineries, steel mills, or airplane cockpits so resemble each other in different countries with different political and social arrangements, and the job structure and occupations of such work places, and even the relative occupational ordering of wage rates, are so similar. In these facets of an industrializing society the influence of technology is dominant, leaving relatively little room for other influences.

This view does not mean that other influences are entirely absent at the work place. Thus, a weaver's job may be characteristically a woman's job in many societies while it may be a man's job in most Muslim countries. Or, a strong ideology may dictate for a period that piece rates be used for a job classification rather than leaving the choice of methods of wage payment to more practical considerations of efficiency and the influence of supervision. The relations between training in a formal school system and on the job at the work place may vary in some respects among countries. But the larger truth is that the iron hand of technology tends to create relative uniformity in job structure, compensation differentials and technical training. These uniformities are enhanced by migration and international flow of capital equipment and specialists.

Beyond the work place, technology also has a direct and immediate impact upon the household and consumer through the standardization of many consumer goods, to which any world traveller even in backward areas would attest. The automobile, the tin can and the soft drink are ubiquitous. Forms of western dress are widespread. In more developed areas, various consumer durables such as refrigerators and washing machines have spread widely. Technology has also had no less an impact on citizens everywhere through forms of mass transportation, the mails, radio and television. It is little wonder that leaders in different social and political systems are so concerned to try to control the consequences of these means of communication.

Technology also appears to have some influence, although it is less confining, on the general education system. Technological developments have also contributed to changes in the extended family characteristic of traditional societies and to changes in class relationships.

But technology has less deterministic consequences on a society in other areas. Higher educational systems among countries reflect greater diversity than do steel mills, despite the levelling influence of industrialization. Legal education shows greater diversity than the education of engineers and chemists. As we noted (p. 49), industrialization creates an urban dominance everywhere and a decline in the position of traditional agriculture. While metropolitan areas show increasing similarity around the world, they also reflect significant differences in cultural heritage and the consequences of different policies. We also noted that higher incomes under industrialization necessarily tended to produce everywhere more intellectuals. But the roles and activities of such intellectuals vary a great deal, indeed, we referred to them as a floating force in society (pp. 89–92).

Thus, there are some features of the transformation of society through industrialization in which the role of technology is dominant and narrowly conformist such as in the standardization of many aspects of the work place and some consumer goods. There are, however, other features of the march towards industrialism over which technology has much less constraint. These are the areas where our analysis holds the decisions of the industrializing élites to be decisive, and the impact of earlier cultural forms to be important.

Postscript

The Need for Internal Consistency

Our analysis held that the industrial society, like any established society, develops a distinctive consensus 'which relates individuals and groups to each other and provides an integrated body of ideas, beliefs, and value judgements' (p. 53). We argued that in the industrial society 'science and technical knowledge have high values'; 'taboos against technical change are eliminated'; 'education has a high value'; 'industrialization calls for flexibility and competition'; 'goods and services have a high value'; and 'the work force is dedicated to hard work, a high pace of work, and a keen sense of individual responsibility for performance of assigned norms and tasks'. We stressed that 'the function of making explicit a consensus and of combining discrete beliefs and convictions into a reasonably consistent body of ideas is the task of intellectuals in every society' (p. 54).

We also recognized that each individual case of industrialization involved important internal conflicts, tensions and issues of consequence among disparate interests and groups. But there are necessarily limits to the degree of disharmony and tension. If consensus is not sufficiently preserved, the dominance of the particular élite may be jeopardized or the institutions of the society may not be able to perform their assigned functions. Economic and social progress of the society is consequently affected adversely.

A number of questions have been raised, in the shadow of events of the late 1960s, concerning the capacity of industrializing societies to maintain a requisite consensus. It is held in some quarters that a fundamental crisis of consensus may be developing in the United States and some other countries, as evidenced by university dislocation, racial violence and other class conflict, so intense as to force major alignments in the society. For some such developments are looked upon with keen anticipation and for others with deep fear. Irrespective of one's views, these discussions compel a review of the degree of consensus that is requisite to a successful course towards industrialism.

A consensus, or an ideology, in part serves as a means of control over conduct in a society. Shared ideas constitute a substitute for controls and formal organizations to direct activity and to resolve conflict. As we observed, 'strict supervision imposed on a lethargic work force will not suffice; personal responsibility for performance must be implanted within workers, front-line supervisors and top managers' (p. 53). Thus, one consequence of the breakdown of a consensus is an increase in the need for formal mechanisms of control and administration. The less the consensus, in a given industrializing society, the greater the extent and penetration of bureaucratic controls. But these have limits to coerce conduct.

The consequences of a decline in consensus depend very much on the subjects upon which there is a loss in shared understanding or ideology, and the criticality of these understandings to the particular élite. The capacity of any élite to govern, to command respect, to formulate policies and to carry them out is most critical. The capacity to prevent open conflict and violence on any substantial scale is likewise pivotal. The decline of consensus on some other features, such as the work ethic, the valuation of goods and services, or the respect for science, may require (depending on the degree of dissent) a long period to adjust to any decisive consequences. But in the long run a rejection of these values may be expected to slow the march to industrialism or to change the character of the leaders.

The central role of intellectuals in the formulation of a consensus, and in 'restating the major values, premises, and consensus of a society from time to time' (p. 54) may have been to a degree exaggerated in our earlier formulation. Intellectuals often are badly divided and consequently partially discredited. Political leaders may take on more of the assignment of formulating new propositions for acceptance. While they may no doubt use the services of some intellectuals, political and other active leaders of groups and associations may come not only to exercise the major role of reconciling conflicting interests but also formulating new acceptable compromises in the society and theories to explain and justify them.

But industrializing societies, for varying periods, may be

Postscript

characterized by considerable conflict, disharmony and even a temporary breakdown in consensus.

Convergence of Systems

We set forth in *Industrialism and Industrial Man* the view that industrial systems, regardless of the cultural background out of which they emerge and the path they originally follow, tend to become more alike over an extended period of time; that systems, whether under middle-class or communist or dynastic leadership, move towards 'pluralistic industrialism' where the state, the enterprise or association, and the individual all share a substantial degree of power and influence over productive activities. The process of convergence moves sometimes faster and sometimes slower and is, on occasion, reversed, but it is a long-run development of fundamental significance. It points the general direction of change.[6]

We noted the 'diversity' of arrangements that are possible within pluralistic industrialism. This diversity lies between the alternatives of pure state socialism and pure market capitalism, both of which emphasize the role of the manager; and between the guild socialism of G. D. H. Cole and private anarcho-syndicalism, both of which emphasize the role of the working group. Each of these four possibilities constitutes a 'pure' model with clear sovereignty for one group or another. Pluralistic industrialism, by contrast, emphasizes mixed sovereignty and there are many possible mixtures.

Pluralistic industrialism, then, may take several forms and by its nature is likely to undergo constant adaptations to the demands of the several semi-sovereign elements. We see pluralistic industrialism as a range of alternatives rather than a single arrangement. A pure system is, by definition, more rigid.

We would like to suggest, as illustrations, four generalized models of pluralistic industrialism:

1. Where the state, under a single doctrine and leadership, permits and encourages substantial independence to enterprises to determine products and to set prices and wages in response to

consumer demand and labour-market conditions. The state has a general capital investment plan and determines the general directions of economic growth.

2. Where the enterprise has an elemental sovereignty based on private ownership, with the state more in the role of support of rather than domination over the general productive process. The state preserves law and order and protects property rights, but also takes responsibility for policies intended to stabilize the price level, provide full employment, assure growth, and provide social security.

3. Where the workers and consumers through their own organizations and their political influence in the state are strongly protected from exploitation by the state and by the enterprise. Through legislative efforts, bargaining agreement, legal action and individual initiative, the interests of organized employees and consumers are given a high order of importance.

4. Where productive efforts in many fields, such as agriculture, handicrafts and the services, are organized through largely self-governing groups of workers or consumers or both. The state provides central services of defence, welfare, and so forth.

In each of these illustrative forms, the state, the enterprise or the association, and the individual have considerable influence; but the influence will vary. In the first, the state is more dominant; in the second, the enterprise manager (and the individual consumer); in the third, the associated workers and consumers, but as workers and consumers; and in the fourth, the workers and consumers as owners. The first is a modified market socialism or state capitalism; the second and third are modified forms of social capitalism, and the fourth is a modified form of state syndicalism.

There will not be one single and inevitable result; there will be no purity of theory and design; and there will be constant movement in specific arrangements. Convergence is towards a range of alternatives rather than to a single point. The pluralism of the state, the enterprise or association, and the individual is matched by the industrial relations system of the state, the manager and worker associations which we set forth in our Chapter 7. The two are counterparts of each other, responding to the same general forces.

There are 'limits' and may even be 'exceptions' to convergence as T. H. Marshall has noted.[7] In particular, we accept the view of Goldthorpe[8] that 'political' considerations will have more impact on the 'life chances' of persons in a strongly statist pluralism and that the 'class situation of individuals and groups, understood in terms of their economic power and resources' will have more effect on the 'life chances' of persons in a more market-oriented pluralism. But we reject Goldthorpe's interpretation that we see a 'one-way total convergence' towards capitalism; rather, in the words of Dunning and Hopper, we see a 'two-way partial convergence' between market capitalism and state socialism with the possible addition of some syndicalist elements.[9]

Our doctrine of convergence does imply that economic forces for relative similarity are more powerful in the long run than political forces for absolute diversity – but not totally overwhelming; and that, among various forces, the world-wide identity of the most effective technology is persuasive. There is one best technology; this affects economic relations, and economic relations affect political realities – but to a lesser extent and in different ways than Marx thought were written into the inexorable laws of the universe.

Discontinuities in the Later Stages of Industrialization

Some critics have questioned whether the road to industrialism is as continuous as *Industrialism and Industrial Man* seemed to imply. While that analysis recognizes that there are many obstacles and constraints confronting an industrializing élite, it is sometimes argued that major discontinuities may arise world-wide, or be created by the industrializing process itself, to alter dramatically the strategy of the élite or leadership group in all countries. Individual developments may arise in a particular country, of course, which alter discretely the prospects of industrial development, such as the discovery of oil in Libya, or the forcible seizure of power by communist leaders, but the question at issue concerns the possibility of major distortions in the future in the industrialization process universally.

We recognized that 'pluralistic industrialism will never reach a final equilibrium. The contest between the forces for uniformity and for diversity will give it life and movement and change' (p. 277). But the view has been strongly advanced that society is in for cataclysmic changes. A sense of this emphasis is seen in the following extract from Daniel Bell writing for the American Academy's Commission on the Year 2000:

... More and more we are becoming a 'communal society' in which the public sector has a greater importance and in which the goods and services of society – those affecting cities, education, medical care, and the environment – will increasingly have to be purchased jointly. Hence, the problem of social choice and individual values – the question of how to reconcile conflicting individual desires through the political mechanism rather than the market – becomes a potential source of discord. The relation of the individual to bureaucratic structures will be subject to even greater strain ... The growth of a large, educated professional and technical class, with its desire for greater autonomy in work, will force institutions to reorganize the older bureaucratic patterns of hierarchy and detailed specialization ... The new densities and 'communications overload' may increase the potentialities for irrational outbursts in our society ... Society becomes more functionally organized, geared to knowledge and the mastery of complex bodies of learning. The culture becomes more hedonistic, permissive, expressive, distrustful of authority and of the purposive, delayed-gratification of a bourgeois, achievement-oriented technological world. This tension between the 'technocratic' and the 'apocalyptic' modes, particularly among the intellectuals, may be one of the great ruptures in moral temper, especially in universities.[10]

1. One view is that the rate of technological change may be so rapid or that some one dramatic innovation may make such a quantum jump that the whole industrialization process will be altered. But the evidence to date on atomic energy or the computer, for instance, would not find these technological developments to be so cataclysmic in their impact. (Nuclear war is a separate matter.) While the cumulative effects of technological change over a generation are very substantial, it appears that significant in-

novation takes a number of years to generate and to introduce, and a variety of smaller changes and adaptations seem to characterize industrialization rather than a few major distortions. Moreover, technological change grows out of past change and the economy is studded with diffuse points of innovation. It is always possible, of course, that some unforeseen mutation may arise quickly but the evidence at hand would seem to make such a development most unlikely.

It may also be possible that the rate of technological change may accelerate to such rates that the society cannot readily absorb such changes or make the required adaptations. There is some evidence that the rate of increase of productivity may have accelerated slightly in the post-war world, but the magnitude thus far is not large. But continuing responses to a continuing series of small changes may prove no less disruptive to industrialization than a major single change.

2. It may be argued that industrialization is creating a new class of technocrats which may come to constitute an entirely new élite directing the industrialization process. *Industrialism and Industrial Man* emphasizes the tendency towards professional management in all societies. 'In professional management, technical ability, experience, education, knowledge of the organization, and ability to impress people who make decisions are more important than relationships to a family or a political régime' (p. 154). We stated, 'Every industrializing élite will require technicians, administrators, and bureaucrats' (p. 35n). Technological competence is essential to industrialization and the leaders of each country will necessarily draw such competence into their ranks. Technocrats, whatever the term may mean, are not a separate élite but rather an element of the leadership group of each society. Generally, however, the technical improvement of leadership is necessary.

3. The spread of higher education widely throughout a society, it is urged, has created considerable pressures for full participation of workers and citizens in the decisions affecting their economic and political lives. These developments, it is thought, may be so dramatic as to change the forms of organization and the roles of workers and managements at the work place and the forms of

government in the larger community. The widespread and rapid adoption of the principle of 'maximum feasible participation' in the industrial and political spheres might have dramatic consequences for the character of industrialization.

We have shown that in the course of industrialization, organizations of workers arise to constitute in varying degrees a form of participation in industrial and community life. We noted the various forms in which workers, managers and the state may each 'share in the making of rules' (p. 228). It is, of course, possible that existing organizations at the work place and in community life may be so rigid or so insensitive to the shifting interests of workers and citizens for greater participation, that wholly new institutions may arise to fulfill these aspirations. But these interests may also be absorbed by existing organizations or by the creation of professional associations where they do not exist. Moreover, serious interest in intensive participation appears to be limited to a minority of the work force and citizenry, albeit this proportion may show some secular rise with industrialization. The careful studies of worker participation that have been made both in eastern and western countries do not suggest that any sustained interest in participation at the work place has compelled drastic changes in worker organizations. The impact of participation in the political community is more difficult to assess but appears no more far-reaching.

4. The industrialization process may create new cultural forms and new styles of life, so dramatic and pervasive, that the devotion to work is corrupted. We said of the industrial society, 'The work force is dedicated to hard work, a high pace of work and a keen sense of individual responsibility for performance of assigned tasks and norms. Industrial countries may differ with respect to the ideals and drives which underlie devotion to duty and responsibility for performance, but industrialization requires an ideology and an ethic which motivate individual workers' (p. 53).

It may well be that the new humanism, discussed in the next section, will corrode the inner dedication of workers and managers to performance and thereby affect, even significantly, the course of industrialization. But the evidence to date indicates that wage-earners everywhere are still so interested in increased consumption that they are not likely to be significantly affected. The national leaders seem to be able to provide strong additional incentives. It may be that some of the most highly educated employees, and even some associated white-collar workers, may be so alienated from traditional values that their incentives are significantly altered. But the performance of a work force, we have previously argued, is substantially influenced by the quality of management, and there appears to be little evidence yet for sufficient disaffection to reduce appreciably the supply of competent managers. The new elements of the work force present significant challenges to the new managers. But this potential discontinuity is by no means evident; the question warrants continuing scrutiny.

In each of these four areas, we see continuing adjustments rather than sudden and dramatic changes.

The New Humanism versus Industrialism

A decade ago we called attention to the 'new bohemianism' as one of the major factors potentially affecting the 'road ahead' to pluralistic industrialism. In the intervening decade, the 'cultural revolution', with its 'counter-culture', has spread rapidly. Related to it has been an attack on the 'consumptionist society' with its emphasis on material goods, and on the 'one-dimensional man' ruled by technology and those who manage technology. Bohemian attitudes have spread and deepened significantly. We thought we saw bohemianism as a largely off-the-job phenomenon. Now it seems to be penetrating some jobs in society, particularly white-collar jobs, causing a more casual attitude towards performance. Furthermore, some persons refuse employment altogether in favour of a way of life separated as far as possible from the discipline of industrialism, if not from its useful products.

The old theme of distrust of technology and of revulsion against the machine has taken on new emphasis as the new Luddites reject the industrial system the way the old Luddites rejected the individual machine.

This is a countervailing force rising in reaction to the more pervasive force of technology, and it is an objective feature of the post-modernized society. It raises questions about the constant rise of the G.N.P. and the centrality of productivity per man-hour. Humanization is now again the cry as it was when the 'deserted village' was being mourned; and when Marx wrote what are now known as *The Manuscripts of 1844*. It emphasizes the individual versus the machine and versus the managerial élites who control it. It involves a move towards the syndicalism of the small participatory group as against the large corporation of the middle-class leadership, the centralized state of the communists, and the paternal firm of the dynastic élite. Syndicalism is now challenging other forms of society as it has not done for nearly a century. The corporation, the state, and the trade union all combine against more open syndicalism.

Some explorations are already taking place as to how to increase participation and to provide more individual options in response. Technology itself provides new opportunities, if not for participation, certainly for options, as variety in products and in arrangements for work become possible with more adaptive machines, including the computer.[11]

The new humanism also urges a 'life-long' view which may not be entirely consonant with the necessities of industrialization. Education might be more continuous than the pattern of compression into the early years. The life-time pattern of earnings which took greater account of family needs does not readily fit into conventional wage-setting by job content. The new humanism impels quite different and variable combinations of work and leisure throughout a life-time.

Underneath this humanist reaction and these preliminary adjustments to it, lies a central problem in industrialism: society requires more discipline to go along with the greater interdependence that the new technology brings, but the more highly educated labour force wants more freedom for spontaneous individual action within the work environment, as well as outside it. Thus technological society might carry the 'seeds of its own destruction' – not in class versus class, but in the discipline that the technology requires versus the spontaneity of the labour force that it helps to create. Some of the requirements of the new society run into conflict with the new man it spawns.[12]

Thus we would give greater emphasis, one decade later, to the force of the new humanism and to the potentialities of intense conflict between what we called the 'semi-managers' and the 'semi-managed' (p. 259). The university campus is feeling the first great impact of this force and this conflict. We believe, however, that pluralistic industrialism will adjust to this new theme and not be destroyed by it. The leadership groups and the 'semi-managers' alike will need to be more alive to humanistic, as against material-istic, factors.

The Survival of Industrialism

We have noted earlier that our 1960 prediction of the 'road ahead' was pluralistic industrialism. Among other things, this meant that 'the complexity of the fully developed industrial society requires, in the name of efficiency and initiative, a degree of decentraliza-tion of control, particularly in the consumer goods and service trades industries; but it also requires a large measure of central control by the state and conduct of many operations by large-scale organizations' (p. 270).

At the time we were writing, some of the questions now raised about the survival of industrial societies did not have their present urgency. Apart from the threat of nuclear war (which would render all other considerations invalid), there are increasingly serious questions posed by the population explosion (discussed earlier); increasing pollution and waste; rapid usage of the world's natural resources; and the cultural revolution of youth in advanced countries, affecting the will to work. Do these con-siderations make us less optimistic about the long-run future of pluralistic industrialism? The answer is a qualified 'Yes', but not so pessimistic as some have suggested.

The world-wide population explosion is manageable tech-nologically and culturally, but it will take some time to bring population increase rates down in many of the developing countries where the average is now above 2·5 per cent a year and still rising.

The responsibility of governments in these countries for mounting greater efforts towards population limitation is clear.

But an advanced industrial society has the other problems mentioned: increasing pollution of water resources and the air, increasing waste disposal problems, and the pressure to discover new supplies of natural resources as existing supplies dwindle. Strip mining in coal which desecrates the land is one example; drilling for new oil and gas offshore and frequent pollution of sea water is another. Furthermore, some areas and some people in an affluent industrial society seem to be blighted and left behind: the urban ghettos of large metropolitan areas in the United States or the slum areas outside cities in other countries, and the 'disadvantaged' whose deficiencies in environmental development and education often make them misfits for many of the jobs of an industrial society. All of these factors, as well as others resulting from their own chosen life-styles, have led to alienation of the young, many of them students, in many industrial societies.

Rebellion, not always as 'quiet' as we suggested (p. 277) but no less desperate, has already developed in these societies. Perhaps each new generation of rebelling youth will moderate with maturity and family responsibilities; but a continuing minority may permanently reject the work ethic which is basic to the concept of continued economic growth, as we noted in preceding sections. The prospect, however, is that a substantial majority of the population of labour-force age will continue, through work and the income it provides, to move towards their individual goals in the society.

As for the other consequences attributed to advanced industrialism, their urgency is not moderated, although it is put in better perspective, by the historical fact that (as in the less developed societies today) those societies now more advanced had in their earlier history more poverty, more unemployment, more inhumane treatment of individuals, more polluted water, and many fewer amenities than rebellious youth often take for granted now.[13]

Advanced industrial societies will have continuing problems with the consequences of pollution, waste, and natural resource exhaustion, and with the problems of blighted cities and the disadvantaged. But only the advanced industrial society, with its innovative resources in science, technology and administration, has the capacity to deal with these problems. Political pressures will inevitably build up to force governments to take corrective action and to fund research on new solutions.

For example, René Dubos has suggested that a new technology based on the virtue of recycling resources will have to be developed, and new energy sources sought which have fewer possibilities of pollution, solar energy being the clearest example. He is, however, pessimistic about the 'growth myth'. 'The impact of technology has effects that are irreversible. Whether we want it or not, we can't survive unless we reform, reconstruct, and re-evaluate our industrial system.' Quality, rather than quantity of production, should be the criterion of success, he believes.[14]

Dubos' prescription would involve a substantial re-ordering of priorities, which the pluralistic industrial state is better equipped to do than the less advanced society. The survival capacity of the advanced industrial society, despite its problems, is substantial, because of the technical and human resources it can mobilize to deal with these problems. All societies over the range of recorded history have had problems, including the pre-industrial ones. There never was and probably never will be a Golden Age society.

Clark Kerr John T. Dunlop Frederick H. Harbison
Charles A. Myers

1971

Appendix:
The Inter-University Study of Labor Problems in Economic Development

Organization and Orientation

Industrialism and Industrial Man is only one of many publications growing out of the 'Inter-University Study of Labor Problems in Economic Development'. This informal organization was formed by the four authors of this volume in 1954 to bring together people, projects, and funds for the purpose of making studies of human agents in the industrialization process. The study, and the preliminary investigations which led to it, have received financial support from the Ford Foundation.

In its first eight years of existence, the Inter-University Study has sponsored more than forty projects involving work in thirty-five countries. A total of seventy-eight persons of eleven different nationalities have been involved in some phase of the research. Those associated with the Inter-University Study have published 20 books, and a Reprint Series contains twenty-nine articles. A number of other articles have also appeared, and additional books are in the press or in manuscript. The publications are listed and the books and articles in the Reprint Series are annotated in this appendix.

From 1954-9 the Inter-University Study was concerned primarily with industrialization, managerial organization and ideology, the development of industrial working forces, and the role of labour organizations. Studies of 'labour problems' as thus broadly defined were undertaken in industrially advanced countries such as Germany, Japan, the Soviet Union, and Italy. The range of underdeveloped economies and newly industrializing societies included India, Egypt, and Indonesia. The 'cross-cut', or topical, studies have dealt with managerial ideologies, management organization and development, wage structures, the problems of worker protest, labour organizations, the recruitment and commitment of working forces, and the comparative analysis of industrial relations systems.

In collaboration with other research and educational institutions, the Inter-University Study has held conferences on labour and management problems in economic development in Turkey, Lebanon, Iran, Pakistan, India, Indonesia, Japan, Colombia, Brazil, Argentina, Chile, Nigeria, and the United States. Thus, through publications, jointly sponsored research projects, and international conferences, the Inter-University Study has sought to establish a means of communication – and a common language – among those who have a professional interest in the labour and management problems of modern societies.

The arrangements for financial support of various projects have been as diverse as the number of countries in which inquiries were made. In some cases, such as, for example, the country studies of India and Egypt, as well as the cross-cut analysis of industrial relations systems, the entire cost was underwritten by the Inter-University Study. In other cases, grants from the Inter-University Study were matched with resources already available to individuals or institutions. In a few instances, the Inter-University Study took care only of the marginal cost of projects which were financed mostly with other resources. The conferences were financed jointly by the Inter-University Study, the Ford Foundation, and institutions in the various countries.

During the course of the next several years, the Inter-University Study hopes to continue and extend both its cross-cut and country studies. In the future, more emphasis will be given to policy issues and to the communication of research findings in conferences. One of the new concerns is the comparative analysis of patterns of utilization of high-level manpower in societies at various stages of development and the critical examination of the role of education in the modernization process. The two objectives of this new interest are to find a means of making long-range projects of human resource requirements in newly developing countries and to establish guide-posts for determining a strategy of investments in human resource development which are most appropriate for such countries. This part of the project will proceed with the support of a recent grant from the Carnegie Corporation of New York.

In the future, as in the past, therefore, the objective of the Inter-University Study will be to promote and sponsor comparative studies of the role of human resources in the processes of economic development. The purpose is both to conduct research and to help to develop people in different countries as experts in the analysis of industrial relations and manpower development problems. The Inter-University Study has been interested in the past and will be concerned in the future with both research and operations, with fundamental knowledge and policy applications. *Industrialism and Industrial Man*, therefore, is not the final volume of our joint enterprise. It is rather an interim report.

We are deeply indebted to all the persons associated with the Inter-University Study for their contribution to the project in general and to our thinking in particular. Their names and the institutions of their affiliations at the time of their association with the project appear below. We wish to express at this time our particular debt to a few additional persons who contributed directly in conversations and writing to the central ideas expressed in this volume. At our request they read earlier drafts of the manuscript and made many detailed and stimulating comments. They are: E. Wight Bakke, Everett E. Hagen, Edward S. Mason, Abraham J. Siegel, and David Williams. During the eight years of this project, we have also benefited greatly from an exchange of views and close association in overseas seminars with Dr Thomas H. Carroll, former Vice-President of the Ford Foundation, who had officer responsibility for its programme in Economic Development and Administration. To Marie Klein, the administrative secretary of the Inter-University Study for the first four years, we owe a special debt of gratitude for holding together the procedural strings of the entire project.

Clark Kerr, John T. Dunlop, Frederick H. Harbison,
Charles A. Myers

November 1962

Appendix

**Individuals Associated with the Inter-University Study
(Academic Affiliation during Work with the Study) (1954–61)**

Ahmedebad Textile Industry & Research Institute, India
    Chowdhry, Kamla, Psychology Division
    Pal, A. K., Human Relations Division
American University of Beirut
    Badre, Albert Y., Economic Research Institute
    Bawarshi, Tewfick, Economic Research Institute
    Klat, Paul J., Economic Research Institute
    Nabulsi, Hikmat, Economic Research Institute
    Sayigh, Yusif A., Economic Research Institute
    Siksek, Simon G., Economic Research Institute
California, University of (Berkeley)
    Anspach, Ralph, Institute of Industrial Relations
    Bendix, Reinhard, Department of Sociology and Institute of Industrial Relations
    Burgess, Eugene W., School of Business Administration
    Conroy, John, Institute of Industrial Relations
    Coontz, Sydney, Institute of Industrial Relations
    Fisher, Lloyd, Institute of Industrial Relations
    Galenson, Walter, School of Business Administration and Department of Economics
    Kerr, Clark, President, University of California
    Kisch, Herbert, Institute of Industrial Relations
    Lange, M. G. (Institut für Politische Wissenschaft, Berlin-Dahlem, Germany)
    Leibenstein, Harvey, Department of Economics
    Linz, Juan, Institute of Industrial Relations
    Morgenstern, Otto, Institute of Industrial Relations
    Roth, Gunther, Institute of Industrial Relations
    Scalapino, Robert, Department of Political Science
    Schran, Peter, Institute of Industrial Relations
    Wachenheim, Hedwig, Graduate Research Economist
Chicago, University of
    Harbison, F. H., Industrial Relations Center
    Hoselitz, Bert F., Division of Social Sciences
    Klein, Marie E., Industrial Relations Center
    Lorwin, Val R., Division of Social Sciences
    Massey, Ralph J., Industrial Relations Center

Nash, Manning, Department of Anthropology
Rottenberg, Simon, Department of Economics
Slotkin, J. Sydney, Division of Social Sciences
Willner, Ann Ruth, Graduate Student in International Relations
Wohl, Richard, Division of Social Sciences

Colorado, University of
Ehrmann, Henry W., Department of Political Science

Council of Personnel Administration, Stockholm, Sweden
Lahnhagen, Rolf, Director
Lohse, Lennart

Florence, University of, Italy
Ferrarotti, Franco, Social Sciences

Harvard University
Berg, Elliot, Department of Economics
Dunlop, John T., Department of Economics
Horowitz, Daniel, Research Associate
Palekar, S. A., Research Associate, Littauer School of Public Administration
Rothbaum, Melvin, Department of Economics
Ulman, Lloyd, Department of Economics

Indian Institute of Technology, Kharagpur, India
Ganguli, H. C.

Institut für Politische Wissenschaft, Berlin-Dahlem, Germany
Lange, M. G.
Stammer, Otto

Liverpool, University of
Matthews, David, Department of Social Science
McGivering, Ian, Department of Social Science
Scott, William H., Department of Social Science

Massachusetts Institute of Technology
Abbott, Harold G., Industrial Relations Section
Baldwin, George B., Department of Economics and Social Science
Bauer, Raymond A., Department of Economics and Social Science
James, Ralph C., Department of Economics and Social Science
Kalacheck, Edward, Industrial Relations Section
Kannappan, Subbiah, Industrial Relations Section
Kotler, Philip, Industrial Relations Section
Munson, Fred C., Industrial Relations Section
Myers, Charles A., Department of Economics and Social Science
Siegel, Abraham J., Department of Economics and Social Science
Williams, David, Industrial Relations Section

T–L

Appendix

Mount Holyoke College
  Hawkins, Everett D., Department of Economics
Northeastern University
  Rosen, Sumner, Department of Economics
Princeton University
  Blumenthal, W. Michael, Industrial Relations Section
  Eason, Warren W., Industrial Relations Section
  Harbison, F. H., Industrial Relations Section
  Hartmann, Heinz, Industrial Relations Section
  Ibrahim, Ibrahim A., Industrial Relations Section
  Klein, Marie E., Industrial Relations Section
  Rimlinger, Gaston V., Industrial Relations Section
  Shearer, John C., Industrial Relations Section
Roosevelt University
  Sturmthal, Adolf, Philip Murray Professor
Rutgers University
  Alexander, Robert J., Department of Economics
Vassar College
  Brown, Emily Clark, Department of Economics
Washington University (St Louis)
  Sobel, Irvin, Department of Economics
Yale University
  Leiserson, Mark, Department of Economics
Miscellaneous
  de Möy, Gérard, Industrial Consultant, Paris, France
  Montjoie, René, Inspecteur de Mines, Metz, France
  Thorner, Daniel, Bombay, India

Publications of Inter-University Study of Labor Problems in Economic Development

Books

Frederick Harbison, Joan Maruhnic and Jane R. Resnick, *Quantitative Analyses of Modernization and Development*, Industrial Relations Section, Princeton University, Princeton, New Jersey, 1970.
Charles A. Myers, *Computers in Knowledge-Based Fields*, Massachusetts Institute of Technology Press, Cambridge, Massachusetts, 1970.
Frederick Meyers, *Training in European Enterprises*, Institute of Industrial Relations, University of California, Los Angeles, 1969, monograph series 14.

E. Wight Bakke, *Revolutionary Democracy – Challenge and Testing in Japan*, Shoe String Press, Hamden, Connecticut, 1968.

Richard D. Robinson, *High Level Manpower in Economic Development: A Turkish Case*, Center for Middle Eastern Studies, Harvard University Press, Cambridge, Massachusetts, 1967, monograph series 17.

Dieter K. Zschock, *Manpower Perspective of Colombia*, Industrial Relations Section, Princeton University, Princeton, New Jersey, 1967. Spanish translation by Ediciones Tercer Mundo (*El Empleo en Colombia: Perspectivas y Futuro*), Bogotá, 1967.

Frederick Harbison and Charles A. Myers, edrs, *Manpower and Education: Country Studies in Economic Development*, McGraw-Hill Book Co., Inc., New York, 1965.

Charles A. Myers, *Education and National Development in Mexico*, Industrial Relations Section, Princeton University, Princeton, New Jersey, 1965.

Frederick Harbison and Charles A. Myers, *Education, Manpower and Economic Growth: Strategies of Human Resource Development*, McGraw-Hill Book Co., Inc., New York and London, 1964. Korean translation by Eulyoo Publishing Company of Korea, under sponsorship of U.S. Information Agency, 1964. Japanese translation by the Diamond Publishing Co., Ltd, Tokyo, 1965. Portuguese translation under auspices of U.S. Information Agency, by Fundo de Cultura, Rio de Janeiro, 1965.

Clark Kerr, John T. Dunlop, Frederick Harbison and Charles A. Myers, *Industrialism and Industrial Man*, Oxford University Press, Inc., 1964. (A revision of the earlier edition published by Harvard University Press, 1960.) Arabic translation by Al-Maktaba Al-Ahlia, Beirut, Lebanon, 1962. Japanese translation by Toyo-Kegai-Shinpo-Sha, Tokyo, 1963. Portuguese translation by Centro de Publicações Técnicas da Alianca, Rio de Janeiro, 1963. Spanish translation by El Instituto de Organización y Administración de la Universidad de Chile and the Editorial Universitaria de Buenos Aires, Buenos Aires, 1963. German translation Europäische Verlagsanstalt, Frankfurt, 1964. Persian translation by Mr Abolghasem Taheri, B.T.N.K., Teheran, 1965.

Adolph Sturmthal, *Workers' Councils: A Study of Workplace Organization on Both Sides of the Iron Curtain*, Harvard University Press, 1964.

Daniel L. Horowitz, *The Italian Labor Movement*, Harvard University Press, 1963.

Walter Galenson, edr., *Labor in Developing Economies*, University of California Press, 1962.

Appendix

Shreekant A. Palekar, *Problems of Wage Policy for Economic Development*, Asia Publishing House, New York, 1962.

Robert J. Alexander, *Labor Relations in Argentina, Brazil and Chile*, McGraw-Hill Book Co., Inc., New York, 1962.

Heinz Hartmann, *Enterprise and Politics in South Africa*, Industrial Relations Section, Princeton University, New Jersey, 1962.

Albert Y. Badre and Simon G. Siksek, *Manpower and Oil in Arab Countries*, Economic Research Institute, American University of Beirut, Lebanon, 1960.

I. McGivering, D. Matthews, and W. H. Scott, *Management in Britain*, Liverpool University Press, 1960.

John C. Shearer, *High-Level Manpower in Overseas Subsidiaries – Experience in Brazil and Mexico*, Industrial Relations Section, Princeton University, New Jersey, 1960.

Frederick Harbison and Charles A. Myers, *Management in the Industrial World: An International Analysis*, McGraw-Hill Book Co., Inc., New York, 1959. Japanese translation by Daiamondo-Sha, Tokyo, 1961. Spanish translation by Ediciones del Castillo, S.A., Madrid, 1962.

Heinz Hartmann, *Authority and Organization in German Management*, Princeton University Press, New Jersey, 1959.

Walter Galenson, edr, *Labor and Economic Development*, John Wiley & Sons, Inc., New York, 1959.

John T. Dunlop, *Industrial Relations Systems*, Henry Holt & Co., New York, 1958.

Frederick Harbison and Ibrahim A. Ibrahim, *Human Resources for Egyptian Enterprise*, McGraw-Hill Book Co., Inc., New York, 1958. Arabic translation by Dar al-Marifah, Cairo, 1961.

Charles A. Myers, *Labor Problems in the Industrialization of India*, Harvard University Press, 1958. Also published as *Industrial Relations in India*, Asia Publishing House, Bombay, 1958 (second printing, 1961).

Henry W. Ehremann, *Organized Business in France*, Princeton University Press, New Jersey, 1957.

Harvey Leibenstein, *Economic Backwardness and Economic Growth, Studies in the Theory of Economic Development*, John Wiley & Sons, Inc., New York, 1957.

Reinhard Bendix, *Work and Authority*, John Wiley & Sons, Inc., New York, 1956.

Val R. Lorwin, *The French Labor Movement*, Harvard University Press, 1954.

*Articles**

'The Labour Problem in Economic Development: A Framework for a Reappraisal', by Clark Kerr, Frederick H. Harbison, John T. Dunlop, and Charles A. Myers, *International Labour Review*, March 1955, Reprint no. 1.

'Modern Management in Western Europe', by F. Harbison and Eugene W. Burgess, *Journal of Sociology*, July 1954, Reprint no. 2.

'The Structuring of the Labor Force in Industrial Society: New Dimensions and New Questions', by Clark Kerr and Abraham Siegel, *Industrial and Labor Relations Review*, January 1955, Reprint no. 3.

'International Comparisons of Wage Structures', by John T. Dunlop and Melvin Rothbaum, *International Labour Review*, April 1955, Reprint no. 4.

'The Trade Union Movement and the Redistribution of Power in Postwar Germany', by Clark Kerr, *Quarterly Journal of Economics*, November 1954, Reprint no. 5.

'Investment Criteria, Productivity and Economic Development', by Walter Galenson and Harvey Leibenstein, *Quarterly Journal of Economics*, August 1955, Reprint no. 6.

'The City, The Factory, and Economic Growth', by Bert F. Hoselitz, *American Economic Review*, May 1955, Reprint no. 7.

'Labour Problems of Rationalisation: The Experience of India', by Charles A. Myers, *International Labour Review*, May 1956, Reprint no. 8.

'Entrepreneurial Organization as a Factor in Economic Development', by Frederick Harbison, *Quarterly Journal of Economics*, August 1956, Reprint no. 9.

'Collective Bargaining in Postwar Germany', by Clark Kerr, *Contemporary Collective Bargaining*, Reprint no. 10.

'Collective Bargaining in Postwar France', by Val R. Lorwin, *Annals of the American Academy of Political and Social Science*, March 1957, Reprint no. 11.

'Public Enterprise in Indian Industry', by George B. Baldwin, *Pacific Affairs*, March 1957, Reprint no. 12.

* Reprint nos. 1–8, 10–18, and 29 out of print. All others available from: Inter-University Study of Labor Problems in Economic Development, P.O. Box 248, Princeton, New Jersey 08540.

Appendix

'Productivity and Labour Relations', by Clark Kerr, *Productivity and Progress*, Reprint no. 13.

'Working-Class Politics and Economic Development in Western Europe', by Val R. Lorwin, *American Historical Review*, January 1958, Reprint no. 14.

'Recent Developments in Management Training in India', by Charles A. Myers, *Indian Journal of Public Administration*, April–June 1958, Reprint no. 15.

'International Differences in the Strike Propensity of Coal Miners: Experience in Four Countries', by Gaston V. Rimlinger, *Industrial and Labor Relations Review*, April 1959, Reprint no. 16.

'Managers and Entrepreneurs: A Useful Distinction?', by Heinz Hartmann, *Administrative Science Quarterly*, March 1959, Reprint no. 17.

'Two Centers of Arab Power', by Frederick Harbison, *Foreign Affairs*, July 1959, Reprint no. 18.

'The Interindustry Propensity to Strike: An International Comparison', by Clark Kerr and Abraham Siegel, in *Industrial Conflict* (McGraw-Hill Book Co., Inc., 1954), Reprint no. 19.

'Lessons from Abroad for American Management', by Charles A. Myers, *Journal of Business of the University of Chicago*, January 1960, Reprint no. 20.

'The Local Union in Soviet Industry: Its Relations with Members, Party and Management', by Emily Clark Brown, *Industrial and Labor Relations Review*, January 1960, Reprint no. 21.

'Autocracy and the Factory Order in Early Russian Industrialization', by Gaston V. Rimlinger, *Journal of Economic History*, March 1960, Reprint no. 22.

'Problems of Manpower and Industrialization in the U.S.S.R.', by Warren W. Eason, *Population Trends in Eastern Europe, The U.S.S.R. and Mainland China, Proceedings of the Thirty-sixth Annual Conference of the Milbank Memorial Fund*, November 4–5 1959, Reprint no. 23.

'Industrialism and Industrial Man', by Clark Kerr, Frederick Harbison, John T. Dunlop and Charles A. Myers, *International Labour Review*, September 1960, Reprint no. 24.

'The Workers' Councils in Poland', by Adolf Sturmthal, *Industrial and Labor Relations Review*, April 1961, Reprint no. 25.

'The Trade Union in Soviet Social Insurance: Historical Development and Present Functions', by Gaston V. Rimlinger, *Industrial and Labor Relations Review*, April 1961, Reprint no. 26.

'Backward-Sloping Labor Supply Functions in Dual Economies – The Africa Case', by Elliot J. Berg, *Quarterly Journal of Economics*, August 1961, Reprint no. 27.

'Social Security, Incentives, and Controls in the U.S. and U.S.S.R.', by Gaston V. Rimlinger, *Comparative Studies in Society and History*, November 1961, Reprint no. 28.

'Human Resources Development Planning in Modernising Economies', by Frederick H. Harbison, *International Labour Review*, May 1962, Reprint no. 29.

'The American System of Industrial Relations: Is It Exportable?', by Charles A. Myers, *Proceedings of the Fifteenth Annual Meeting, Industrial Relations Research Association*, December 1962, Reprint no. 30.

'Students on the March: The Cases of Mexico and Colombia', by E. Wight Bakke, *Sociology of Education*, Spring 1964, Reprint no. 31.

'Education and Employment in the Newly Developing Economies', by Frederick Harbison and Charles A. Myers, *Comparative Education*, June 1964, Reprint no. 32.

'The African University and Human Resource Development', by Frederick Harbison, *Journal of Modern African Studies*, vol. 3, no. 1, 1965, Reprint no. 33.

'Socialism and Economic Development in Tropical Africa', by Elliot J. Berg, *Quarterly Journal of Economics*, vol. 78, November 1964, Reprint no. 34.

'The Development of a Labor Force in Sub-Saharan Africa', by Elliot J. Berg, *Economic Development and Cultural Change*, vol. 13, No. 4, July 1965, Reprint no. 35.

'Roots and Soil of Student Activism', by E. Wight Bakke, *Comparative Education Review*, vol. 10, no. 2, June 1966, Reprint no. 36.

'The Professional and Political Attitudes of Chilean University Students' and 'Field Work in a Hostile Environment: A Chapter in the Sociology of Social Research in Chile', by Myron Glazer, *Comparative Education Review*, vol. 10, no. 2, June 1966, Reprint no. 37.

'Human Resources and World Economic Development: Frontiers for Research and Action', by Charles A. Myers, *International Labour Review*, vol. 94, no. 5, November 1966, Reprint no. 38.

'A Systems Analysis Approach to Human Resource Development Planning', by Frederick H. Harbison, *South Atlantic Quarterly*, Summer, 1967, Reprint no. 39.

'From Ashby to Reconstruction: Manpower and Education in

Nigeria', by Frederick H. Harbison, in *Growth and Development of the Nigerian Economy*, edited by Carl K. Eicher and Carl Liedholm, Michigan State University Press, 1970, Reprint no. 40.

'Postscript to *Industrialism and Industrial Man*', by Clark Kerr, John T. Dunlop, Frederick H. Harbison and Charles A. Myers, *International Labour Review*, vol. 103, no. 6, June 1971, Reprint no. 41.

'Human Resources as the Wealth of Nations', by Frederick H. Harbison, *Proceedings of the American Philosophical Society*, vol. 115, no. 6, December 1971, Reprint no. 42.

Notes

Foreword

1. Frederick Engels, *The Condition of the Working Class in England*, Panther edn, 1969, p. 79.

2. R. M. Titmuss, Introduction to R. H. Tawney, *Equality*, George Allen & Unwin, 1964, p. 11.

3. Jock Young, 'The Role of the Police as Amplifiers of Deviancy, Negotiators of Reality and Translators of Fantasy: some consequences of our present system of drug control as seen in Notting Hill', in Stanley Cohen, edr, *Images of Deviance*, Penguin Books, 1971, p. 55.

4. John H. Goldthorpe, 'Social Stratification in Industrial Society', in R. Bendix and S. M. Lipset, edrs, *Class, Status and Power*, Routledge & Kegan Paul, 2nd edn, 1967, p. 649.

5. Stanley Cohen, edr, *Images of Deviance*, p. 24.

6. Raymond Williams, *The Long Revolution*, Chatto & Windus, 1961, ch. 4.

7. Robert A. Nisbet, *The Sociological Tradition*, Heinemann, 1967.

8. ibid.

9. Ralf Dahrendorf, *Class and Class Conflict in an Industrial Society*, Routledge & Kegan Paul, 1959.

10. Quoted in Barrington Moore, Jr, *Soviet Politics: The Dilemma of Power: The Role of Ideas in Social Change*, Harper Torch Books, 1965, p. 161.

11. J. K. Galbraith, *The New Industrial State*, Hamish Hamilton, 1967.

12. Frank Parkin, *Class Inequality and Political Order*, MacGibbon & Kee, 1971.

13. cf. H. J. Gans, *People and Plans*, New York, Basic Books, 1968, for a discussion of 'potential' and 'effective' environments.

14. C. Kerr *et al.*, *Industrialism and Industrial Man*, Heinemann Educational, 1962 edn, p. 33. The passage quoted has been removed from the 1964 edition reprinted here, but it remains in my view still the most succinct formulation of the authors' central perspective.

Notes

15. C. Kerr *et al.*, 'Postscript to *Industrialism and Industrial Man*', p. 296 in this volume.

16. C. Kerr *et al.*, *Industrialism and Industrial Man*, 1962 edn, p. 285; this passage also has been omitted from the 1964 edition, but see the 1971 Postscript, pp. 291–3 in this volume.

17. ibid., p. 276 in this volume.

18. C. Kerr *et al.*, 'Postscript to *Industrialism and Industrial Man*', p. 298 in this volume.

19. W. E. Moore, *Social Change*, Prentice-Hall, 1963; *The Impact of Industry*, Prentice-Hall, 1965.

20. John H. Goldthorpe, 'Social Stratification in Industrial Society', R. Bendix and S. M. Lipset, edrs, *Class, Status and Power*, Routledge & Kegan Paul, 2nd edn, 1967.

21. Alan Dawe, 'The two sociologies', *British Journal of Sociology*, vol. XXI, no. 2, June 1970.

22. cf. Marshall D. Sahlins, *Tribesmen*, Prentice-Hall, 1968; 'On the Sociology of Primitive Exchange', in M. Banton, edr, *The Relevance of Models for Social Anthropology*, A.S.A. Monograph 1, Tavistock, 1965.

23. Arnold S. Feldman and Wilbert E. Moore, 'Are Industrial Societies Becoming Alike?', in A. W. Gouldner and S. M. Miller, edrs, *Applied Sociology*, New York, Free Press, 1965, p. 263.

24. Alasdair MacIntyre, *Marcuse*, Fontana/Collins, 1970, p. 71.

25. Tom Burns, edr, *Industrial Man*, Penguin Books, 1969, p. 7.

Introduction

1. See, for example, Reinhard Bendix, 'The Lower Classes and the "Democratic Revolution"', *Industrial Relations*, October 1961, pp. 91–116.

Chapter 1: The Logic of Industrialization

1. T. S. Ashton, *The Industrial Revolution 1760–1830*, Oxford University Press, 1948, pp. 125–6.

2. The page citations in the *Manifesto* are to K. Marx and F. Engels, *Manifesto of the Communist Party*, Moscow, Foreign Languages Publishing House, 1955; page citations in *Capital* are to Karl Marx, *Capital*, First edition, Moscow, Foreign Languages Publishing House 1954, English edition. Chapter XV in this first volume of *Capital* is entitled 'Machinery and Modern Industry', pp. 371–507.

3. W. Arthur Lewis, *The Theory of Economic Growth*, George Allen & Unwin, 1955, p. 116.

4. The 32 labour grades in the basic steel industry and the many thousands of jobs described and rated in the manual in use in the United

States are eloquent testimony to the way in which an industrial work force is structured. While the details of the ordering vary among countries, the steel industry of all countries reflects a highly differentiated and ordered work force. See Jack Stieber, *The Steel Industry Wage Structure*, Cambridge, Massachusetts, Harvard University Press, 1959. Compare American Iron and Steel Institute, *Steel in the Soviet Union*, New York, 1959, pp. 287–376.

5. Bert F. Hoselitz, 'The City, The Factory, and Economic Growth', *American Economic Review*, May 1955, pp. 166–84.

6. If industrializing countries are arrayed in groups according to product *per capita*, the proportion of the labour force in agriculture and related industries varies from 61·2 per cent in the least developed group to 14·4 per cent in the group with the highest product *per capita*. See Simon Kuznets, *Six Lectures on Economic Growth*, Glencoe, Illinois, The Free Press, 1959, pp. 44–5.

7. W. Arthur Lewis, *The Theory of Economic Growth*, p. 92.

8. Marion J. Levy, Jr, 'Some Social Obstacles to "Capital Formation" in Underdeveloped Areas', in *Capital Formation and Economic Growth*, A Conference of the Universities – National Bureau of the Committee for Economic Research, New Jersey, Princeton University Press, 1955, p. 461.

9. 'Political power, properly so called, is merely the organized power of one class for oppressing another.' K. Marx and F. Engels, *Manifesto of the Communist Party*, Moscow, Foreign Languages Publishing House, 1955, p. 95. The highest purpose of the state is the protection of private property; it is an instrument of class domination. See also F. Engels, *Origin of the Family, Private Property and the State*, translated by Ernest Untermann, Chicago, C. H. Kerr & Co., 1902, p. 130, and Paul H. Sweezy, *The Theory of Capitalist Development, Principles of Marxian Political Economy*, New York, Oxford University Press, 1942, pp. 243–4.

10. In the good society which Marx believed to be the final and inevitable result of the dialectical process, there would no longer be a division of society into economic classes. Since he held the state to be merely an instrument of class coercion, with the disappearance of classes, there would follow a concomitant 'withering away' of the state. 'The society that is to reorganize production on the basis of free and equal association of the producers will transfer the machinery of state where it will then belong – into the Museum of Antiquities by the side of the spinning wheel and the bronze age.' F. Engels, *Origin of the Family, Private Property and the State*, p. 211.

Notes

11. Daniel Bell, *Work and Its Discontents*, Boston, Beacon Press, 1956. 'Although religion declined, the significance of work was that it could still mobilize emotional energies into creative challenges' (p. 56).

12. Eric Hoffer, 'Readiness to Work' (unpublished manuscript).

13. J. Robert Oppenheimer, *The Open Mind*, New York, Simon & Schuster, 1955, p. 121.

14. G. Myrdal, *An International Economy*, New York, Harper & Brothers, 1956, pp. 9–16.

Chapter 2: The Industrializing Élites

1. Everett E. Hagen, 'The Process of Economic Development', *Economic Development and Cultural Change*, April 1957, pp. 206–14, and 'How Economic Growth Begins: A General Theory Applied to Japan', *Public Opinion Quarterly*, Autumn 1958, pp. 373–90.

2. E. Levasseur, *The American Workman*, Baltimore, The Johns Hopkins Press, 1900, pp. 445–6.

3. Reinhard Bendix, *Work and Authority in Industry*, New York, John Wiley & Sons, Inc., 1956, pp. 22–116.

4. A. J. Meyer, *Middle Eastern Capitalism*, Cambridge, Massachusetts, Harvard University Press, 1959, p. 64: '. . . Cyprus is still economically unviable and a ward of the West for its food and clothing.'

5. See American Iron and Steel Institute, *Steel in the Soviet Union*, New York, 1959, p. 329.

6. Karl Mannheim, *Ideology and Utopia*, New York, Harcourt, Brace & Co., 1949, p. 219.

7. For a discussion of the sources of industrializing élites, see Everett E. Hagen, 'The Process of Economic Development', pp. 193–215.

8. John Scott, *Democracy Is Not Enough: A Personal Survey of the Hungry World*, New York, Harcourt, Brace & Co. 1960, p. 19.

9. W. W. Rostow, *The Stages of Economic Growth, A Non-Communist Manifesto*, Cambridge University Press, 1960, pp. 103, 133.

10. Daniel Lerner, *The Passing of Traditional Society*, Glencoe, Illinois, The Free Press, 1958, uses this term to denote the people on the margin between traditional and modern society.

Chapter 3: Shaping the Industrialization Process

1. See George M. Foster, *Traditional Cultures: The Impact of Technological Change*, New York, Harper & Brothers, 1962, for a recent discussion of cultural restraints and stimulants to economic growth.

2. This is E. B. Tylor's definition, quoted in A. L. Krober and Clyde Kluckhohn, *Culture – A Critical Review of Concepts and Definitions*, paper of the Peabody Museum of American Archaeology and Ethnology, Harvard University, 47.1:43, 1952.

3. Ralph Linton, 'Cultural and Personality Factors Affecting Economic Growth', in *The Progress of Underdeveloped Areas*, Bert F. Hoselitz, edr, Chicago, University of Chicago Press, 1952, p. 83.

4. Edward Norbeck and Harumi Befu, 'Informal Fictive Kinship in Japan', *American Anthropologist*, vol. 60, 1958, p. 116.

5. See C. K. Yang, *A Chinese Village in Early Communist Transition and The Chinese Family in the Communist Revolution*, The Technology Press of the Massachusetts Institute of Technology, distributed by Harvard University Press, Cambridge, Massachusetts, 1960.

6. F. S. C. Northrup, *The Taming of the Nations: A Study of the Cultural Bases of International Policy*, New York, The Macmillan Co., 1952, p. 74.

7. Max Weber, *The Protestant Ethic and the Spirit of Capitalism*, translated by Talcott Parsons, New York, Charles Scribner's Sons, 1948. Talcott Parsons, *The Structure of Social Action*, New York, McGraw-Hill Book Co. Inc., 1937, pp. 500–558. R. H. Tawney, in his *Religion and Rise of Capitalism*, Harcourt, Brace & Co. 1926, was one of Weber's critics, raising the incisive question whether economic factors did not produce the change in religious ideas.

8. Daniel Lerner, *The Passing of Traditional Society: Modernizing the Middle East*, Glencoe, Illinois, The Free Press, 1958, p. 105.

9. For a corroborating view, see Milton Singer, 'Cultural Values in India's Economic Development', *Annals of the American Academy of Political and Social Science*, 305:81–2, May 1956. See also George M. Foster, *Traditional Cultures: The Impact of Technological Change*, pp. 160–62.

10. William O. Douglas, *West of the Indus*, Garden City, New York, Doubleday & Co. Inc., 1958, pp. 445, 481.

11. Rudolf Schlesinger, *Soviet Legal Theory*, New York, Oxford University Press, 1945, p. 258. Vyshinsky quotes Marx as saying, 'Society does not rest on law. That is a phantasy of jurists. On the contrary, law – in contrast to the arbitrariness of the separate individuum – must rest on society, must be an expression of society's general interests and needs . . .' A. Vyshinsky, *The Law of the Soviet State*, New York, The Macmillan Co., 1948, p. 37.

12. Lord Salter, *The Development of Iraq, A Plan of Action*, Iraq Development Board, 1955, p. 2: 'The main limiting factors to progress

Notes

are not material but human.' See Frederick Harbison, 'Two Centers of Arab Power', *Foreign Affairs*, July 1959, pp. 1–12.

13. Alexander Gerschenkron, 'Economic Backwardness in Historical Perspective', in *The Progress of Underdeveloped Areas*, Bert F. Hoselitz, edr, University of Chicago Press, 1952, pp. 3–29 and 'The Rate of Industrial Growth in Russia Since 1885', *The Tasks of Economic History*, supplement, 7:144–74, 1947.

14. 'Rostow on Growth', *The Economist*, 15 August 1959, pp. 409–16 and 22 August 1959, pp. 524–31.

15. Alexander Gerschenkron, 'Notes on the Rate of Industrial Growth in Italy, 1881–1913', *Journal of Economic History*, December 1955, p. 372.

16. Arthur D. Gayer, W. W. Rostow, Anna Jacobson Schwartz, *The Growth and Fluctuation of the British Economy 1790–1850*, vol. II, Oxford University Press, 1953, p. 626; Alvin H. Hansen, 'Factors Affecting the Trend of Real Wages', *American Economic Review*, March 1925, pp. 27–42; E. H. Phelps Brown and Sheila V. Hopkins, 'The Course of Wage Rates in Five Countries, 1860–1939', *Oxford Economic Papers*, June 1950, pp. 226–96.

17. Simon Kuznets, Wilbert E. Moore, and Joseph J. Spengler, edrs, *Economic Growth: Brazil, India, Japan*, Durham, North Carolina, Duke University Press, 1955, pp. 14–15. The quotation is from Chapter 1, 'Problems in Comparisons of Economic Trends', p. 120, by Simon Kuznets.

18. Alexander Gerschenkron, 'Notes on the Rate of Industrial Growth in Italy, 1881–1913', p. 365.

19. Edward S. Mason, *Economic Planning in Underdeveloped Areas: Government and Business*, New York, Fordham University Press, 1958, pp. ix–x.

20. Simon Kuznets, 'International Differences in Capital Formation and Financing', in *Economic Growth: Brazil, India, Japan*. pp. 26, 27.

21. United Nations, Economic and Social Council, E/2901, 21 June 1956, Financing of Economic Development, the International Flow of Private Capital, 1953–1955, *Report by the Secretary General*, p. 9.

22. See A. G. Korol, *Soviet Education for Science and Technology*, New York, Technology Press and John Wiley & Sons, 1957, and N. deWitt, *Education and Professional Employment in the U.S.S.R.*, Washington, National Science Foundation, 1961.

23. See F. Harbison, 'Human Resources Development Planning in Modernizing Economics', *International Labour Review*, May 1962, pp. 435–58.

24. Bert F. Hoselitz, 'Patterns of Economic Growth', *The Canadian Journal of Economics and Political Science*, November 1955, pp. 416–31. Hoselitz uses the terms 'dominant' and 'satellitic' patterns of development to indicate the degree of dependence upon one or more countries.

Chapter 4: Managers of Enterprises: Their Power, Position, and Policies

1. For an elaboration of the definition of management, see Frederick Harbison and Charles A. Myers, *Management in the Industrial World: An International Analysis*, New York, McGraw-Hill Book Co. Inc., 1959, pp. 3–20.

2. Samuel E. Hill and Frederick Harbison, *Manpower and Innovation in American Industry*, New Jersey, Princeton University Press, 1959.

3. Peter Abrahams, *A Wreath for Udomo*, New York, Alfred A. Knopf, 1956, p. 348.

4. David S. Landes, 'Observations on France: Economy, Society, and Policy', *World Politics*, April 1957, p. 336. There are exceptions to this generalization, and the rapid expansion of certain segments of French industry in recent years is associated with changes in the traditional pattern of French management.

5. See Joseph S. Berliner, *Factory and Manager in the U.S.S.R.*, Cambridge, Massachusetts, Harvard University Press, 1957, pp. 9, 202.

6. James Burnham, *The Managerial Revolution*, New York, John Day Co. Inc., 1941. For a more balanced view, with particular reference to the United States, see Adolph A. Berle, Jr, *Power Without Property: A New Development in American Political Economy*, New York, Harcourt, Brace & Co. 1959.

7. Reinhard Bendix, *Work and Authority in Industry*, New York, John Wiley & Sons, Inc., 1956, pp. 162–74.

8. Solomon B. Levine, *Industrial Relations in Postwar Japan*, Urbana, Illinois, University of Illinois Press, 1958, p. 36.

9. Quoted in Charles A. Myers, *Labor Problems in the Industrialization of India*, Cambridge, Massachusetts, Harvard University Press, 1958, p. 96.

10. For a fuller description of this type of democratic-consultative management, see Frederick G. Lesieur, edr, *The Scanlon Plan: A Frontier in Labor-Management Cooperation*, New York, The Technology Press and John Wiley & Sons, Inc., 1958; Allan Flanders and

Notes

H. A. Clegg, *The System of Industrial Relations in Great Britain*, Oxford, Basil Blackwell, 1954, pp. 323–64.

Chapter 5: Developing the Industrial Labour Force

1. For example, the first natives to work in the South African diamond mines in the 1870s were the indentured servants of Europeans. These natives had originally been forced into indenture because of cattle killing and starvation among the tribes. See Sheila van de Horst, *Native Labour in South Africa*, Oxford University Press, 1942, pp. 28ff.

2. P. G. Powlsland, *Economic Policy and Labour*, edited by Walter Elkan, East African Institute of Social Research, study no. 10, Kampala, Uganda, 1957. See particularly pp. 28ff. for a discussion of imposition of forced labour by British administrations and danger to native institutions.

3. Elliot J. Berg, 'French West Africa', in *Labor and Economic Development*, edited by Walter Galenson, New York, John Wiley & Sons, Inc., 1959, p. 194.

4. For a brief account of forced labour in Russia, see Emily Clark Brown, 'The Soviet Labor Market', *Industrial and Labor Relations Review*, January 1957, pp. 190–98.

5. See Solomon Schwarz, *Labor in the Soviet Union*, New York, Frederick Praeger, 1952, pp. 10ff.

6. H. J. Habakkuk, *American and British Technology in the 19th Century, The Search for Labour-Saving Inventions*, Cambridge University Press, 1962.

7. This may occur even in advanced industrializing countries, such as the United States, when new recruits come to northern factory centres from southern or border state rural areas and return frequently for intermittent periods. See James Sidney Slotkin, *From Field to Factory: New Industrial Employees*, Research Center in Economic Development and Cultural Change, University of Chicago, Glencoe, Illinois, The Free Press, 1960, p. 104.

8. Quoted from James C. Abegglen, *The Japanese Factory*, Glencoe, Illinois, The Free Press, 1958, pp. 133–4.

9. See, however, Arthur M. Ross 'Do We Have a New Industrial Feudalism?', *American Economic Review*, December 1958, pp. 903–20.

10. Kingsley Davis, 'The Unpredicted Pattern of Population Change', *Annals of the American Academy of Political and Social Science*, May 1956, pp. 53–9.

11. Bert F. Hoselitz, 'Urbanization and Economic Growth in Asia',

Economic Development and Cultural Change, October 1957, pp. 42–54; Kingsley Davis and Hilda H. Golden, 'Urbanization and the Development of Pre-Industrial Areas', *Economic Development and Cultural Change*, October 1954, pp. 6–24.

Chapter 6: The Workers: Impact and Response

1. T. S. Ashton, *The Industrial Revolution 1760–1830*, Oxford University Press, 1948, p. 99.

2. George Macaulay Trevelyan, *British History in the Nineteenth Century and After*, Longmans, Green & Co., 1941, p. 156.

3. J. L. Hammond and Barbara Hammond, *The Town Labourer 1760–1832; The New Civilization*, Longmans, Green & Co., 1925, p. 19.

4. David Ricardo, *The Principles of Political Economy and Taxation*, Cambridge University Press, 1951, p. 390.

5. Frederick Engels, *The Condition of the Working Class in England in 1844*, George Allen & Unwin, 1950, p. 177. See, however, F. A. Hayek, *Capitalism and the Historians*, University of Chicago Press, 1954.

6. T. S. Ashton, *The Industrial Revolution 1760–1830*, p. 123.

7. Sidney and Beatrice Webb, *The History of Trade Unionism*, Chiswick Press, 1913, p. 22.

8. J. L. Hammond and Barbara Hammond, *The Skilled Labourer 1760–1832*, Longmans, Green & Co., 1920, p. 259.

9. Wilbert E. Moore, *Industrialization and Labor*, Ithaca, Cornell University Press, 1951, p. 122.

10. W. Arthur Lewis, *The Theory of Economic Growth*, George Allen & Unwin, 1956, p. 161.

11. Norman Ware, *The Industrial Worker 1840–1860, The Reaction of American Industrial Society to the Advance of the Industrial Revolution*, reprinted, Gloucester, Massachusetts, Peter Smith, 1959, p. 107.

12. Frederick Engels, *The Condition of the Working Class in England in 1844*, pp. 178–9. For a detailed description of some rules in the United States in the 1890s, see E. Levasseur, *The American Workman*, Baltimore, The Johns Hopkins Press, 1900, pp. 170–77.

13. *The American Workman*, p. 171.

14. Kazuo Okochi, *Labor in Modern Japan*, The Science Council of Japan, Division of Economics, Commerce and Business Administration, Economic Series no. 18, Tokyo, March 1958, p. 15.

15. Charles A. Myers, *Labor Problems in the Industrialization of India*, p. 48.

Notes

16. J. L. Hammond and Barbara Hammond, *The Town Labourer 1760–1832; The New Civilization*, pp. 39, 40.

17. Bert F. Hoselitz, 'The City, The Factory, and Economic Growth', *American Economic Review*, May 1955, pp. 180–81.

18. James Morris, 'The Power of the Street in the Arab World', *The New York Times Magazine*, 18 October 1959, p. 11.

19. Carleton H. Parker, *The Casual Laborer and Other Essays*, New York, Harcourt, Brace & Howe, 1920, p. 76.

20. Charles A. Myers, *Labor Problems in the Industrialization of India*, p. 44.

21. See Elliot J. Berg, 'French West Africa', in W. Galenson, edr, *Labor and Economic Development*, p. 200.

22. Wilbert E. Moore, *Industrialization and Labor*, p. 116. For a discussion of turnover in East Africa, see Walter Elkan, 'Migrant Labor in Africa: An Economist's Approach', *American Economic Review*, May 1959, pp. 188–97.

23. ibid., p. 118.

24. Daniel Katz, 'Satisfactions and Deprivations in Industrial Life', in *Industrial Conflict*, Arthur Kornhauser, Robert Dubin, Arthur M. Ross, edrs, New York, McGraw-Hill Book Co. Inc., 1954, pp. 86–106.

25. *Report of the Commission Appointed to Inquire Into the Unrest in the Mining Industry in Northern Rhodesia in Recent Months*, Lusaka, The Government Printer, 1956, pp. 13–14.

26. Elliot J. Berg, 'French West Africa', in W. Galenson, edr, *Labor and Economic Development*, p. 227.

27. V. I. Lenin, *What Is to be Done?*, New York, International Publishers, 1929, p. 90.

28. Albert Y. Badre and Simon G. Siksek, *Manpower and Oil in Arab Countries*, Beirut, American University Press, 1960, ch. 6.

29. Subbiah Kannappan, 'The Tata Steel Strike: Some Dilemmas of Industrial Relations in a Developing Economy', *Journal of Political Economy*, October 1959, pp. 489–90; also see Morris David Morris, 'Order and Disorder in the Labour Force; the Jamshedpur Crisis of 1958', *The Economic Weekly*, 1 November 1958, pp. 1387–94.

30. The term 'job consciousness' was used by Selig Perlman, *A Theory of the Labor Movement*, New York, The Macmillan Co. 1928, p. 6. The present authors reject the claim for universality made by Perlman: 'It is the author's contention that manual groups, whether peasants in Russia, modern wage earners, or medieval master workmen, have had their economic attitudes basically determined by a con-

sciousness of scarcity of opportunity . . . Starting with this consciousness of scarcity, the "manualist" groups have been led to practising solidarity . . .' Perlman also uses the concept of job control (see pp. 7, 263–79). For the present authors job control finds its origins not in universal scarcity, nor in universal characteristics of the mentality of manual workers, but rather in the characteristics of the middle-class élite and the middle-class-led society.

31. John Clarke Adams, 'Italy', in *Comparative Labor Movements*, Walter Galenson, edr, New York, Prentice-Hall, Inc., 1952, p. 419.

32. For a more detailed treatment, see Clark Kerr and Abraham J. Siegel, 'Industrialization and the Changing Nature and Impact of Worker Protest' (unpublished manuscript).

33. 'Bonn Socialists Meet on Revision', *New York Times*, 14 November 1959, p. 5.

34. Arthur M. Ross, 'The Natural History of the Strike', in *Industrial Conflict*, pp. 23–36.

Chapter 7: Industrial Relations Systems and the Rules of the Work Place

1. Clark Kerr and Abraham J. Siegel, 'The Structuring of the Labor Force in Industrial Society: New Dimensions and New Questions', *Industrial and Labor Relations Review*, January 1955, pp. 151–68.

2. Harvey Leibenstein, *Economic Backwardness and Economic Growth, Studies in the Theory of Economic Development*, New York, John Wiley & Sons, Inc., 1957, pp. 62–76.

3. Quoted in R. B. Davison, 'Labor Relations in Ghana', *Annals of the American Academy of Political and Social Science*, March 1957, p. 139.

4. Elliot Berg, 'The Recruitment of a Labor Force in Sub-Saharan Africa', 1960 (unpublished manuscript).

5. 'Wages and Related Elements of Labour Cost in European Industry, 1955: A Preliminary Report', *International Labour Review*, December 1957, pp. 558–87.

6. John T. Dunlop and Melvin Rothbaum, 'International Comparisons of Wage Structures', *International Labour Review*, April 1955, pp. 3–19.

7. 'The Interracial Wage Structure in Certain Parts of Africa', *International Labour Review*, July 1958, pp. 20–55.

8. International Labour Office, *Problems of Wage Policy in Asian Countries*, Studies and Reports, new series, no. 43, Geneva, 1956,

pp. 24–7; Lloyd G. Reynolds and Cynthia H. Taft, *The Evolution of Wage Structure*, New Haven, Yale University Press, 1956, pp. 355–60.

9. Clark Kerr, 'The Prospect for Wages and Hours in 1975', in *U.S. Industrial Relations: The Next Twenty Years*, Jack Stieber, edr, East Lansing, Michigan, Michigan State University Press, 1958, pp. 169–204; Pamela Haddy and N. Arnold Tolles, 'British and American Changes in Inter-Industry Wage Structure under Full Employment', *Review of Economics and Statistics*, November 1957, pp. 408–14; Melvin Rothbaum, 'National Wage-Structure Comparisons', in *New Concepts in Wage Determination*, George W. Taylor and Frank C. Pierson, edrs, New York, McGraw-Hill Book Co. Inc., 1957, pp. 299–327.

10. Arthur M. Ross and Paul T. Hartman, *Changing Patterns of Industrial Conflict*, New York, John Wiley & Sons, Inc., 1960.

Chapter 8: Pluralistic Industrialism

1. Barbara Ward, *Five Ideas that Changed the World*, New York, W. W. Norton & Co. Inc., 1959, p. 87.

2. See W. W. Rostow, *The Stages of Economic Growth*, *A Non-Communist Manifesto*.

3. For a discussion of this point with reference to management in the United States, see Adolf A. Berle, Jr., *Power Without Property: A New Development in American Political Economy*, New York, Harcourt, Brace & Co. 1959.

Postscript

1. The advanced industrial society is particularly characterized by a vast expansion of service industries of all kinds, so that white-collar employment often exceeds blue-collar employment.

2. Adapted from information in Appendix VII in F. H. Harbison, Jane Resnick, and Joan Maruhnic, *Quantitative Analyses of Modernization and Development*, Industrial Relations Section, Princeton University, New Jersey, 1970. These data were calculated from other data in Unesco Statistical Yearbooks.

3. *The World Employment Programme*, Report of the Director-General to The International Labour Conference, International Labour Office, Geneva, 1969.

4. See pp. 47–8, 128–9, and Frederick Harbison and Charles A. Myers, *Education, Manpower and Economic Growth: Strategies of Human Resource Development*, McGraw-Hill Book Co., Inc. New York and London, 1964.

5. See, for example, F. H. Harbison, Jane Resnick and Joan Maruhnic, *A Quantitative Analysis of Modernization and Development*, and Everett E. Hagen and Oli Hawrylyshyn, 'Analysis of World Income and Growth, 1955–1965', *Economic and Cultural Change*, October 1969.

6. There has been a very considerable discussion of convergence in both eastern and western countries. See William A. Faunce and William H. Form, edrs, *Comparative Perspectives on Industrial Society*, Boston, Little, Brown & Co. 1969.

7. T. H. Marshall, 'A Summing Up', in *The Sociological Review: Monograph No. 8: The Development of Industrial Societies*, October 1964.

8. John H. Goldthorpe, 'Social Stratification in Industrial Society', ibid.

9. E. C. Dunning and E. I. Hopper, 'Industrialization and the Problem of Convergence', *Sociological Review*, July 1966.

10. 'The Year 2000 – The Trajectory of an Idea', *Daedalus*, Summer 1967.

11. For example, see Derek C. Bok and John T. Dunlop, *Labor and the American Community*, Simon & Schuster, New York, 1970, ch. 12, especially pp. 351–60; and Charles A. Myers, *Computers in Knowledge-Based Fields*, Massschusetts Instiute of Technology Press, Cambridge, Massachusetts, 1970.

12. John Kenneth Galbraith called attention to this same conflict at the conference organized by the International Association of Cultural Freedom at Princeton University in 1969. See François Duchêne, 'The Continuous Millennium', *Survey*, Autumn 1969, quotes Galbraith pp. 8–9.

13. See, for example, Charles Booth (1891–1903), *Life and Labour of the People in London*, 17 vols., New York, A.M.S. Press, Inc. (library binding 1902–1903).

14. *The New York Times*, 18 June 1970. Dr Dubos, a Rockefeller University biologist, made these remarks at a conference on 'Industry and Environment' in New York. In a later article, he observed, 'Human beings can almost certainly survive and multiply in the polluted cage of technological civilization, but we may sacrifice much of our humanness in adapting to such conditions.' *Life*, 24 July 1970.

Index

Index

Index

Index

Penguinews and
Penguins in Print

Every month we issue an illustrated magazine, *Penguinews*. It's a lively guide to all the latest Penguins, Pelicans and Puffins, and always contains an article on a major Penguin author, plus other features of contemporary interest.

Penguinews is supplemented by *Penguins in Print*, a complete list of all the available Penguin titles – there are now over four thousand!

The cost is no more than the postage; so why not write for a free copy of this month's *Penguinews*? And if you'd like both publications sent for a year, just send us a cheque or a postal order for 30p (if you live in the United Kingdom) or 60p (if you live elsewhere), and we'll put you on our mailing list.

Dept EP, Penguin Books Ltd, Harmondsworth, Middlesex

Note: *Penguinews* and *Penguins in Print* are not available in the U.S.A. or Canada